"Critically important and advancing disability research with concrete examples of the ethnographic turn, Barton's participatory research methods and conclusions witness persons with intellectual disability as 'people inextricably caught up in one another' in the communion of the faithful, as the image of God, and by a baptismal hermeneutic of inclusion as members of the Body of Christ/the Church. Practical, insightful, and liberating, Barton's work is welcome to the corpus of Baylor's commitment to disability studies."
—**Mary Jo Iozzio**, Professor of Moral Theology, School of Theology and Ministry, Boston College

"Dr. Barton's scholarly yet accessible book about our baptismal theology and the reality of disabilities is a timely work that needs to be read and discussed by clergy and lay leaders, and indeed all who take seriously Jesus' Way of Love."
—**Michael Curry**, Presiding Bishop of The Episcopal Church and author of *Love Is the Way* and *The Power of Love*

"To read this book is to receive, with its author, the baptismal witness of Christians with intellectual disabilities. That witness illumines, inter alia, the Gospels' accounts of Jesus' baptism, the *Book of Common Prayer*'s baptismal choreography, and the practice of pastoral care."
—**Lauren F. Winner**, Associate Professor of Christian Spirituality, Duke Divinity School

"Barton has written a though-provoking book at the intersection of liturgical and disability theology, looking at a core practice of the church and taking seriously the perspectives of people with intellectual disabilities. This is breaking new ground. Anyone working in disability and liturgical theology, whether academically or practically, would do well by letting Barton and her research partners speak into their thinking and praxis."
—**Armand Léon van Ommen**, *Worship*

SRTD
STUDIES IN RELIGION, THEOLOGY, AND DISABILITY

SERIES EDITORS

Sarah J. Melcher
Xavier University, Cincinnati, Ohio

John Swinton
University of Aberdeen, Aberdeen, Scotland

Amos Yong
Fuller Theological Seminary, Pasadena, California

Becoming the Baptized Body
Disability and the Practice of Christian Community

Sarah Jean Barton

BAYLOR UNIVERSITY PRESS

© 2022 by Baylor University Press
Waco, Texas 76798

All Rights Reserved. No part of this publication may be reproduced, stored in a retrieval system, or transmitted, in any form or by any means, electronic, mechanical, photocopying, recording, or otherwise, without the prior permission in writing of Baylor University Press.

Unless otherwise stated, Scripture quotations are from the New Revised Standard Version Bible, copyright 1989, Division of Christian Education of the National Council of the Churches of Christ in the United States of America. Used by permission. All rights reserved.

Cover Design by Kasey McBeath
Cover Art: Ivanka Demchuk, "Baptism of Christ," mixed technique on canvas and wood
Book Design by Diane Smith, Baylor University Press

First issued in paperback in 2024 under ISBN 978-1-4813-1688-0

The Library of Congress has cataloged the hardcover as follows:

Names: Barton, Sarah Jean, 1986- author.
Title: Becoming the baptized body : disability and the practice of Christian community / Sarah Jean Barton.
Description: Waco, Texas : Baylor University Press, 2022. | Series: Studies in religion, theology, and disability | Includes bibliographical references and indexes. | Summary: "Explores how baptismal theologies and practices shape Christian imagination, identity, and community, through privileging the perspectives and stories of Christians with intellectual disabilities"-- Provided by publisher.
Identifiers: LCCN 2021050083 (print) | LCCN 2021050084 (ebook) | ISBN 9781481316873 (hardback) | ISBN 9781481316903 (pdf) | ISBN 9781481316897 (epub)
Subjects: LCSH: Baptism. | Church work with people with mental disabilities.
Classification: LCC BV814 .B37 2022 (print) | LCC BV814 (ebook) | DDC 234/.161--dc23/eng/20220204
LC record available at https://lccn.loc.gov/2021050083
LC ebook record available at https://lccn.loc.gov/2021050084

This book is the fruit of doing theology together, and I dedicate it to all those whose witness made it possible, and to those who still yearn for a community of baptismal belonging.

Series Introduction

Studies in Religion, Theology, and Disability brings newly established and emerging scholars together to explore issues at the intersection of religion, theology, and disability. The series editors encourage theoretical engagement with secular disability studies while supporting the reexamination of established religious doctrine and practice. The series fosters research that takes account of the voices of people with disabilities and the voices of their family and friends.

The volumes in the series address issues and concerns of the global religious studies/theological studies academy. Authors come from a variety of religious traditions with diverse perspectives to reflect on the intersection of the study of religion/theology and the human experience of disability. This series is intentional about seeking out and publishing books that engage with disability in dialogue with Jewish, Christian, Buddhist, or other religious and philosophical perspectives.

Themes explored include religious life, ethics, doctrine, proclamation, liturgical practices, physical space, spirituality, and the interpretation of sacred texts through the lens of disability. Authors in the series are aware of conversation in the field of disability studies and bring that discussion to bear methodologically and theoretically in their analyses at the intersection of religion and disability.

Studies in Religion, Theology, and Disability reflects the following developments in the field: First, the emergence of disability studies as an interdisciplinary endeavor that has impacted theological studies, broadly defined. More and more scholars are deploying disability perspectives in their work, and this applies also to those working in the theological academy. Second, there is a growing need for critical reflection on disability in world religions. While books from a Christian standpoint have dominated the discussion at the interface of religion and disability so far, Jewish, Muslim, Buddhist, and Hindu scholars, among those from other religious traditions, have begun to resource their own religious traditions to rethink disability in the twenty-first century. Third, passage of the Americans with Disabilities Act in the United States has raised the consciousness of the general public about the importance of critical reflection on disability in religious communities. Lay readers are looking for scholarly discussions of religion and disability as these bring together and address two of the most important existential aspects of human lives. Fourth, the work of activists in the disability rights movement has mandated fresh critical reflection by religious practitioners and theologians. Persons with disabilities remain the group most disaffected from religious organizations. Fifth, government representatives in several countries have prioritized the greater social inclusion of persons with disabilities. Disability policy often proceeds based on core cultural and worldview assumptions that are religiously informed. Work at the interface of religion and disability thus could have much broader purchase—that is, in social, economic, political, and legal domains.

Under the general topic of thoughtful reflection on the religious understanding of disability, Studies in Religion, Theology, and Disability includes shorter, crisply argued volumes that articulate a bold vision within a field; longer scholarly monographs, more fully developed and meticulously documented, with the same goal of engaging wider conversations; textbooks that provide a state of the discussion at this intersection and chart constructive ways forward; and select edited volumes that achieve one or more of the preceding goals.

Contents

Foreword by John Swinton		xi
Acknowledgments		xv
Introduction		1
1	Entering the Conversation	21
2	Drawing from a Multitude of Witnesses	47
3	The Bible and Baptism	87
4	A New Creation *Paul and Baptismal Identity*	103
5	Baptismal Liturgy and Disability	121
6	Practicing and Proclaiming Baptismal Identity	139
7	Practices of the Baptized Body *Preparation, Testimony, and Reaffirmation*	153
Conclusion		181
Notes		187
Bibliography		213
Scripture Index		231
Thematic and Author Index		233

Foreword

I have always been fascinated by the question of what kind of knowledge theology provides us with. Is it simply intellectual knowledge that, for the most part, remains in the hands of intellectuals to construct and reflect upon? Or is it something that involves practice and engagement with what God is doing in creation in the present? The answer of course is that theology provides us with knowledge of both. It can help us to think faithfully about God and to practice faithfully in the power of God's Holy Spirit. They are both part of the same movement. Although the academy has a tendency to separate intellectual from practical knowledge, the point of theology is transformation and transformation requires bodies. We have to learn how to use our minds (Matthew 22:37), but our bodies are the place where that which we know enters into the materiality of God's creation. Knowing God is an intellectual and a social practice (Jeremiah 22:16). It is into this complex interplay between theory and practice that the theologian attempts to find clarity and understanding about who God is and who human beings are before God.

    Such a task requires an approach that can hold the tension between theory and practice, God as a concept or a series of ideas and God as a living presence in our lives. In this book Sarah Jean Barton embarks upon this complex task by exploring baptism in the light of the experiences of people living with intellectual disabilities. To do this, she draws on the emerging approach of Theological Ethnography. Theological Ethnography attempts to utilize qualitative research methods for theological ends. Although Sarah does not describe her work in this way, her approach clearly resonates with this theological approach. Theological Ethnography is distinct from social scientific approaches to the study of religion in that it generates a theological attitude to empirical methods. It is also distinct from traditional theological method in that while it utilizes doctrinal and systematic forms of knowledge and reasoning it does this in a combination with empirical methods of inquiry. Although it emerges from Practical Theology, it remains distinct from it in that it is both theological and empirical without being correlational. In other words, it does not structure the relationship between social science and theology as stages in a correlated conversation.[1]

This approach has shifted attention in theology from a focus solely on abstract forms of reasoning, toward the various ways that theology is situated within the lived experience of communities and individuals. By paying close attention to particular contexts and communities, the method of Theological Ethnography enables scholars to explore the multilayered dynamics of personal belief, communal expression, and practice. This kind of research is not an alternative to more systematic forms of reasoning in theology, but it does offer a challenge for scholars to engage with the complexity of particular communities and the richness and contradictions that are characteristic of faith as it is practiced and lived. Theological Ethnography has the possibility to clearly, critically, and carefully attend to the ways in which the presence of God is experienced by particular individuals and religious communities and the ways in which that presence affects and impacts upon our knowledge of God.

And this is precisely what Sarah does in this fascinating and important book. Her central focus is on a group of people for whom relatively little attention has been paid in relation to theological construction and the impact of beliefs on the discipleship of "forgotten" individuals. While paying close attention to theological tradition, and carefully and clearly locating herself within the doctrinal history of baptism, Sarah opens up space to ask the questions: What does baptism look like if we take seriously the experiences of people with profound intellectual disabilities? What does the church mean when it claims that intellectual understanding is necessary for the efficacy of baptism? How can this be if baptism is primarily the work of the Holy Spirit? What difference does it make if we listen carefully and attentively to the baptismal stories of people with intellectual disabilities and allow that knowledge to interact with what we thought we knew about baptism? By taking seriously doctrinal knowledge and knowledge of how God is acting in the present, Sarah's work presents a rich, deep, challenging and sometimes beautiful reframing on baptism and the theology of baptism. This book breaks new ground in terms of theological method and gives voice to a group of people who are rarely listened to within the process of theological development. Sarah Jean Barton is an important emerging disability scholar, and this book deserves to be taken seriously.

John Swinton
October 2021

Acknowledgments

I am unspeakably grateful for the stories, challenges, and witnesses extended to me by the individuals and church communities who participated in the research for this book. I will continue to carry their profound baptismal stories of joy, challenge, and wonder with me.

The team at Baylor University Press, especially managing editor Cade Jarrell, and Sarah Melcher, a series editor for Studies in Religion, Theology, and Disability, offered frequent encouragement and support throughout the development of this book. Sarah's assistance throughout the revision process helped me to embrace my own authorial voice. Before I submitted the initial proposal for this book to Baylor, Jill Harshaw offered kind and thorough feedback on my preliminary manuscript.

Nathan Longfield, a former student of mine at Western Theological Seminary, provided innumerable hours of support throughout the revision process and assisted me with the technological details of compiling this book's bibliography and index. The book would not be here today without his support of the project and his technological skills where my own failed. Amid wrangling Microsoft Word documents, it was a joy to share conversations about baptismal theology with a friend so deeply attuned to the transformative realities of baptismal discipleship. Jordan Hildenbrand, who worked as my research assistant during the 2020–2021 academic year at Duke University, also provided support during revision of chapter 2.

Several years ago, this book began as a dissertation at Duke Divinity School. Warren Kinghorn, one of the coadvisors for my dissertation, and now a dear colleague, has been an advocate, mentor, and source of encouragement to me since our first conversation in 2011. His careful guidance profoundly influenced the unfolding of this project. My other coadvisor, John Swinton, who I also first met in 2011, has continually pushed me in my development as a theologian. I am grateful for his kindness, humor, as well as his willingness to share his deep wisdom about taking on qualitative research as a theologian. I am humbled and honored that he authored this book's foreword. While completing initial work on this project at Duke Divinity School for my Doctor of Theology degree, Susan Grove Eastman, Fred Edie, and Willie James Jennings also offered generous feedback, helping to make this project more responsive to the life of the church. I designed and took an independent study course on baptismal theologies with Randy Maddox, whose influence also helped bring this book to life.

The process of bringing a book into the world (especially in the midst of a global pandemic!) was made possible, and even enjoyable, by wise colleagues and fellow authors who offered space for conversation around the writing and publishing process. These conversation partners included Keith Dow, Bethany McKinney Fox, Barb Hooper, Jerusha Neal, Rebecca Spurrier, Devan Stahl, Tyler Tate, Wylin Wilson, Lauren Winner, and Norman Wirzba. Many friends also sustained and encouraged me throughout the long season of writing that brought this book into being. Thank you especially to Adam DePrimo, Chauncey Handy, Bryon Hansen and Britt Olson, Amy, Matt, Luke, and Will Jantzen, Evie, Jonathan, and Eleanor Jespersen, Bethanie, Chris, Caedmon, and Eden Overland, Dorothy Porcello, Imogen, Giles, George, and Wilfred Rhodenhiser, Sarah and Devin Shea, and Regina Wenger.

Duke Divinity School formed me as a disciple and a theologian. I am in debt to my colleagues, students, and friends there. I am also deeply grateful to the following faculty, staff, and students at Western Theological Seminary where I served as a Henri Nouwen Fellow from 2018–2020: Carol Ann Bailey, Ben Conner, Anne Elzinga, Emily Holehan, Rachel Klompmaker, Shari Oosting, Sue

Rozeboom, David Stubbs, Emily Ulmer, and Allison Van Liere. They each cheered me on throughout the writing process. My colleagues at Duke Health, especially all those in the Pediatric Occupational Therapy and Physical Therapy division, provided friendship and support of my work as an occupational therapy practitioner and as a theologian. And I cannot begin to express my gratefulness to the families I have come to know and those I continue to work with at Duke Health: they are those who first taught me to ask the questions that occupy the heart of this book. My colleagues at Duke University's Occupational Therapy Doctorate Program continually supported my writing process. My mentors and friends at the Institute on Theology and Disability continue to nurture my heart and my scholarly development.

St. Joseph's Episcopal Church in Durham, NC has provided me with a church home for nearly a decade. I give thanks to God for all the faithful ministers at St. Joseph's who serve God together in the Durham community. Grace Episcopal Church in Holland, MI provided a church home away from North Carolina and a community of encouragement during my two-year academic fellowship in western Michigan. The brothers at Saint Augustine's House, a Lutheran monastery in Oxford, MI, provided me with gracious hospitality and a grounding rhythm of prayer for a week in October 2018 while I completed an intensive writing retreat that produced the first version of chapter 2. Unashamed thanks to the staff of Elmo's Diner in Durham, NC who provided me with more meals than I can mention throughout the process of writing this book. And of course, the Barton and Phillips families offered their love as I spent long hours writing, often missing out on family gatherings.

I am grateful to The Louisville Institute, for their support of me both as a Doctoral Fellow (2015–2017) and then as an Honorary Dissertation Fellow (2018–2019). I am especially thankful for my wonderful cohort colleagues in the Doctoral Fellowship for their encouragement, both during the fellowship and beyond, as well as my 2019 Winter Seminar group who asked some clarifying questions that shaped this project. The Calvin Institute on Christian Worship provided me with research grant funding that made it possible to compensate my research participants, purchase equipment for interviewing, and complete travel for interviews and site visits over the course of the data gathering process. I am grateful for their commitment to exploring how to faithfully support the participation of disabled Christians in worship. In addition, I give thanks to those who participated in my workshop offerings at the Calvin Institute's 2019 Symposium on Worship, especially for how their questions helped me craft chapter 7 of this book. Finally, the Episcopal Church Foundation named me an Academic Fellow in their Fellowship Partners Program in 2018. Their financial support allowed me to spend dedicated time writing what was first my doctoral dissertation, and is now this book.

Finally, to my spouse, Andrew, and to our tiny dogs, Jed and CJ: I am unspeakably grateful for your constancy in loving me. Andrew, thank you for taking care of me and our family throughout the past years of writing and for being a faithful partner in all our adventures. I am grateful to God that you are my most beloved partner on this pilgrim journey.

Introduction

In 2014, I met a young woman named Hallie[1] and her mother, Heather, at a specialty clinic for children and adolescents with intellectual disabilities. One day, between Hallie's visits with different providers on the interdisciplinary healthcare team, Heather and I struck up a conversation. She asked me how long I had worked as an occupational therapist and what I enjoyed doing in my free time.

Heather and I began to discuss my work as a theologian—specifically, my research at the intersection of Christian practices of baptism and the experience of disability. As soon as I mentioned my research on baptism, something lit up in Heather's eyes. She expressed to me her anguish over her and Hallie's experiences in church. Heather longed to see Hallie baptized. She recounted going to church after church, seeking a community to call home. But instead of finding a place of belonging, Heather and Hallie encountered rejection, in both explicit and subtle ways, at every church they visited.

Heather explained that the pastors' explanations for these rejections varied slightly, but the root cause was always the same: Hallie was too loud, too disruptive, and too distracting. And besides, *Hallie could never understand what happened in baptism because of her intellectual disability*, as one pastor told Heather. Baptizing Hallie, therefore, *wouldn't really matter*. Heather sighed and with tears in her eyes told me that she and Hallie had not been to a church in months.

RECEIVING THE WITNESS OF WOUNDS: THE SHAPE AND SCOPE OF THIS PROJECT

Hallie and Heather's story of longing for baptism and belonging, met by repeated exclusion and dismissal from Christian churches, presented me with an open wound I could not ignore. Their story invited me into a deeper commitment to doing theology from within wounds—an approach to theological exploration that springs out of a pressing notion that faithful reflection and action cannot wait.[2]

As a scholar with a deep commitment to practical theology, I knew that a faithful response to the open wound of Hallie and Heather's story could not be a work primarily completed on my own. Understanding practical theology as "a shared endeavor"[3] among Christians from a diversity of contexts and identities, I began to reflect on how I might seek out the experiences, stories, and insights of Christians with intellectual disabilities in relationship to Christian theologies and practices of baptism. Through participatory qualitative research, I sought to take part in storytelling and worship with other Christians across diverse denominational affiliations, especially around the intersections of baptism and disability, in order to collectively generate a faithful response to the wound of the repeated denials of Hallie's baptism.[4] And beyond the particular wounds made palpable in the lives of Hallie and Heather, my research participants also embodied faithful baptismal responses to their own stories of woundedness and exclusion from the church, realities also testified to by a growing body of research among social scientists of religion.[5] This practical and participatory approach to theology with others sought active transformation through "working in wounds, working with wounds, and working through wounds."[6]

Key Concepts: Baptism

This book offers the fruit of doing theology about baptism and living out baptismal vocation alongside, with, and led by people experiencing intellectual disabilities. But what kind of shared perspectives on baptism ground this project? My research participants and I shared an understanding of baptism as the traditional initiatory practice of the church, as well as a source of Christian unity, with its roots in Jesus' baptism, ministry, death, and resurrection.[7]

While different research participants from a variety of confessional traditions emphasized particular distinctives in their doctrines and practices of baptism, we found consensus in affirming the rite of baptism as involving water and administration in the Triune name of the Father, the Son, and the Holy Spirit. Whether understood as sacrament or ordinance, my research partners also affirmed baptism as constitutive for both individual and communal Christian identity.

Practical theologians Craig Dykstra and Dorothy Bass argue that "part of the work of Christian theologians in every age is to reflect on the shape and character of the way of life Christians enter when we rise from the watery death of baptism. How should the new selves we have been given walk in newness of life?"[8] As we will explore throughout the pages to come, the work of theologizing about baptism with my research partners—Christian adults with intellectual disabilities along with their loved ones and clergy leaders—witnessed to a myriad of ways that baptismal practices and theologies can renew our imaginations about who we are and how we might inhabit individual and communal lives marked by what St. Paul calls "new creation." It is my hope that this project's work of bringing together disability and baptism in critical theological reflection enlivens faithful responses to the work of the Holy Spirit in the vocations of all the baptized.

Key Concepts: Intellectual Disability

Before further exploring the contours of this book's participatory and practical approach to theological reflection on baptism, I want to offer some definitional sketches for who I have in mind when I describe the witness of my coresearchers and other individuals with intellectual disabilities. The majority of medical definitions of intellectual disability identify two core areas of deficit among people given this diagnostic label: issues with intellectual functioning (for example, skills like problem-solving or learning) and barriers to adaptive functioning (for example, life skills such as self-care or communication).[9] This definition of intellectual disability from modern Western medicine has often been accompanied by the assignment of a "severity level," describing the impact of an individual's disability on their daily functioning as mild, moderate, severe, or profound.[10]

While these medically rooted definitions of intellectual disability can offer partial descriptions of the lives of people with intellectual disabilities, I want to caution us that they are not sufficient in and of themselves. Defining disability from a medical perspective risks an overemphasis on negative notions of deficit and insufficiency.[11] Medical definitions also fail to recognize the strikingly heterogenous lived experiences of people with intellectual disabilities. For example, while many people within this population communicate fluently with spoken language and enjoy life activities such as full-time employment, marriage, and independent living, others may require 24-hour support or communicate apart from any spoken language. My disabled research participants represented a range of these lived experiences: some living independently and involved in committed romantic relationships and paid employment, and others who were nonspeakers with high support needs, living with family members or in a group home setting. While many professionals tend to describe my latter research participants as those with "profound intellectual disability," self-advocates with intellectual disabilities have challenged the assignment of disability severity levels, instead calling for a renewed focus on empowerment when describing their lives.[12]

Therefore, I offer the term intellectual disability[13] throughout this book not primarily as a kind of medical label, but rather in recognition and respect of its current widespread use among self-advocates with intellectual disabilities, including this project's research participants. Additionally, my writing moves between the use of identity-first language (e.g., disabled people) and person-first language (e.g., person with a disability) as a means of reflecting the variance of preferences among my coresearchers, as well as the general population of people with intellectual disabilities and a diversity of other disability identities.[14]

Frameworks for Disability

Theologians reflecting on disability, as well as scholars in the field of disability studies, engage a wide range of conceptual models for thinking about disability. As will quickly become clear, no commonly accepted definition for disability exists in academic, community, or ecclesial settings.[15] Therefore, in what follows, I want to offer a brief survey of prominent approaches to conceptualizing disability and highlight my own preference for approaching the phenomenon of disability from an integrated approach that considers how both the beauties and challenges of disabled life inform communal connections and action.

The "medical model" provides one contemporary framework for disability, though it is rejected as the preferred mode of narrating disability by most theologians. The medical model envisions disability as an intrinsic, individualized, and inherently negative "problem." This medical construal of disability, for adherents to the medical model, ought to evoke responses that seek to remediate, minimize, or eliminate disability through therapeutic fixes (e.g., surgery, rehabilitation, or medication).

In response to the negative valence surrounding disability in this medical framework, early disability rights activists and scholars offered a new framework for understanding disability: the social model. In this model of disability, an inherently negative impairment no longer disables individuals—rather, the contexts, environments, and societies that disabled people inhabit serve as the primary disabling factors.

Take this simple scenario as an example: if a society eliminated stairs and instead built ramps for navigation of all indoor and outdoor structures, whether private or public, people using wheelchairs might no longer be considered "disabled" in these contexts of architectural access and mobility. As disability studies and feminist scholar Alison Kafer concisely argues, disability is a "product of social relations."[16] Disabled people challenge communally and socially understood visions of "normative" bodies and minds—whether they read with Braille, communicate without the use of spoken language, or navigate the world on wheels. The social model of disability posits that the constructions of our shared society discriminate against people with disabilities—societal barriers for access and participation are what disables people, not particular differences in individual minds and bodies. In this social model for disability, the impetus for change falls not upon individuals with particular impairments, but upon societies as a whole, to enact systemic justice and access.

The minority framework offers another well-known approach to disability, closely related to the social model. In the minority model, disability is primarily understood as a shared identity that aligns those of us who identify as disabled with all other people with disabilities. This widely heterogeneous group of people (with identities marked by intellectual, learning, psychiatric, physical, and sensory disabilities) share a minority identity by virtue of the collective discrimination and prejudice they face within society. A uniting factor of discrimination establishes a basis for solidarity of identity across diverse groups of disabled people.

Drawing upon these three popular models of disability, Kafer offers the "political/relational" framework for disability as a synthetic approach. From this political/relational lens for disability, Kafer argues that "the problem of disability is located in inaccessible buildings, discriminatory attitudes, and ideological systems that attribute normalcy and deviance to particular minds and bodies. The problem of disability is solved not through medical or surgical normalization but through social change and political transformation."[17] Kafer's model draws needed attention to the social and ideological contexts of normalcy that not only construct understandings of disability, but actively marginalize disabled people in the contemporary world.

Early thinkers in the field of disability studies established theoretical foundations for this concept of normalcy. For Rosemarie Garland Thomson, normalcy builds upon an understanding of the "normate": a socially constructed figure that individuals attempt to represent themselves as (through cultural capital and particular performances of embodiment). Through these strivings to represent oneself as the normate, individuals seek to obtain further social authority and subsequently wield power.[18] In this schema of the normate, disabled people with marked differences in their bodies and minds can obtain only limited power. Lennard Davis traces the historical roots of normalcy to the nineteenth-century concept of norms. Normalcy implies that the majority of any particular population ought to somehow participate in a given set of norms—be they certain intellectual capacities or the possession of certain physical features to complete daily activities in a particular way.[19]

Kafer's model resists and even disassembles commitments to these forms of normalcy in contemporary society. Instead of prioritizing alignment with established norms related to embodied capacities, Kafer identifies disabled experience as a site that gathers diverse people together for practices of "collective reimagining."[20] In other words, the political/relational framework envisions relationships with and among people experiencing disability as key places where creative questions are generated to renew our imaginations and practices. Disability is no longer a reality marked by deviance, static definitions, or an ongoing commitment to normalcy.[21] Instead, communities marked by disability are spaces of coalition. In these coalitions, people are not primarily bound to one another by their specific impairments, but rather through shared action to creatively resist, reimagine, and reconstruct the social and political landscapes that perpetuate discrimination against disabled people.

I find Kafer's coalitional framework for disability a helpful aspiration for cultivating partnerships between disabled and nondisabled people in Christian communities. Understanding experiences of disability as generative sites for reimagination supports the work of theologizing in community. In the context of this project, a coalitional framework for disability supports the robust integration of stories and perspectives from Christians with intellectual disabilities to not only guide theological reflection on practices and theologies of baptism, but to spur on church communities to the holy and creative task of reimagining both present and future realities that embrace diverse baptismal vocations among disabled and nondisabled people who seek to follow Jesus together.

Participatory Research as Theological Method

My commitment to theological reflection involving a communal response to wounds aligns with my embrace of the "ethnographic turn" in this project's theological method. Joining other theologians who engage in qualitative research methodology as a mode of theological inquiry, I share a sense that theology ought not only be *applied* to particular wounds and situations, but actually "take flesh within them."[22] In other words, qualitative research provides the methodological context in which "the meanings of the word 'God'" might be discovered "by watching what this community does when it is acting, educating or 'inducting,' imagining and worshipping."[23]

Pursuing qualitative research offered me an avenue not to abandon more traditional doctrinal approaches to theological questions at the intersections of baptism and disability, but instead to prioritize the perspectives of disabled Christians and attend to these perspectives in lively conversation with existing theological work. In this way, my book endeavors to illustrate the gift of the ethnographic turn for practical theology, especially as it concerns welcoming and respecting a diversity of interpretations of Christian practice from communities with little previous access to theological discourse.[24] It is my conviction that this kind of theological exploration results in the critical expansion and enrichment of our shared theologies and practices. Through exploring baptismal theologies and practices with my coresearchers, especially Christians with intellectual disability, I seek to raise new questions that help us attune ourselves to the holy and often unexpected work of the Holy Spirit in the new lives of all the baptized.[25] Doing theology in this way provides not only a rich, descriptive account of lived theologies and practices among Christians with intellectual disabilities, their loved ones, and clergy, but also a generative witness that offers an expansive challenge to assumptions and practices in Christian communities related to identity and vocation.[26]

WE ALL SPEAK FROM SOMEWHERE: MY "WAY IN" TO DISABILITY CONVERSATIONS

"All research is, to an extent, autobiography."[27] As we embark together to explore insights arising from the stories of baptismal practices, theologies, and identities of Christians with intellectual disabilities, I want to offer a few further details about my own identities and lived experiences that inform my working in, with, and through wounds alongside other Christians.[28]

As the opening words of this introduction suggest, my vocation involves not only the work of a practical theologian but also that of a pediatric occupational therapist. This bivocational trajectory was deeply shaped by my experiences in college as a caregiver for children with intellectual disabilities, as well as through ongoing community-based advocacy work alongside people with intellectual disabilities. While I am not a person with an intellectual or developmental disability, I live with a nonperceptible chronic and intermittently disabling health condition. These experiences have shaped me into a person who affirms significant limitation as an unsurprising aspect of being human.[29] My relationships and identities related to disability have also shaped me as one who appreciates the deep delight that can emerge from the mundane and unexpected realities of disabled daily life.[30]

My work is also deeply informed by my confessional tradition in The Episcopal Church. The weekly rhythms of my life include lay leadership in my local parish and a central commitment to a baptismal way of life exemplified in *The Book of Common Prayer*'s Baptismal Covenant: an affirmation of Christian faith in the words of the Nicene Creed, and with God's help, discipleship marked by practices of service, peace, resisting evil, continuing in the teachings and fellowship of the apostles, and respecting the dignity of every human being.[31] Resonant with my Anglican identity, I also hold a core conviction that baptism in the name of the Triune God is a deep well for Christian unity across diverse ecumenical traditions.

Finally, I am a white, upper-middle class, cisgender, heterosexual woman. These facets of my identity, alongside my bivocational and ecclesial orientation to the world, shape the way I listen to and receive the wounds of others. As I explore further in chapter 2, these realities of my lived experience present me with continual sites for critical self-reflection and reflexivity in order to carefully, yet never definitively, uncover how my biases and assumptions shape my theological reflection. While my lived experiences are one source that shape my practical theological approach to wounds and their accompanying questions, they are not the experiences I seek to prioritize or even center in this book. Held together with the identities and lived experiences of my research participants for this project, I hope to demonstrate an approach to theological reflection on disability that honors the complexities and co-creatings that arise from the presumption that "our lives with God, neighbor, and world cannot be understood independently of one another."[32]

DISABILITY THEOLOGY AS WITNESS

I began this theological project with the expectation and assumption that the witness of baptismal stories, theologies, practices, and identities from a disability perspective could provide a crucial avenue for Christians to renew their imaginations about identity. According to John Swinton, research in the field of disability theology seeks to "understand and interpret the gospel of Jesus Christ, God, and humanity against the backdrop of the historical and contemporary experiences of people with disabilities."[33] Building on Swinton's foundational definition, I approached the task of disability theology as one of receiving witness, critically and continuously informed by lived human experiences of disability. In the following section, I want to identify some potential hazards and questions related to disability theology as an act of receiving and amplifying witness and offer a further articulation of how I conceive of this project's framework of witness.

Theological explorations of intellectual disability raise important questions surrounding issues of representation. Who has the right to speak about the experience of disability? Whose voices should carry the greatest weight? How might theologians faithfully and rigorously support the central maxim of the disability rights movement—"nothing about us without us"?[34] Among most theologians of disability, the challenge of "nothing about us without us" leads to self-disclosure about their own positionality. Additionally, theologians engaging the topic of disability strive to prioritize stories emerging from individuals with lived experiences of disability. However, this prioritization of disabled voices in the task of theological witness can become complex when collaborating with people with intellectual disabilities, especially those with more profound experiences of disability.

Charles Taylor warns not only of the complexity of representation, but also its dangers, particularly for historically underrepresented people:

> Our identity is partly shaped by recognition or its absence, often by the misrecognition of others, and so a person or group of people can suffer real damage, real distortion, if the people or society around them mirror back to them a confining or demeaning or contemptible picture of themselves. Nonrecognition or misrecognition can inflict harm, can be a form of oppression, imprisoning someone in a false, distorted, and reduced mode of being.[35]

Taylor's thesis here raises many important questions for this project. Although my research approach seeks to center ways of doing theology together among Christians with and without intellectual disabilities, my use of qualitative interviewing notably privileged disabled participants who use words to communicate. Nonspeakers, people who do not communicate with speech, raise an important challenge to the field of disability theology as well as my work—what realities and questions must we attend to in receiving the witness of disabled people, including those who are nonspeakers?

Within existing literature on intellectual disability in the field of disability theology, scholars offer numerous answers to these questions of representation and receiving witness. Reflecting on the spiritual experiences of people with profound disabilities, Jill Harshaw warns of the grave danger of assuming the "right to speak from a position of certainty of the spiritual experience of people who cannot speak for themselves."[36] Harshaw largely opposes qualitative theological research as an appropriate avenue to provide descriptive spiritual experiences of people with intellectual disabilities who are nonspeakers, citing issues of obtaining consent, verifying validity, and the nonnegotiable use of spoken language in the majority of qualitative research methods.[37]

Harshaw critiques other theologians, notably John Swinton, who have suggested that research within faith communities can provide insights into the witness and vocation of people with intellectual disabilities in ecclesial life. She instead turns toward reflection upon the nature of God's self-revelation as the basis for exploring the spiritual lives of profoundly disabled people. According to Harshaw, because qualitative interviewing is inappropriate for the participation of people with profound disabilities, and because she wishes to affirm the personal spiritualities of people with profound impairments (spiritual lives not wholly captured or facilitated through community), she argues that while human beings experience a myriad of limitations in their understanding of their neighbors, God is unencumbered by these limitations.[38] God's self-disclosure of God's self is unhinged from any kind of human limitation; God is an accessible God who graciously and accessibly provides "a God-designed bridge which spans the otherwise unbridgeable gap between the infinite God and a finite humanity."[39]

While I take seriously Harshaw's critique of misapplying qualitative methodologies among people with profound intellectual disabilities and also affirm her theological emphasis on the incarnation, Harshaw's interpretation of the field of disability theology's overemphasis on faith communities strikes me as misguided. In an attempt to avoid speaking descriptively and definitively of the spiritual experiences of people with intellectual disabilities, especially those who are nonspeakers, Harshaw misses an opportunity to describe *the witness* of the lives of people with intellectual disabilities within Christian faith communities.[40] In contrast to Harshaw, I see the witness and presence of disabled Christians who are nonspeakers as a necessary and nonnegotiable site for theological reflection and challenge.

Theologian Brian Brock affirms a witness-based approach to disability theology, emerging from his own disability experience centered upon his relationship with his son with multiple disabilities, Adam Brock. For Brock, Adam is a powerful witness: his life renews beauty and reveals new questions and complications about the world they inhabit together.[41] Writing of his approach to disability theology, Brock proclaims: "I tell Adam's story as a witness to his witness."[42]

Like Brock, I offer this book as a practice of receiving and amplifying the witness of other Christians, whose witness I am indebted to in my own ongoing formation as a Christian disciple. Christian practices are those embodied expressions that bear witness to the good news of Jesus through "communicative modalities beyond speaking words."[43] Differentiated from techniques that try to exert social control, Christian practices instead provide the "means of grace in which the Holy Spirit transforms people in ways that are unpredictable but are oriented toward our witness in the world."[44] Throughout the coming pages, we will explore how these individual and collective acts of witness can renew our attention to the work of the Holy Spirit in empowering all the baptized to embody a vocation of discipleship. In short, these witnesses will lead us into theological exploration of baptismal identity and its implications for the formation of Christian community. I receive these witnesses and join them with my own voice in service of the church.

THE BAPTIZED BODY: A RENEWED VISION FOR CHRISTIAN IDENTITY

Christian theologies and practices of baptism provide a central site for gathering, forming, and sustaining the church—the baptized body of Jesus.[45] In this book, amplifying the insights and stories from research participants, I argue that a baptismal hermeneutic can expansively enliven our imaginations and ecclesial practices as they intersect with the human experience of disability. This argument will unfold through placing my research participants' perspectives into conversation with multiple partners: theologians of disability, scriptural accounts of baptism and anthropology (particularly in the Pauline Epistles), baptismal liturgies, practical and liturgical theologians, and disability studies scholars. In these conversations, I highlight a common difficulty among contemporary churches: robustly supporting, embracing, and learning from and alongside people with intellectual disabilities in a shared life of Christian discipleship. In response to this difficulty, I explore baptismal theologies and practices of baptismal preparation, testimony, and reaffirmation as key loci for the transformation of ecclesial imaginations about Christian identity, as well as practices that embrace the full discipleship of people with intellectual disabilities.

While conversations connecting baptism and intellectual disability are not new to the field of disability theology,[46] I will explore how the baptismal stories and practices from this project's participants expand key paradigms within theological accounts of disability, such as God's image, friendship, and inclusion. As I will argue, some accounts of disability have tended toward theological abstraction,[47] briefly highlighting potential linkages between theological proposals and Christian practices, instead of offering deeply integrative accounts of how a theological exploration of disability can enliven central Christian practices.

Highlighting the witness of my research participants, I will argue that baptismal theologies and practices, sites of radical affirmation of the profound interdependence of human persons on Jesus Christ and the community of Jesus' body, as well as a deeply embodied and Spirit-enabled participation in discipleship, are critical for the renarration of Christian identity in contemporary churches. These theologies and practices of baptism not only provide a foundational means to reshape the church's anthropological imagination toward a Jesus-centered, communal, and participatory vision for all human creatures, but also offer concrete avenues of participation for all people to serve and follow Jesus, including those with intellectual disabilities.

BAPTISM AND DISABILITY: ATTENDING TO HISTORICAL TRAJECTORIES OF IDENTITY

Before concluding with a summary of the overall trajectory of this book's argument, I want to offer some brief historical contextualization regarding the identity of intellectually disabled people in Western liberal democracies. This historical trajectory will help to underscore both the urgency and relevance of baptismal identity for theological conversations about disability. In other words, appreciating historical factors that have shaped imagination about identity among people with intellectual disabilities can help us attune ourselves more carefully to attend to the wounds like those experienced by Hallie and Heather, and commit to the work of reimagining Christian identity from a baptismal hermeneutic.

Among social contexts in the modern West, both in academic discourse as well as among the wider public, the uniqueness of human identity is often understood to lie within one's rationality or "intelligence." In their research on intellectual disability and identity, Robert Bogdan and Steven Taylor succinctly observe, "the ability to think—to reason, understand, and remember—has sometimes been presented as defining humanness. Intelligence is what separates people from animals."[48] In a similar vein, philosopher Peter Singer asserts in his 2011 edition of *Practical Ethics*, "the fact that a being is a human being, in the sense of a member of the species *Homo sapiens*, is not relevant . . . it is, rather, characteristics like rationality, autonomy, and self-awareness that make a difference."[49]

This powerful narrative that human identity is centrally constituted by intelligence largely emerges from the historical development and eventual widespread deployment of intelligence testing in North America throughout the twentieth century. In *The Mismeasure of Man*, Stephen Jay Gould contends that intelligence quotient (IQ) tests established intelligence as a "single number capable of ranking all people on a linear scale of intrinsic and unalterable mental worth"[50] with a "genetically fixed" foundation.[51] The widespread adoption of formal IQ testing in the American educational system, as well as its early popularity as an assessment among immigration and military officials, created a foundation for the widespread influence of IQ testing on the anthropological imagination of the contemporary United States.

Before the rise of IQ testing, a foundation of biological determinism had already animated a hierarchy of identity among human groups, rooted in false interpretations of race, class, and sex. Gould defines this biological determinism as the notion that "shared behavioral norms, and the social and economic differences between human groups—primarily races, classes, and sexes—arise from inherited inborn distinctions and that society, in this sense, is an accurate reflection of biology."[52] The rise of IQ testing propelled the lives of the "feeble-minded"[53] onto the stage of biological determinism. People with intellectual disabilities, with lives marked by minimal social productivity, the need for support in carrying out day to day activities, and in some cases with limited spoken language and symbolic reasoning, were perceived as deserving the lowliest position in society. Their intelligence, rendered through IQ testing as a single number correlated to an identity of severely decreased worth, suggested a biological basis for denying them the goods and protections of "typical" citizens.

The tethering of human identity to the "unitary mental process" of intelligence became a driving force across American society for the determination of one's capacity and efficiency as an economic producer. Higher IQ testing scores correlated with higher productivity, and therefore an assignment of greater societal worth. The interconnections between productivity and human capacity began to emerge as a central marker of human identity in the American anthropological imagination. Affirming this, Dorothy Roberts emphasizes the dangerous moral implications resulting from use of IQ testing in America: "intelligence became a shorthand for moral worth as well as cognitive capacity."[54]

In addition to IQ testing, shifts in modern notions of time also influenced the development of negative and deficiency-oriented perceptions of the identities of people with intellectual disabilities. Throughout the twentieth century, Thomas Baynton suggests that societies in the modern West increasingly understood time and its influence upon human lives "as a race . . . an unending struggle for existence."[55] This emerging understanding of time was paralleled by changes in disability terminology. Instead of retaining previous and widely utilized vocabulary to describe commonalities of human life (such as "affliction" or "fragility"), new words such as "handicapped" and "disabled" emerged as a way to distinguish disabled people from nondisabled groups that wholly abandoned any self-descriptors related to limitedness.[56] This new vocabulary for disability highlighted the disadvantages disabled people, especially those with intellectual disabilities, faced in the "race for life," cultivating conceptions of disability identity apart from universally experienced human realities of fragility.[57] In these emerging contexts that paired human identity and societal worth with efficiency, nondisabled people could maintain their social standing by dedicating increased attention to urgent economic production. In contrast, most people living with intellectual disabilities encountered increased vulnerability in their identities,[58] especially notable in decreased possibilities for workforce participation.

The entanglement of intellectual disability with an identity of lesser worth remains alive and implicit within contemporary anthropological imaginaries across Western societies. As we will see in the next chapter, this distorted view of identity among people with intellectual disabilities came to bear upon ecclesial practices. This project claims a powerful, alternative narrative about Christian identity and disability—one rooted in the work of the Holy Spirit, alive and active in the lives of all the baptized, including those who are disabled.

MAPPING THE COURSE AHEAD

This book unfolds through a process of receiving the baptismal witness of Christians with intellectual disabilities, their loved ones, and pastors. Through the witness of their stories and reflections, I will argue for a practical theology of baptism as critical for reshaping and renewing our imaginations about Christian identity and vocation for all God's children, with and without disabilities. This conviction will primarily emerge from a disabled perspective—one that affirms the Jesus-centered, communal, and participatory life of Christian discipleship rooted in unity to Jesus and his life of death and resurrection, and renewed through the Spirit's power in ongoing practices of baptismal preparation, testimony, and reaffirmation.

In chapter 1, I explore existing conversations in the field of disability theology that address the intersections of intellectual disability and identity, as well as current texts that engage with the Christian practice of baptism as it relates to disability. I argue that many of these theological accounts of disability largely remain within the realm of abstraction—in other words, they lack robust connection to lived practices within Christian communities. Drawing upon arguments from theologians of color on baptism, identity, and Christian practices to help establish the necessity of resisting abstraction in theological reflection, I then illustrate how this book's methodological approach of inclusive qualitative research helps expand the current field of disability theology.

Chapter 2 explores further details of the research process with my participants who witnessed to me through shared worship, storytelling, and reflection on baptism and its impact upon their lives. I offer a detailed discussion of my process for designing and implementing a theological research process with disabled and nondisabled participants focused on access. The second half of the chapter is dedicated to exploring the main descriptive findings of the research project. Here I present key stories, themes, and interpretations emerging from the research interviews and times of participant observation, including participant descriptions of baptism, core commitments to community, Jesus, and materiality in baptismal identity, meaningful baptismal practices, as well as resonances between Christian Scripture and baptismal imagination.

In chapters 3 and 4, guided by the witness of this project's research participants, I highlight areas of Christian Scripture related to baptism, and my participants' interpretations of these passages, as they raise new questions at the nexus of disability, identity, and Christian practice. In chapter 3 this exploration focuses on the Gospel accounts of Jesus' baptism and Paul's understanding of baptism throughout his New Testament letters as sources of thinking more expansively about baptismal identity, with attention to how a disability perspective enriches the impact of these passages upon Christian community. In chapter 4, again guided by insights from my research partners, I argue that Paul's construction of human identity in relationship to baptism, particularly his framework of "new creation" in 2 Corinthians 5, provides important insights for how disability theologians, as well as how contemporary Christian churches, imagine identity for all the baptized.

We turn from the biblical text to baptismal liturgies in chapter 5 in order to analyze, critique, and expand how baptismal liturgies might support Christian imagination with regard to identity among people with intellectual disabilities. In conversation with liturgical theologians, my research partners' experiences, and the 1979 *Book of Common Prayer*'s rite of "Holy Baptism," we will explore how liturgical forms open fresh theological insights about the communally constitutive work of liturgical participation as it relates to the belonging of all the baptized.

Building upon insights for refining and transforming baptismal liturgies in chapter 5, chapter 6 considers concrete practices of baptism within the lives of people with intellectual disabilities. In this chapter, I expand upon the insights of my research participants to advance practical frameworks related to accessibility, pastoral care, and ecumenical sensitivity. In addition, I highlight how the lives of people with intellectual disabilities present both possible challenges and expanded opportunities related to baptismal practices. I also offer further discussion of how baptismal practices can support the renewal of ecclesial perspectives on baptismal identity at the heart of embracing the gifts and vocation of all the baptized, especially people with intellectual disabilities.

Finally, in chapter 7, the witness of my research participants will illustrate rich avenues for cultivating belonging and careful attention to the work of the Holy Spirit in the lives of the baptized body. Focusing on the practices of baptismal preparation, baptismal testimony, and baptismal reaffirmation, this constructive chapter seeks to enliven readers' imaginations about the possibilities for embracing communal baptismal identity and its accompanying practices that strengthen communal belonging. Our theological exploration of ecclesial wounds will come to its conclusion with the stories of my coresearchers. They proclaim to us new ways to embrace the powerful work of the Holy Spirit in making us a "new creation" baptismal people.

1

Entering the Conversation

As we saw in the opening story of Hallie's repeated denials of baptism, Christian ecclesial communities often fail to cultivate spaces of belonging for people with intellectual disabilities. What lies at the root of these difficulties to form communities marked by belonging, neighbor love, and hospitality for all of God's people? And what faithful responses might theologians and churches embrace to turn toward patterns of baptismal belonging?

In this chapter, I begin with an exploration of how many Christian theological accounts of intellectual disability tend toward abstraction—creating a disjuncture between theological propositions and core Christian practices. Drawing upon literature at the nexus of Christian identity, the racial imagination, and baptism, I highlight further evidence regarding the dangers of theological abstraction as it relates to the creation of ecclesial imagination around anthropology—what it means to be a human being before God. These accounts of Christian identity as they relate to core ecclesial practices will also give us a clearer view of the ecclesial exclusion experienced among many people with intellectual disabilities.

After attending to these questions regarding theological abstraction, I next highlight how theologians of intellectual disability have attempted to bring together Christian doctrine and practice. To do so, I explore three key themes in Christian theological accounts of intellectual disability: God's image, friendship, and the inclusion paradigm. I illustrate how these key themes resist both theological abstraction as well as practices of ecclesial exclusion, instead encouraging communal transformation through a commitment to the centrality of Christian identity among people across the spectrum of disability identities. We will also survey existing work in contemporary theology that addresses the intersections of baptism and disability. Beginning with historical theological analyses, followed by denominational perspectives on the intersections of baptism and disability, we will uncover the pressing need for new ways of doing theology, rooted in practice and disability experience, that not only resist theological abstraction but usher us into a more expansive appreciation of the work of the Holy Spirit in enabling all the baptized for ministry.

As we enter existing conversations at the nexus of theology and disability throughout this chapter, I will seek to highlight the growing need to prioritize collaborative modes of theologizing. In other words, I will suggest that theological exploration in close partnership with people experiencing intellectual disabilities, within and through ecclesial wounds, uncovers previously underexplored insights and constructive practices. This approach to the work of theology both resists abstraction and provides a critical avenue for reshaping the church's theological imagination. I close this chapter with an introduction to my distinctive methodological approach to the work of theologizing together in and through disability experience.

THE CHALLENGE OF THEOLOGICAL ABSTRACTION

Reflections on disability in contemporary theological scholarship seek to offer an expansive theological anthropology. These theological explorations of disability look to support the belonging of disabled people within ecclesial settings and the recognition of disabled people as faith leaders. A natural question arises when surveying these texts in the field of disability theology—what kind of on-the-ground practices accompany theological anthropologies informed by disability, enabling belonging and inclusion within congregations? How do themes of the *imago Dei* and friendship connect to, challenge, and even enhance core practices of the Christian faith? How do these theological accounts of disability resonate with the grammar and distinct lived practices of Christian discipleship?

In her assessment of the field of disability theology, Jill Harshaw laments a persistent and "inadequate connection between theological theory and ecclesial practices."[1] As Harshaw argues, the insufficient connections between theological propositions and Christian practice result in minimal transformation within contemporary ecclesial communities with regard to disability. To put it differently, without robust connections to core church practices, theological accounts of disability, even those rooted in distinctively Christian accounts of the *imago Dei*, friendship, and inclusion, largely fail to support transformation of churches' lived practices. Even within congregations that are alive to needed practices of repentance and transformation related to the belonging of people with disabilities, guarding against potential discrepancies between theological proposals and Christian practices remains crucial: cultivating ongoing connections at the theology-practice nexus allows communities to remain attuned to God's ongoing work in their midst, as well as the theological and pastoral necessity of grounding theology in practice.[2]

Without an explicit connection to practices, imagination about identity within Christian communities is left vulnerable to the priorities of modern Western liberal democracies. As we explored in this book's introduction, the priorities of contemporary Western societies often imagine people with intellectual disabilities as dispensable within the context of community life. As a result, churches struggle to inhabit an imagination that envisions the core practices of their life together supporting the full flourishing and meaningful participation of people with disabilities. A disconnection between ecclesial practices and theological claims renders churches diminished in their capacity to recognize and affirm the discipleship of people with intellectual disabilities.

The disjuncture between core Christian practices and theological propositions produces a resultant theological abstraction within some contemporary theological accounts of disability. As I have suggested here, the abstraction of theological reflection from ecclesial practices is not only a problem in scholarly methodology—theological abstraction also poses a quandary and even a danger for Christian communities. When practices and lived experiences of disability are avoided, or addressed only anecdotally, they fail to sustain interpretive weight that can shape a community's core practices as well as their imagination about disability. Theological abstraction results in an impoverished ecclesial imagination about the work of the Holy Spirit among all the baptized. In short, without robust connections between practice and doctrine, Christian communities remain entrenched in patterns of belonging that relegate disabled people to marginalized positions within the church, or worse, exclude them entirely.

Defining Core Christian Practices

Before further exploring the dangers of theological abstraction as it relates to cultivating communities of belonging, I want to make explicit what I mean by the core or key practices of Christian ecclesial life. Craig Dykstra and Dorothy Bass offer a general definition of Christian practices as "things Christian people do together over time to address fundamental human needs in response to and in light of God's active presence for the life of the world."[3] These Christian practices encompass a wide range of faithful actions in a life of following Jesus, such as keeping the Sabbath, practicing hospitality, offering healing, making pilgrimage, and initiating discernment. They also include practices related to worship and liturgical expression: confession, repentance, giving, and singing.

But what constitutive practices sit at the heart of Christian discipleship? In other words, what core practices orient, ground, and shape distinctively Christian embodiments of the practices such as hospitality and healing mentioned above? I understand core ecclesial practices as those that sustain and constitute the corporate worship of Christian communities—the foundational practices that help Christians praise God and attend to God's ongoing work in the world. In short, key ecclesial practices are the basic yet distinctive things that suggest membership in a Christian community.[4]

These orienting practices of Christian life are prayer, the sacraments (Eucharist and baptism), and practices of receiving and proclaiming Christian Scripture.[5] Within these key Christian practices, baptism is distinctive in providing the constitutive practice that joins the lives of Christians with the life of Jesus Christ, through Jesus' death and resurrection as Paul describes in Romans 6. Baptism is an initiation into Jesus' body and the church. In this way, baptism as a core ecclesial practice provides both initial connection as well as ongoing orientation to a life of discipleship joined to Jesus' death and resurrection.⁶ Baptism establishes the individual lives of Christians and the communal life of the baptized body in the hope of new creation and new life, rooted in Jesus' resurrection.⁷

THE DISTORTION OF IDENTITY IN CHRISTIAN PRACTICE

As I will illustrate in this section, issues related to theological abstraction cannot simply be solved by an uncritical invocation of core ecclesial practices. In other words, Christian practices do not automatically bring about faithful transformation. Because of sin, distinctive Christian practices, including baptism, hold a "propensity for violence, for curvature, for being exploited for the perpetuation of damage."⁸ This capacity for deformation within the practices of Christian communities should alert us to carefully consider how the bringing together of theological propositions with lived practice might contribute to the destruction, rather than the healing, of community. We will survey here how theological abstraction can shape ecclesial imagination about identity, and subsequently, ecclesial practices. These accounts not only make clearer the troublesome history of ecclesial exclusion emerging from theological abstraction and the deformation of Christian practices, but also press us further into the urgency to bring together doctrine and practice in exploring the nexus of disability and theology.

Historical and Contemporary Examples: Deformation of Identity in Baptismal Practice

In *The Black Christ*, theologian Kelly Brown Douglas exposes how dominant social imaginaries regarding identity shaped Christian practices within the nineteenth-century white, evangelical culture of the American South. In the sphere of "slaveholding Christianity," Douglas notes the distortion of baptismal practices in order to ensure "the slaves understood baptism was not synonymous with earthly freedom."⁹ In order to maintain the status quo of an anthropology that designated those of African descent as subhuman, enslaved people were forced to publicly affirm baptism as a ritual "merely for the good of [their Souls]" rather than a promise of freedom "from the Duty and Obedience you owe to your Master while you live."[10] This sobering example of ritual manipulation illustrates not only the power of social imaginaries about human identity to shape ecclesial practice, but also the grave dangers of theological abstraction.

In Douglas' account of baptismal practices in the context of "slaveholding Christianity" in the American South, white slaveholding Christians held to theological propositions about freedom in Christ. This commitment to freedom extended to their theologies of baptism, yet for those they held captive as enslaved people, the theological centrality of freedom in Christ became partial and strictly spiritual in nature. Allegiance to societal norms surrounding slavery bolstered an imagination about human identity that blocked their ability to hold together a theological commitment to freedom in Christ with ecclesial and social practices that would have enacted freedom for those held in captivity.

M. Shawn Copeland also analyzes the deeply disrupted practices of baptism in the context of slavery in the American South. Copeland contends that white slaveholders bristled at the theological underpinning of baptism: the affirmation that all human beings share a common, nonviolable, and nonhierarchical nature. This radical theological assertion rooted in baptism—that slaves and slaveholders alike share a mutual human identity—"represented a threat to the power differential, which sustained the positions of master and slave."[11] However, this baptismal pressure on the dominant anthropological imaginary of the historical American South did not ultimately change the course of white evangelical practices; white slaveholders continued to subject the people they enslaved to distorted practices of baptism, resonant with no measure of earthly freedom.

The baptismal practices among slaveholders in the historical American South did not serve a theological telos of affirming the *imago Dei* and freedom in Christ at the heart of the Holy Spirit's proclamatory work in baptism; instead, these practices, abstracted from their theological roots, "sought to unmake the God-image of Africans."[12] Affirming theological commitments to freedom within ecclesial practices of baptism was so threatening to a group of Virginian Anglicans in the time period of slavery in the American South that parishioners threatened to kill their priest after he officiated a baptismal service where both enslaved Black children and free white children were baptized at the same time.[13]

Demonstrating the impact on baptismal practices from theologies embedded within colonial missionary work among European Christians, both within the historical United States and beyond, Willie James Jennings argues that a narrative of whiteness becomes the primary way to tell the story of all people, including their lands and ways of life.[14] In this formative narrative of whiteness, baptism becomes a practice through which homogeneity rather than diversity is affirmed and perpetuated. Just as the anthropological imaginaries among white slaveholding Christians displaced theological affirmations of Christ's freedom imparted to all the baptized, Jennings contends that the narrative of whiteness resists baptism as a radical practice of belonging—the Triune God's work of drawing together in Jesus' body those who were once far apart.

In baptisms abstracted from the theological centrality of belonging in Jesus' body, Jennings contends that we rob this ecclesial practice from its central message of joining in Jesus' suffering, death, and resurrection life.[15] In other words, theological abstraction leads to a hyperemphasis on the local particularity of the baptizand being drawn into the body of Jesus, without an affirmation of the new life and radical integration into the body of Jesus at the heart of the church's practice of making Christians.[16] When our theologies do not align with the core practices of Christian life, our imaginations about our neighbors' identities become distorted. And yet, even when we seek intentional integration of theology and practice, the practices of our faith remain vulnerable to what Lauren Winner names as "sin's wiliness"[17]—the propensity for distortion shared across all creation on this side of God's good future—even in our enactment of core practices of the Christian faith.

With American slavery as just one example, popular ways of imagining the foundations of human worth and identity directly influence access to and participation in Christian practices of baptism. As we will see, despite theological commitments embodied in signage and website headings that declare "all are welcome here!" or "come as you are, no exceptions," many ecclesial practices remain abstracted from these theological commitments to Christian hospitality. This form of theological abstraction leads to belonging within church communities marked by readily apparent affinities. For those without readily apparent affinities to an existing congregation, such as people with intellectual disabilities, only a restricted welcome may be extended (if any welcome is offered at all). As popular societal imaginaries about human identity come into competition with theological affirmations about human identity before God, Christian practices of welcome often illustrate where the allegiance of a community lies. Communities marked by homogenous belonging, to the exclusion of disabled people, illustrate another reality of the dangers of theological abstraction.

In relationship to Christian practices of baptism, Western liberal democratic constructions of human identity often spur questions regarding the appropriateness of baptism for some people with intellectual disabilities.[18] Theologians of disability note that debates regarding the administration of the sacrament or ordinance of baptism among people with intellectual disabilities are not only a problem of modernity: both Catholic and Protestant traditions offer historical evidence of debates regarding access to baptism among people with cognitive impairments.[19] Churches in the post-Enlightenment era, especially traditions aligned with credobaptism, must contend with the heightened importance of intellectual assent as it relates to their baptismal practices.[20] Even in the context of paedobaptist traditions, when individuals with intellectual disabilities may be baptized as an infant or young child, the promises of post-baptismal support in a child's life may ring hollow—though someone is baptized, they find exclusion within their church community. Societal commitments to particular human cognitive capacities as central for human identity have led churches to dismiss people with intellectual disabilities from their ecclesial communities, or, such as in this book's opening story of Hallie and Heather, deny baptism.

In addition to Hallie and Heather's story, research partners for this book recalled to me painful stories of ecclesial exclusion and baptismal delay. Barbara, a faithful layperson in The Episcopal Church, recalled a pastor's wife approaching her when Barbara's young son with Down Syndrome, Bob, was three years old. The pastor's wife asked Barbara about her plans for Bob in the coming year when he would age out of the church's nursery program. Barbara reflected and responded: "I don't know. I mean . . . we will probably keep him in Sunday nursery school for a bit." The pastor's wife then firmly responded, "Well, Bob can't come to church anymore." Barbara was shocked. Her assumption about Bob's continued support needs were met not with hospitable grace, but frank rejection. Barbara conveyed to me that this was the first, but not last, experience of rejection she faced with Bob as they navigated finding a church home where they could belong and Bob could be baptized.

Steve, a teacher and lay leader, recounted to me a story about his experience as a regular guest preacher at First Avenue Baptist Church. Every time Steve preached at this church, he observed a young man with intellectual disabilities named Aaron who always "handed out bulletins at the back of the church, and helped ladies find their ways to the pews." After a multiple year relationship with this congregation, Steve asked the church's regular pastor whether or not Aaron had been baptized. The pastor answered quickly and emphatically: "Oh, no! We don't baptize intellectually disabled people." Steve pushed back: "Why don't you baptize Aaron? He obviously has a role within the congregation. He's a welcomer. Everyone knows him. Do you think he's supposed to know what is happening when he's baptized?"

This conversation sparked ongoing dialogue among multiple church leaders at First Avenue Baptist Church. Steve's questioning about Aaron's role in the congregation ultimately led the church leadership to discern that they would proceed with Aaron's baptism. After the baptism, Steve remembers speaking with Aaron's parents who were absolutely overjoyed. But, as Steve recounts, Aaron's parents had remained silent for years about their deep desire for Aaron's baptism: "they had never wanted to make it a controversial matter."

Another story emerged during my conversation with a United Methodist pastor named Ambrose. Ambrose discussed with me the formation of some of his initial questions about baptism. At the time, Ambrose was a young adult attending a nondenominational church where "baptism was always presented as this choice that you must make. You must rationally say you understand you are a sinner and that you have put your faith in Jesus." At this same time in his young adulthood, Ambrose worked as a caregiver at a group home for adults with significant intellectual disabilities. Ambrose lovingly remembered one particular resident he worked with:

> A guy named Fred. It was my job to watch John Wayne movies with him. Make a meal. Take him to the bathroom. Clean him. Shower him. Get him ready for bed. Drive him to dialysis.... and it occurred to me with Freddie, one day in the shower—water! It was like "aha!"—Fred is never going to walk down the aisle in our church and say "I've decided to give my life to Jesus. I want to be baptized."

Reflecting on this reality in Fred's life as a nonspeaking adult with intellectual disabilities, Ambrose continued,

> The math worked out real quick for me that my church's baptismal theology did not have room for someone like Fred. They would say: "he doesn't need to be baptized." I knew that the baptismal theology I had been given did not have room for people with disabilities. And that really set me on a hunt. It was Fred that taught me that my theology of baptism was too shallow. God has shown me that God's baptismal theology is really for all of God's people—all of God's children.

RESISTING DISTORTED ACCOUNTS OF IDENTITY: APPROACHES FROM THE FIELD OF DISABILITY THEOLOGY

In response to contemporary emphases on autonomy, rationality, and intellect at the heart of Western ecclesial anthropologies that distort Christian practices, many disability theologians have taken up the task of reimagining theological anthropology, identity, and Christian practice for "all of God's children." Even outside of the field of disability theology, theological accounts of Christian identity informed by disability have been offered in service of resisting theological abstraction. For example, in her constructive work on Christian identity, Medi Ann Volpe considers an expanded vision of Christian identity that maintains classical descriptions of faith and practice, but includes "those whose ability to practice or express the faith is limited."[21] Volpe's reimagined account of Christian identity holds together theological doctrine and practice by stressing the centrality of formation: the lifelong journey of following Jesus in Christian community.[22] For Volpe, narrating Christian identity through a framework of discipleship squares doctrine with an ongoing, relational practice of formation that centers God's creative work in uniting Christians to Christ in the Holy Spirit.[23] The relational and theocentric embodiment of doctrine in practices of Christian formation begins at baptism, unfolding within a lifetime of baptismal living.

Volpe's effort to reframe Christian identity through an integrative account of Christian doctrine and practice provides an example of the kind of work that theologians writing about intellectual disability have also attempted to produce. Theological accounts of identity in the field of disability theology, in their resistance of theological abstraction, draw together theological propositions with suggestions for embodied Christian praxis. These integrative proposals rely on thematic frameworks that emphasize concepts such as human vulnerability, limitation, and interdependence. In the following section, I will attend to four prominent themes within contemporary, theological reflection on intellectual disability: God's image, friendship, inclusion, and embodiment. In exploring these four themes, we will attend to how these accounts attempt to resist damaging imaginaries about human identity as well as how they seek to bridge Christian doctrine and practice.

The Invocation of the Image of God

In theological writings focused on intellectual disability, many authors explore the image of God as somehow normative for their claims related to Christian identity. Through careful attention to defining the *imago Dei*, disability theologians attempt to turn from the notion of God's image as intrinsically connected to individual human capacity.[24] Instead, disability theologians advance a relational and egalitarian theological foundation for God's image that firmly situates disabled people as image bearers equal with nondisabled people. This equality in bearing the *imago Dei*, regardless of disability status, calls for practices of care, dignity, and respect, in both ecclesial settings and beyond.[25]

Theologians Amos Yong, Tom Reynolds, and Hans Reinders each advocate for a "relational" account of the *imago Dei* in their theological accounts of intellectual disability. This relational understanding of God's image seeks to move beyond structural (or substantive) perspectives—theologies of God's image that prioritize inherent human characteristics such as cognitive capabilities and morality as somehow reflective of God's nature.[26] A relational vision of the *imago Dei* also diverges from a functional perspective, which understands not only innate human capacities as a necessary component of imaging God, but also prioritizes participation in responsible dominion over nonhuman creation—the image of God manifests itself in what human creatures actually *do*.[27]

Yong champions a Christological view of God's image, working from Scripture's emphasis on Jesus as "*the* image of the invisible God."[28] With this Christological focus, Yong proposes:

> The imago Dei is less about some constitutive element of the human person and more about God's revelation in Christ and in the faces of our neighbors; yet the life of Jesus provides a normative account of what it means to be human, and the Holy Spirit creatively enables and empowers our full humanity in relationship to ourselves, others, and God, even in the most ambiguous of situations.[29]

Similarly, Thomas Reynolds also offers a relational narration of the *imago Dei*, arguing that God's image is constituted by three key dimensions: human openness to creativity with others, relation to others, and availability for others.[30] For Reynolds, this theological affirmation of the image of God calls forth human imitation: "the *imago Dei* as *imitatio Dei*."[31] Imaging God by imitating God requires actions equally accessible among people with intellectual disabilities as well as nondisabled people: an openness to others, being in relation with human neighbors, and finally, being available for others. Reynolds' doctrine of God's image becomes embodied in human neighbor relations that seek to imitate God's radical openness and availability.

Hans Reinders nuances a relationally grounded notion of God's image, arguing that the *imago Dei* exists completely *external* to human creatures. God's image is rooted in the Christian doctrine of the Trinity. The Triune God's community of love, which lovingly spills into the lives of human creatures as God's children, replaces human characteristics or capacities as the constitutive foundation of God's image.[32] This theological understanding of God's image calls forth Christian practices that seek friendship between disabled and nondisabled people in a pattern that parallels God's Triune community of love that spills into the lives of God's human creatures. These friendships among people of various disabilities enliven Christian imagination about identity as rooted in reciprocal and bidirectional relationships rather than particular human capacities such as intellectual acumen.

The Friendship Framework

As we see emerging in Reinders' account of the *imago Dei*, relational accounts of the *imago Dei* in disability theology often parallel strong emphases on friendship between human neighbors. Reinders and Jason Greig both advance a concept of friendship that centers relational practices marked by bidirectional vulnerability as a key avenue for constructing an alternative imagination about Christian identity that resists the contemporary primacy of individualization and efficiency in accounts of human identity.[33]

Reinders, building on previous work from Stanley Hauerwas, offers the foundational argument for friendship as the key element of thinking faithfully about intellectual disability. Reinders asserts that friendship constitutes "the ultimate good of being human."[34] This teleological reorientation toward friendship roots human dignity and identity in being received by God and others, rather than identity based in a particular set of capacities. Considering the reality that God chooses to befriend human beings, Reinders claims that friendship with other human beings is the core vocation of Christians.[35] As we explored above, a triune understanding of God's nature establishes God's relationship of unconditional and loving friendship with human beings.[36] Reinders highlights the incarnation as the fullest expression of this love between God and human creatures.[37] For Reinders, a commitment to the theological proposal that all human creatures receive the Triune God's unconditional love presses Christians to embrace practices of celebration. Friendships provide the most fitting context to practice the celebration of difference and encounter love.[38]

Building on the foundational arguments around friendship advanced by Reinders, Jason Greig's work on friendship and disability draws upon the witness of L'Arche communities.[39] Like Reinders, Greig offers a theological account of friendship as an open and mutually transformational relationship marked by hospitality to all people, regardless of disability identity.[40] For Greig, relationships of friendship find their roots in the Christian telos of friendship with God,[41] as well as an ecclesiology that understands the church as a community of friends.[42] The theological understanding of church as a "community of friends" grounds Greig's related affirmations of Christian identity: rather than defining human identity around capacities or achievements, being human is "a gift granted by God within the relationships in the community of the church."[43] Beyond affirming this theological perspective on the nature of the church, Greig advances a Christian praxis of receiving and honoring others as gifts, rather than receiving and honoring others based on achievement.

The Inclusion Paradigm

Theological reflection on inclusion, often intersecting with considerations of God's image and friendship, constitutes another major theme in theologies of intellectual disability. Scholars who center an inclusion paradigm, including Erik Carter and Jill Harshaw, help suggest practices of formation that allow communities to imagine human identity in new ways. These practices of Christian formation bring to life what these scholars establish as the theological basis for belonging within ecclesial communities.

Erik Carter's interreligious work on inclusion emphasizes religious education programs as well as the importance of collaboration with service providers and other community allies.[44] For Carter, practicing inclusivity with regard to the spiritual needs of people with intellectual disabilities attends to a critical gap in contemporary faith communities.[45] Carter further contextualizes his inclusive approach, arguing that church leaders ought to facilitate conversations around inclusion utilizing both theological and biblical language. Making theological and Scriptural commitments to inclusion explicit within ecclesial dialogue not only affirms a community's theological commitments but helps embed inclusion in language and practice.[46]

Expanding on Carter's pragmatic approach to issues of inclusion among people with intellectual disabilities in faith settings, Harshaw centers her discussion of inclusion on the relationship of people with intellectual disabilities to God (not just other human neighbors).[47] Harshaw's engagement of an inclusion framework focuses her overarching argument about the accessibility of God: "ultimately, it is not human incapacity in any form that matters, but God's infinite capacity to accommodate his revelation to it."[48] Harshaw's theological claims about God's inclusive nature, manifest in God's revelatory accommodation to all people, connect to her recommendations for Christian practice. These practices include emphasizing God's connection to and empowerment of people with various disabilities in the sacraments, as well as in how churches pattern their lives after the Scriptural narrative of the Holy Spirit's work, expectant for how the Spirit may be at work in church members with even significant disabilities.

The Body in Disability Theology

One final approach to drawing together doctrine and practice within the contemporary field of disability theology has been a turn to the body. Embodied proclamations of God's love present sites for rich theological interpretation.[49] For example, Greig highlights how L'Arche communities regularly practice a sacred ritual of foot washing as a formative practice of hospitality that includes people living with profound disabilities.[50] This ritual of foot washing forms L'Arche communities not in patterns of intellectual assent, but rather, into an embodied *habitus* of love, friendship, and welcome.[51] Like Greig, Yong emphasizes the importance of kinesthetic practices and other forms of multisensory, nonverbal participation in the life of Christian worship and discipleship.[52] Yong later claims that people with disabilities in their presence and participation in church communities serve as "conduits for the presence and activity of Christ."[53]

From a Roman Catholic perspective, theologian Elizabeth Antus argues for renewed attention to embodied participation in the sacraments among people with and without disabilities "as a site of vulnerability, porosity, spontaneity, and sometimes even disruption."[54] Instead of perceiving disabled forms of liturgical participation as disruptions and "negative erosions" of Christian worship, Antus argues for a praxis of inclusion: "those whose bodies are despised and deemed out of control find special welcome in the sacraments, especially the Eucharist."[55] Frances Young, reflecting on the life of her son Arthur who lives with multiple disabilities, also argues that attending to the body is crucial for deciphering a diversity of ways to participate in Christian worship apart from intellectual understanding. Young illustrates how she witnesses Arthur being caught up in the inbreaking reign of God through silence, facial expressions, and rapture during music.[56]

The emphasis on bodily participation in Christian practice as a locus for theological reflection on disability resonates with Stanley Hauerwas' foundational claim that "liturgy is social action."[57] In other words, embodied participation in worship shapes Christians into who they are—Christians cannot be Christian without enacting the church's core practices. As such, Hauerwas proposes that people with intellectual disabilities provide a "test case" for Christian communities in their faithful telling of the Christian story—how are people with intellectual disabilities cared for in Christian communities? Are their bodies included in the practices of the church—especially worship, communion, and baptism?[58] And if they are included, does this inclusion explicitly resonate with core doctrinal commitments of the gathered community?

RECONCEIVING CHRISTIAN IDENTITY AND COMMUNITIES OF BELONGING: BAPTISM AS A BRIDGE

Throughout theological writings on disability, readers will intermittently encounter small excurses about core ecclesial practices such as baptism or Holy Communion. These anecdotal offerings can typically be found in brief concluding or constructive sections within larger arguments related to the themes we explored above: *imago Dei*, friendship, and inclusion.[59] Considering core Christian practices can help encourage new approaches to theological reflection that extend beyond strictly cognitive modes of theological work.[60] These anecdotes can also help spur imagination about lived practices within particular church communities. In order to illustrate the importance of Christian practices for theological reflection on disability, some scholars turn specifically to baptism to support their various claims: the primacy of God's prodigal hospitality,[61] the indispensability of disabled people for the life of the church,[62] baptism as the paradigmatic Christian sign of inclusion,[63] and baptism as a central illustration of the communal nature of the church's life of discipleship.[64] In the following subsections, we will explore article-length works that engage the specific intersections of disability and baptism, beginning with historical theological reflections on both Roman Catholic and Protestant thought, followed by contemporary reflections from denominationally specific resources. In these explorations, we will consider how accounts of baptism within theologies of disability act as a bridge in drawing together Christian doctrine and practice.

Analyses from Historical Theology

In *Disability in the Christian Tradition*, Miguel J. Romero writes on Thomas Aquinas' theological anthropology as it connects to the sacrament of baptism, focusing on the flourishing of those Aquinas considered *amens*: people who experience "a corporeal infirmity in which the lower powers of the human body necessary for the operation of reason (sensation and phantasm) do not cooperate with the immaterial intellect."[65] With careful caveats related to disability language and the nature of anachronism, Romero suggests that the *amens* in Aquinas' lifetime were similar to people with profound intellectual disabilities in contemporary Western societies.[66] Centrally, in Romero's interpretation of Aquinas, no experience of bodily affliction or disability can ultimately thwart friendship with God—the highest good and teleological end of human beings.[67] In Aquinas' sacramental theology, those who are baptized receive sanctifying and restorative grace to participate in this life of loving friendship with the Triune God.[68] Aquinas' baptismal logic underscores that the grace bestowed on human creatures in baptism does not depend upon a person's capacity for reason or intellectual understanding—it is bestowed through God's grace alone.[69] Romero's engagement of

Aquinas creates connections between the key theme of friendship in contemporary theologies of disabilities, while also situating this theme within a Thomistic theology and practice of baptism.

Richard Cross offers an additional account of Aquinas' view on baptism as it intersects with disability. Cross argues that while Aquinas affirms that the Holy Spirit imparts a "disposition of faith" to all the baptized, regardless of disability, individuals with profound impairments are unable to participate in "corresponding acts" of that faith, making necessary that these corresponding acts of faith come from other individuals, without profound disabilities, in the church.[70] In contrast to Aquinas, Cross reviews Duns Scotus' argument that the act of baptism itself imparts implicit faith which is sufficient for participation in faithful discipleship.[71] For Scotus, Cross suggests that the habit of faith initiated in baptism does not consist of a cognitive state or conceptual understanding.[72] Cross concludes that Scotus helpfully critiques and expands Aquinas' baptismal theology, by suggesting that no person, regardless of disability, is reliant on the faith of another for the completion of their salvation—even those with the profoundest impairments participate in a reciprocal relationship with God by nature of their baptism.[73]

Finally, Harshaw explores the baptismal logic of Reformation theologians through a disability hermeneutic, resisting the notion that cognitive capacities are necessary for salvation. She highlights Martin Luther's claim that demonstrating a volitional act of faith should not serve as a deciding factor when discerning if someone ought to receive baptism.[74] Harshaw also expands on Luther's notion of *fides aliena* as a relevant baptismal concept for constructing a theology of disability inclusive of people with more profound intellectual disabilities.[75] She defines *fides aliena* as faith which "originates in God, outside the individual" without requirement of "any overt response to revelation."[76] Harshaw argues that any lack of perceptible evidence of the faithfulness of people with intellectual disabilities does not negate the effects of baptism, nor does it disqualify these people from rich relationships with God.

These explorations of historical Christian theologies of baptism as they relate to people with intellectual disabilities share an emphasis on affirming the longstanding Christian practice of baptizing people with significant intellectual disabilities (as well as this practice's theological justification). Drawing on the witness of Christian leaders and theologians throughout the centuries, these scholarly works highlight redefined boundaries about baptismal qualification and what counts as faith, demonstrating a thoroughgoing commitment to God's grace as the efficacious action in the Christian practice of baptism. Extending the arguments of these historical Christian voices, we will turn now to more contemporary reflections from specific denominational writings that address the intersections of disability and baptism.

Denominational Reflections at the Intersection of Sacraments and Intellectual Disability

The Roman Catholic tradition, in addition to a wealth of general resources on engaging disabled people in the life of the church,[77] contributes several notable resources at the intersection of baptism and the lives of people with intellectual disabilities in Edward Foley's edited volume *Developmental Disabilities and Sacramental Access: New Paradigms for Sacramental Encounters*. Paul Wadell's essay in this collection frames baptism as rooted in God's action in Jesus Christ, rather than human merits that warrant the reception of baptism.[78] In contrast to a framework that emphasizes human understanding as necessary to approach the divine, Wadell emphasizes God's action to extend God's accessible love to all human creatures.[79] Mark Francis embraces a similar emphasis in his essay on shifts in sacramental theology after the Second Vatican Council, arguing that assent to propositional theology does not bear on the efficacy of baptism. This efficacy rests alone in the sufficiency of God's action in Jesus.[80] In contrast to intellectual understanding, participation in baptism generates embodied knowledge, nondependent on "analytic, linear, and logical" ways of knowing.[81] This accounting of baptismal theology calls forth baptismal celebrations among people with and without disabilities that emphasize God's action and reflect God's sacramental work of grace in everyday human life.[82]

John M. Huels, O.S.M., argues that the Catholic Church's tradition of baptizing infants who "lack the use of reason" makes it clear that baptism affirms all people as God's children, regardless of particular capacities and abilities.[83] Joseph Bernardin also calls churches to welcome people with intellectual disabilities as full and equal participants in the baptismal and broader liturgical life of the church.[84] In this way, Bernardin frames ecclesial practices of baptism with people experiencing intellectual disabilities as a challenge for church communities: if disabled people are not included in the church's sacramental life, where else might they find meaningful belonging?[85] Bernardin argues for nourishment of the baptismal identity of all people through practices of accessible catechesis as well as flexible opportunities for liturgical participation.[86] In sum, Bernardin's account draws upon the importance of embodied experience, a key theme connecting doctrine and practice in contemporary theologies of intellectual disability.

In addition to these perspectives from Roman Catholicism, contemporary Protestant faith leaders offer insight to theological and pastoral questions related to baptism and intellectual disability. Melissa Florer-Bixler, a Mennonite pastor and longtime participant in the disability community, draws attention to pressing questions related to disability and baptism within credobaptist traditions, such as: what does the acknowledgment of repentance and the reception of forgiveness mean among adults without symbolic language and reasoning skills that allow for grasping concepts such as sin and evil?[87] Florer-Bixler invites a shift away from evaluating the cognitive capabilities among individuals with intellectual disabilities as part of discerning baptism, appealing to the witness of Scripture: "baptism makes us into the people of God by compromising all competing allegiances to God's kingdom. The Gospels tell us that rival allegiances include family, nation, wealth, and even capabilities."[88] In this baptismal making of community, the gifts of all the baptized are welcomed to contribute to God's ongoing work in the world. For adults with profound intellectual disabilities, Florer-Bixler emphasizes their particular gifts to the building of God's work within the world as dependence and vulnerability.[89] In light of this gift framework, Florer-Bixler argues that a community's discernment of an individual's gifts for "conforming the church more closely to the image of God," and not a particular verbal confession of faith, ought to be the primary indication for baptismal readiness.

In another article concerning intellectual disability, Florer-Bixler advances a proposal for situating noncoercive moral formation at the center of baptismal practices and theologies, rather than cognitive assent.[90] Florer-Bixler roots this argument within critiques of the elevation of cognitive ability, found both in Menno Simon's 1539 treatise *Concerning Baptism*, as well as the contemporary concept of supported decision-making for individuals with intellectual disabilities.[91] Since moral formation in Christian community is never a solitary endeavor, Florer-Bixler illustrates how a communal "supported decision" framework for baptism is called forth from the witness of people with intellectual disabilities, but is an appropriate framing of baptism for all people. She writes, "baptism is for all people, regardless of their intellectual capacity, a supported decision. They are assisted into moral formation by witnessing and mimicking the faith of those who make up the church."[92]

Offering another perspective, Greig suggests that the experiences of people with intellectual disabilities challenge churches in the Anabaptist tradition to reimagine their theologies and practices of baptism. Greig puts forth three ways to reimagine this nexus of baptismal theology and practice, informed by disability: reemphasize the centrality of God's action in baptism, recenter the church (vs. individual self-consciousness) as the subject of faith, and reenliven rich symbols and embodied modes of participation in the ordinance of baptism.[93] Greig's article does not advocate for a complete deconstruction or erasure of Anabaptist theological convictions. Rather, Greig helpfully demonstrates how considering the experiences of people with more profound intellectual disabilities can assist in the process of reinterpreting doctrinal commitments, and in turn, make constructive suggestions for Christian practice.

Jason Whitt, a theologian and Baptist pastor, raises similar questions to Florer-Bixler and Greig in his essay on profound intellectual disability and baptism. Whitt asks, if baptism is symbolic of a preexisting volitional act of obedience to Jesus, what is the place of people with profound intellectual disabilities in credobaptist traditions?[94] Whitt argues that the ordinance of baptism reinforces the belonging of all baptized people within a church community, as well as forms a church's identity as people who live in the life, death, and resurrection of Christ.⁹⁵ For Whitt, these practices of belonging and formation are not merely symbolic in nature. He is therefore advancing a sacramental account of the credobaptist tradition.

Additionally, Whitt challenges arguments within credobaptist traditions that equate the baptism of nonspeaking adults experiencing intellectual disabilities with the practice of baptizing infants.⁹⁶ Churches welcoming people with profound intellectual disabilities do not anticipate a day when these people will make obedient and volitional faith commitments with symbolic language. Instead, like Florer-Bixler and Greig, Whitt challenges churches to carefully attend to the gifts, presence, and teaching brought forth by people with intellectual disabilities, instead of narrowly focusing on their capacity for spoken profession of faith.⁹⁷ To spur his readers' imaginations, Whitt offers a nonexhaustive list of what some of these gifts among people with intellectual disabilities might be: a presence marked by silent ministry, distinctive gentleness, an enhanced capacity for wonder, or the gift of peace.⁹⁸

In conclusion, Whitt humbly suggests that churches in the credobaptist tradition ought to joyfully baptize those with profound disabilities as a way for the believing community to together affirm not only the person's gifts but also their unique place of belonging in Jesus' body.⁹⁹ Practicing baptism among nonspeaking people with intellectual disabilities within Baptist traditions provides a practice of radical belonging for all followers of Jesus, a commitment Whitt emphasizes in its consonance with traditional Baptist tenants of baptism. Whitt understands the complexities of his exhortation and concludes his essay by encouraging credobaptist communities to take up his suggestions within the context of significant local discernment and reflection.¹⁰⁰

A final denominational resource that addresses baptism and disability comes from Myk Habets, a reformed scholar in the paedobaptist tradition. Habets explores questions about baptism among people with profound intellectual disabilities in light of Paul's vision of justification by faith in Romans 5. In resonance with other thinkers in both contemporary and historical theological contexts, Habets argues that in baptism the faith of Jesus is the faith that is sufficient and effective, for both disabled and nondisabled people of all ages.[101] For Habets, this Christological view of faith clarifies Paul's exhortations to the Romans about the nature of their baptismal lives of transformation—the faith of Christ is the source of the transformed postbaptismal life.[102] Building on this account of faith, Habets emphasizes that people with profound disabilities should be baptized as a strong witness to the inclusion of all of God's children in God's covenant of grace. Habets demonstrates an approach of drawing together biblical theology to bear upon ecclesial practices in a way that faithfully responds to disability.

Throughout these denominational resources, we see a common pattern emerge: countering realities of ecclesial exclusion among disabled people through theological, scriptural, and pastoral justifications for access to and robust participation in baptismal life. Across both traditions of paedobaptism and credobaptism, a unified call to baptize people with even the profoundest disabilities emerges. These authors share a compelling vision of a church where people with intellectual disabilities participate alongside all other baptizands in the community of God's people—a community initiated, sustained, and empowered by the love and action of the Triune God. For these scholars, the Christian practice of baptism offers a bridge between upholding doctrine and cultivating vibrant church communities of belonging for people with disabilities.

CONSIDERING A NEW APPROACH: MY METHODOLOGICAL INTERVENTION IN DISABILITY THEOLOGY

As I have highlighted above, the lives of people with intellectual disabilities provide a source of significant theological reflection, especially within contemporary theological scholarship. Additionally, questions of how baptismal practices intersect with disability experiences raise new questions for theological reflection among modern scholars and pastors. Why might more need to be said? And what sources for offering integrative theological proposals remain untapped or underexplored?

Though the vast majority of the theological accounts of disability in this chapter flow out of meaningful and prolonged personal experience with disabled Christians, or even authorial identity as a disabled person, the primary conversation partners engaged throughout published scholarship continue to be acknowledged sources of authority from the academy and church. In addition to resisting theological abstraction by bridging together Christian theological proposals with core ecclesial practices, my reading of scholarship within the field of disability theology highlights the need for inquiry driven by disabled Christians—centering their theological reflections, their stories, and their practices. This notable gap in existing scholarship asks for a new kind of theological methodology—one that allows the stories, experiences, and theological reflections of disabled Christians to drive and orient arguments, and to respond to, challenge, and expand existing authoritative work within the Christian tradition.

In the pages that follow, this is indeed the methodological challenge I choose to take up. By employing an approach of theological qualitative research, I seek to discover and describe core theological commitments and practices surrounding baptism among Christians with intellectual disabilities. My method, however, does not end with description alone. Partnering with my research participants, disabled Christians as well as their loved ones and pastors, I place their claims about baptism into dialogue with existing theological scholarship in order to raise new integrative theological proposals about Christian identity and practice. The questions, critiques, and new directions I propose, therefore, are not mine alone to claim. They instead illustrate the fruit of theology done in partnership, and in particular, disabled partnership. This approach to theological scholarship intervenes in the field of disability theology not only as a method for counteracting theological abstraction, but also as an embodiment of theologizing together in and through Christian experiences of disability.

My approach of theological qualitative inquiry provides a communal avenue into situations of woundedness. As we will explore in the next chapter, this mode of doing theology honors and amplifies the lived experiences of my research partners. This collaborative approach to theological work resists abstraction and uncovers new sources of embodied wisdom. Attention to perspectives on baptismal theologies and practices among people with intellectual disabilities, their clergy, and their loved ones, will help us critically reflect on how theological understandings of Christian identity are worked out in baptismal practices, toward an end of supporting the church's embrace of the discipleship among all the baptized and cultivating communities of belonging across the disability spectrum.

CONCLUSION

As the theological accounts of disability above suggest, a turn to Christian practice yields emerging resources for faithful Christian praxis. Within theological work on disability that specifically considers the practice of baptism, we see general assertions that draw together doctrinal commitments with practical advice for the life of the church, such as encouragement to cultivate belonging, make catechesis accessible, and provide different avenues for liturgical participation among people with intellectual disabilities.

Yet despite these initial turns to Christian practice and subsequent arguments for the practices that constitute faithful application of these theological proposals, the reality of the continued disconnection between scholarly dialogue in disability theology and ecclesial transformation persists. The accounts we explored in this chapter raise necessary questions for future inquiry, but at times lack the specificity to invite readers into new ways of attending to God's work amidst their baptismal communities. And while anecdotes and first-person accounts from disabled individuals surface across many theologies of disability, issues of theological abstraction seem to persist.

The rallying cry of the disability rights movement in North America—"nothing about us without us"—still poses a notable challenge for theologians of intellectual disability.[103] How can theologies both resist abstraction while also privileging the perspectives of individuals with intellectual disabilities as sites of theological wisdom? What methods and approaches to bridging theological reflection and ecclesial practices can ensure that people with intellectual disabilities are serious and ongoing interlocutors?

In the next chapter, I take up this challenge by offering a theological methodology that both seeks to resist abstraction while also committing to the work of theologizing in close partnership with people experiencing intellectual disabilities. I will explore the methodological opportunities, challenges, and questions that arise through a more intentional partnership with people with intellectual disabilities in the work of integrating theological theory and practice. In addition to navigating the pragmatic contours of participatory and qualitative theological research, my primary focus will be delving further into firsthand accounts of how my research partners with intellectual disabilities, as well as their loved ones and clergy, embody baptismal theologies and practices as central to their identities as Christians.

My research partners' baptismal stories will serve as the primary hermeneutical lens through which we will consider disability and Christian identity in the remaining chapters of the book. Throughout these chapters, I illustrate how a baptismal hermeneutic emerging from theological coalitions among people with and without disabilities powerfully highlights God's work in contemporary church communities, a kind of work with the power to reframe and transform our considerations of disability and Christian identity. In turning to practices of baptism not only concerning people with intellectual disability, but storied with and by them, I argue for baptismal practices as a key avenue to the transformation of churches' imaginations about Christian identity, as well as pathways for the participation and flourishing of disabled people in contemporary congregations.

My research partners' baptismal stories from across the ecumenical spectrum thicken and concretize the key themes present in contemporary and historical theologies of intellectual disability. In addition, these stories from qualitative research raise new key themes for consideration in theological accounts of disability: engagement of Scripture beyond the *imago Dei*, particularly the story of Jesus' baptism and Paul's theology of participation, considering Christian practices as constitutive of Christian identity, and the role of communal participation in Christian practices for sustaining authentic belonging among all the baptized.

2

Drawing from a Multitude of Witnesses

The witnesses of others shape our vision of life together in Christian community. As we seek to embrace the witnesses of Christians with intellectual disabilities, how might we faithfully explore their perspectives? How might theological inquiry honor the disability community's call for "nothing about us without us"? And what ways of doing theology can robustly integrate theological propositions and lived practices in order to push against the abstraction we explored in chapter 1?

In this chapter, I will illustrate a theological research process rooted in qualitative methodologies in order to amplify the baptismal stories of people with intellectual disabilities. In addition to describing the pragmatic aspects of theological research in partnership with individuals with intellectual disabilities, this chapter will offer a first taste of the narrative themes and theological insights generated by people with intellectual disabilities, emerging from their own communities and experiences of baptismal vocation. These baptismal stories will become key conversation partners throughout the book's remaining chapters, as we explore how resisting theological abstraction through doing theology in partnership helps raise new critical categories for Christian life and theological reflection. Qualitative theological research provides one fitting pathway to not only richly describe lived baptismal theologies from a disability hermeneutic, but to also construct a witness that can challenge the parameters of our current imaginations. Drawing from a multitude of witnesses in this chapter will begin to enliven how we perceive and support the baptismal identity and discipleship of Christians with and without disabilities.

WHERE THIS CHAPTER WILL LEAD US

In this chapter, we will explore both my process for participating in theological qualitative research at the nexus of baptism and intellectual disability, as well as the key findings of this research partnership. Often referred to as the "ethnographic turn" in theology, I will demonstrate how this particular methodology offers an avenue for resisting theological abstraction by centering the witness of people with intellectual disabilities to break open new perspectives and practices for Christian communities who seek to more faithfully live out their baptismal vocations. In order to contextualize the firsthand accounts of baptism among my research partners, I will first offer a brief introduction to ethnographic research among Christian theologians and ethicists. Next, I will outline my particular framework for theological research within this broader turn to ethnography, exploring key opportunities and challenges that surface in the work of theological research in partnerships with people with intellectual disabilities. Before introducing you to my research partners and their baptismal stories, I will describe the methodological details of this particular project, including my approach to data collection and analysis, as well as my responsiveness to concerns related to research ethics and practices of self-reflexivity. The remainder of the chapter will be devoted to highlighting key categories of the research findings. This introductory overview will usher us into the forthcoming chapters, where we will draw on the insights generated among my research partners as they help expand and critique theological accounts of baptismal identity and formation—through scriptural imagination, liturgical participation, and lived baptismal practices.

THE "ETHNOGRAPHIC TURN" IN CHRISTIAN THEOLOGY

With goals of listening to the work of God in the everyday and probing sources beyond theological texts for critical analysis, Christian theologians and ethicists have increasingly turned to qualitative research methodologies to explore situations of woundedness.[1] Scholars engaging theology in this manner acknowledge the deeply formative practice of encountering individuals, communities, and situations in the context of qualitative inquiry. This inquiry spans a group of interrelated practices now largely accepted as a normative methodological approach in Christian theological and ethical inquiry: fieldwork, participant observation, participatory research, as well as diverse forms of qualitative interviewing.[2] The turn to qualitative methodology provides not only an avenue to take more seriously the lived experiences of individuals and ecclesial communities, but also a mode of theological inquiry that complexifies the privileges and assumptions held by many academics, through dialogue with populations traditionally underrepresented in theological work.

The turn to qualitative methodology in Christian theology and ethics helps us to imagine and enact forms of theologizing beyond texts alone. In the ethnographic turn, the richness of human experience is brought forth as a site for theological reflection. The everyday lives and practices of Christians provide the space where theological ethnographers seek to listen to the work of God and to make evident how theological commitments find their grounding.[3] In this way, theology's ethnographic turn holds a deep commitment to drawing theological reflections out of the complexities of lived reality—a process that often prevents the theological abstraction we considered in the previous chapter.[4]

Many Christian scholars who engage theological qualitative research seek to support church communities in their faithful performance of the Gospel.[5] My attention to stories of baptism as experienced by people with intellectual disabilities, their clergy, and their loved ones, seeks to probe how theological understandings of Christian identity are worked out in baptismal practices, toward an end of supporting the church's embrace of the lives of discipleship among all the baptized. In the next section, I offer a further framing of this methodology that seeks to honor and amplify a multitude of witnesses in the work of theologizing disability.

A METHODOLOGY OF WITNESS: FRAMING MY QUALITATIVE RESEARCH

My theological approach is rooted in partnership to amplify witnesses. My embrace of this methodology emerges from a variety of interdisciplinary sources, including my work as an educator, theologian, and occupational therapist. These overlapping embodiments of my vocation allow me to bring together stories, questions, and bodies of scholarship related to pressing wounds, such as this book's opening story of Hallie's repeated baptismal denials, as well as the issues of theological abstraction we explored in the previous chapter. As Christian ethicist Ryan Juskus puts it, theological ethnography embodies a process of "witnessing witnesses to aid and multiply witnesses."[6]

Through my qualitative theological research, I sought to explore the concrete realities of baptismal practice and witness in the lives of my research partners. Through my research process, I also tried to contextualize how my research partners' witnesses might influence baptismal practices and theologies within other ecclesial communities. Put simply, in amplifying the stories of my research partners in this chapter and beyond, I am not laying out an exact blueprint for all Christian communities in all times and places.[7] Rather, I am illustrating how the stories of my research partners and their own Christian communities can enliven our imaginations about how disabled experience might be honored and critically engaged as we embrace shared Christian identity, worship, and discipleship.

While qualitative theological research anchored by the lives of people with intellectual disabilities is not completely absent from current work in the broader field of theology, only a few published studies exist.[8] Though sparse, these existing works powerfully illustrate the novel critiques, expansive possibilities, and liberatory practices that emerge from theological partnership with disabled Christians. These works of theological ethnography exist as counterstories[9]—witnesses that challenge implicitly negative assumptions about disabled people in the life of the church.

Adding my own theological scholarship to those who have paved the way before me, I highlight next how my approach in partnership alongside Christians with intellectual disabilities responds to a distinct set of benefits and challenges. I also detail some evidence-based best practices from a variety of disciplines that influenced my work as a theological ethnographer attempting to faithfully receive and subsequently amplify the witness of other Christians.

Benefits of Disability-Focused Research

My research on the baptismal witness of people with intellectual disabilities not only offers a novel approach to disability theology, but also sought to prioritize additional research outcomes, such as supporting the wellbeing and flourishing of people with intellectual disabilities.[10] My research process itself consisted of supportive opportunities for my participants, such as the chance to have a new experience, gain financial compensation, and contribute to a project where their stories were listened to and respected.[11]

More broadly, the research for this book expanded the current body of research literature around participation in faith communities among disabled people. In response to quantitative and mixed-method studies calling for improved opportunities for ecclesial participation among people with intellectual disabilities, my research illustrates potential pathways for increased accessibility and belonging from a baptismal perspective. Additionally, it provides a thick description of the experiences of people with intellectual disabilities—a perspective often unaccounted for in quantitative and mixed-methods studies.[12] Theological ethnography resourced me to faithfully tell stories of witness as an act of Christian discipleship—an act impossible apart from partnership.

Challenges of Disability-Focused Research

Throughout my research process, I attempted to anticipate and prepare for potential barriers to carrying out an inclusive and disability-informed research process. One well-documented challenge in inclusive research is the potential for research partners with intellectual disabilities to desire an ongoing relationship with the researcher following the conclusion of formal research activities.[13] To address this challenge, I committed to designing my study with clearly articulated boundaries about the nature of the research relationship for participants.[14] For example, I created a simple and accessible "study information guide" that included visual cues. The guide concluded with a picture of a home, indicating that both myself and the research participants would return home at the conclusion of the interviews and, when applicable, church events that I attended as a participant observer.

Another barrier I anticipated was the possibility of research complications presented by the presence of nondisabled caregivers during my interviews with intellectually disabled research partners. While individuals in caring roles can play supportive roles, their presence can also complicate interviews: obscuring genuine responses from disabled individuals, implicitly or explicitly expecting deference from the disabled participant, or "correcting" reports from the participant with whom they are in a relationship of care.[15] In my research process, I invited answers from participants with intellectual disabilities before any other participants present answered the same question. I also explicitly invited disabled participants to rephrase, correct, or expand upon answers provided by their parents, other family members, or caregivers throughout the interview process. My skills and experiences engaging family units within both ordinary and high-stakes clinical situations as an occupational therapy practitioner aided my awareness of navigating family dynamics in the interview setting. In addition, my formation from disabled leaders and disability studies scholars on self-determination guided my prioritization of perspectives from people with intellectual disabilities throughout my research process.[16]

A MULTITUDE OF WITNESSES: THE SPECIFICS OF MY RESEARCH PROCESS AND PARTNERS

My approach to receiving the witness of Christians with intellectual disabilities, their loved ones, and their clergy emerged in alignment with best practices in qualitative research. Though theological research in partnership with disabled individuals continues to be rather novel, "inclusive research" that centers collaborations with people across the spectrum of disability identities is an established practice across a wide range of disciplines.[17] The research process I discuss here embraces evidence-based practices advanced by methodologists in inclusive research.

Study Design

The heart of this book's research project sought to answer the following questions: What are the experiences of baptism among people with intellectual disabilities across diverse communities of Christian faith? How do baptismal practices and theologies shape communities' beliefs about identity, belonging, and worship? Due to my study's novel research questions, I utilized an exploratory case study design to describe individualized perspectives as well as collective resonances across my participants' reflections on baptism and disability.[18] I framed the study's activities of participant observation, field notes, and in-depth interviews within the relational approach of narrative inquiry.[19] This framing emerged from my desire to respectfully capture and reflect upon "ordinary lived experience"[20] throughout the research process. I designed my qualitative interviews with both semi-structured questions and opportunities for open-ended dialogue, in resonance with best practices advanced in inclusive research literature.[21]

Recruitment and Sampling

I recruited study participants using purposive sampling through hard copy and emailed flyers (distributed at my academic institution as well as local churches and community-based disability organizations). To capture a broad representation of Christian denominations among potential participants, I distributed 95 email invitations to regional clergy and lay leaders, representing 22 different Christian denominations. Following these initial recruitment efforts, I provided follow-up communication through both email and phone.

Ethical Considerations

I sought to integrate best practices for ethical, inclusive research throughout my project, beginning with approval of the full research protocol through Duke University's Campus Institutional Review Board. After conducting the recruitment process, I empowered my potential participants by scheduling interviews at sites, dates, and times selected by the participants themselves. This provision sought to decrease potential barriers related to transportation and also provided me with the chance to conduct interviews in maximally familiar and comfortable settings for my research partners. Allowing my participants to select the scheduling and location details of our interviews also allowed them to self-accommodate for any access or comfort needs they did not wish to disclose during the recruitment process.[22]

Exploring and obtaining informed consent was a vital component of my research process. My protocol included obtaining consent or assent, depending on the access needs of my participants and their legal guardianship status.[23] Before each interview, I verbally reviewed the study information guide with all participants present. This practice allowed the participants and me to get clear about the interview process and to discuss any participant questions or hesitations regarding the research. Participants with intellectual disabilities not under legal guardianship, their participating family member(s), clergy, and lay leaders, all provided verbal consent prior to interviewing. I utilized a visual consent guide to support all participants.[24] My research partners with intellectual disabilities who were not under legal guardianship could consent to either an individual interview process or opt for the presence of a support person during their interview.[25]

An additional interviewee was present during interview activities for people with intellectual disabilities under legal guardianship, as well as people with intellectual disabilities not under legal guardianship who were unable to provide informed consent and still desired to participate in the study. For participants under guardianship, their parent(s) or sibling provided permission for participation in the research process.[26] This permission granting was integrated into the guardian's informed verbal consent process.

Individuals with intellectual disabilities under guardianship next completed the assent process prior to the initiation of the research interview. In the case of people with intellectual disabilities unable to provide informed consent or assent, I requested their presence throughout the duration of the interview with their guardian(s). I invited participants with intellectual disabilities who demonstrated limited spoken language to communicate as desired via assistive communication devices or with interpretation from a guardian, following permission for their participation in the study.[27]

As part of the informed consent and assent processes, all participants selected a pseudonym for use in publications of their stories. In the case of individuals with limited communication, I consulted with their guardian to select a pseudonym.[28] Additionally, clergy participants in the study selected pseudonyms for their faith communities.

In order to protect confidentiality, I fictionalized identifiable personal and institutional information from the interviews and my field notes during the process of data analysis. Per requests from multiple research participants with intellectual disabilities, I also withheld participant-reported racial identities, to further protect anonymity.

I mirrored this supportive approach to navigating consent during the study's interview activities. I designed my interview guides in coherence with Plain Language principles and Universal Design for Learning.[29] In addition, I provided visual cue cards to all participants to support heightened engagement in the interview process. These visual cue cards provided a means of communicating confusion about research questions, access needs related to repetition of information or a slower pace, as well as a way to request breaks throughout the interview process.[30] Cards contained simple pictorial representations accompanied by a word or phrase related to the interview process such as "Help" or "I don't understand" or "I need a break."

These practices helped me anticipate a wide range of access needs and preferences for participation. For example, some participants communicated in short phrases or fragments, others made no eye contact during the interview, while others needed frequent breaks to leave the room or even the building. As I prepared for each interview visit, I renewed my commitment to flexibility within the research process. This flexibility helped me to honor what I initially considered fragmented research contributions but grew to understand as equal and indispensable perspectives within the research project.[31] My own fieldwork as a participant observer, as well as my practices of reflexivity (discussed in the following section), supported my methodological flexibility.[32]

Finally, I made an intentional effort to explicitly demonstrate respect and support for all of my research participants, especially those with intellectual disabilities.[33] One practice I took up to embody this commitment was providing cash compensation to all research partners.[34] Participants with intellectual disabilities who chose to withdraw from the study for any reason, or whose interviews were unable to be used during final analysis, were still provided with equal cash compensation.

Participants

Thirty-three total adult participants[35] took part in the study. The participant ages ranged from 24 to 77 years. 13 participants were individuals with intellectual disabilities, 8 were parents or siblings of a participant with an intellectual disability, 5 were lay leaders, and 7 were clergy. The Christian traditions represented among participants were Churches of Christ, The Episcopal Church, the Southern Baptist Convention, the Cooperative Baptist Fellowship, and The United Methodist Church. Among these denominations, participants were involved with 15 individual congregations. Of these 15 churches, I gained institutional consent to attend events as a participant observer at 1 United Methodist church, 3 Episcopal parishes, and 1 combined Southern and Cooperative Baptist congregation. Each of the 29 participants who completed the interview portion of the research is represented by their chosen pseudonym in Table 1.

Name (Pseudonym)	Age	Participant Category	Baptismal Tradition	Associated Church (Pseudonym)	Participant Observation	Church of Baptism (if different than Associated Church)
Al	33	Person with an intellectual disability (PWID)	Confessional	St. Barnabas Episcopal Church	Yes	First Southwestern Church of Christ
Andrew	67	Parent	Confessional	St. Barnabas Episcopal Church	Yes	First Southwestern Church of Christ
Robert	73	Lay Person	Paedobaptist	St. Barnabas Episcopal Church	Yes	

Name (Pseudonym)	Age	Participant Category	Baptismal Tradition	Associated Church (Pseudonym)	Participant Observation	Church of Baptism (if different than Associated Church)
Eric	61	Parent	Confessional	St. Matthew's Baptist Church	Yes	
Elisabeth	62	Parent	Confessional	St. Matthew's Baptist Church	Yes	
James	23	PWID	Confessional	St. Matthew's Baptist Church	Yes	
Soren	56	Clergy	Confessional	St. Matthew's Baptist Church	Yes	
Daniel	44	Clergy	Confessional	St. Matthew's Baptist Church	Yes	
Danny	66	PWID	Confessional	St. Matthew's Baptist Church	Yes	
Charley	36	Clergy	Confessional	St. Matthew's Baptist Church	Yes	
Paula	45	Clergy	Paedobaptist	St. Mary's Episcopal Church	Yes	
Jim	70	Parent	Paedobaptist	St. Mary's Episcopal Church	Yes	

Name (Pseudonym)	Age	Participant Category	Baptismal Tradition	Associated Church (Pseudonym)	Participant Observation	Church of Baptism (if different than Associated Church)
Hope	62	Lay Person	Paedobaptist	St. Mary's Episcopal Church	Yes	
Alicia	42	Clergy	Paedobaptist	Holy Angels Episcopal Church	Yes	
Mary	43	Sibling	Paedobaptist	Holy Angels Episcopal Church	Yes	
Lea	67	Parent	Paedobaptist	Holy Angels Episcopal Church	Yes	
Hikari	32	PWID	Paedobaptist	Holy Angels Episcopal Church	Yes	
Anna	64	Lay Person	Paedobaptist	Holy Angels Episcopal Church	Yes	
Ava	25	PWID	Confessional	Christ UMC	Yes	
Randy	24	Lay Person	Paedobaptist	Christ UMC	Yes	
John	40	Clergy	Paedobaptist	Christ UMC	Yes	
Ambrose	35	Clergy	Paedobaptist	Holiness United Methodist Church	No	
Adam	39	PWID	Paedobaptist	Trinity Episcopal Church	No	

Name (Pseudonym)	Age	Participant Category	Baptismal Tradition	Associated Church (Pseudonym)	Participant Observation	Church of Baptism (if different than Associated Church)
Parke	76	Parent	Paedobaptist	Trinity Episcopal Church	No	
David	34	PWID	Confessional	Redeemer Baptist Church	No	
Jason	34	PWID	Confessional	Third Baptist Church	No	
Henry	37	PWID	Confessional	Second UMC	No	
Bunny	41	PWID	Confessional	Sunshine Baptist Church	No	
Steve	77	Lay Person	Paedobaptist	Grace Episcopal Church	No	First Avenue Baptist Church

Data Collection

My data collection included individual or small group interviews with my participants (21 total interviews), as well as taking field note data from participant observation experiences with 5 of the churches where my participants worshiped. With 29 research participants, I conducted in-person, in-depth, qualitative interviews (4 of the 33 total participants withdrew participation during the interview stage). Interview length ranged from 7 to 89 minutes, with an average interview length of 39 minutes. Using open-ended interview questions, I prompted my research partners to explore stories of baptism in close connection with their own or another's experience of disability. In my interviews, I sought to evoke feelings, memories, and impressions associated with my participants' experiences surrounding baptismal practices. My interview questions also invited participants into theological reflection on baptism ("What does baptism mean to you?"; "What happens when someone is baptized"?). In addition, I created space within the interviews for my research partners to explore how baptism influenced their understanding of human beings, the church, and the nature of God. Throughout the interviews, I invited participants to reflect on stories from Scripture that resonated with them in relation to baptism and disability.

As a participant observer, I attended a minimum of two gatherings at the five faith communities who consented to institutional participation in this study. I took detailed field notes following attendance at each gathering, with specific attention to contextual and environmental factors at the faith community, the content and structure of the worship service or other event, patterns of participation among those present, and any other notable factors that either supported or impeded access and disability inclusion.

Data Analysis

After completion of each of the twenty-one interviews, I reviewed the full audio files and then securely delivered them to a professional transcriptionist who produced transcripts for each interview. I next reviewed each full transcription synchronously with its recording at least three separate times, writing handwritten analytic memos to identify emergent themes, questions, and connections throughout the data.[36] In these memos, I also sought to capture what struck me as the most poignant and meaningful reflections among my participants. Identifying these reflections fueled my self-reflexive journaling process throughout data analysis. During this initial stage of data analysis, I also reread my field notes, making new comments and adding self-reflexive notes in additional analytic memos.

After completing these initial steps of data review, I began a more systematic approach to data analysis of my interview and field note data, following a thematic analysis framework. I created an initial code list[37] and then proceeded with first-cycle coding of the interviews and field notes, focusing on both descriptive coding[38] as well as In vivo[39] and process coding.[40] Next, I engaged in a subsequent round of coding with a focus on thematizing the descriptive codes.[41] I recorded first-round and subsequent levels of coding within NVivo Qualitative Data Analysis Software (Version 12.1.0, QSR International, 2018).[42] After completion of coding, I cross-tabulated the code assignments to identify emerging themes across the interview data. This process of analysis led me into further conceptualization of prominent intersecting codes across the data, important baptismal themes and practices shared among different categories of research participants (people with intellectual disabilities, their families, lay leaders, and clergy), specific concepts related to disability and baptism that resonated most clearly with a single category of participants, and conceptual differences and similarities between my research partners from paedobaptist and credobaptist contexts.

Reflexivity and Cocreation in Theological Qualitative Research

Throughout the research process, I processed my experiences—whether familiar, challenging, or surprising—through several self-reflexive practices, including journaling and prayer. These practices helped me to appreciate, unpack, and examine my own contributions that influenced the cocreation of research data with my participants.[43] My social location as a white, cisgender woman, a Christian, an occupational therapist, a theologian, a lay leader in The Episcopal Church, and a person living with chronic health conditions, reflect key components that informed my approach to this research process. Throughout my research, I tried to cling to the following exhortation from John Swinton: "the honest methodological position from which Christians should begin their ethnographic practices is not neutrality but prayer."[44] Instead of attempting to neutralize my identities and life experiences, I attended to them throughout the research process as important sources of influence. At times my journal notes were filled with great joy and excitement, and at other times, with discomfort and distress. The notes that recounted my discomfort often reflected on claims about disability, either implicit or explicit, that I encountered throughout the research process.

Following Swinton's exhortation above, part of my process of self-reflexivity was to prayerfully[45] acknowledge to God my own limits and to confess my temptation to limit what another might authentically wish to share with me about baptism. I needed grace to approach the research process with an open perspective: ready to listen and learn. Prayer helped me to identify and attempt to surrender the limits that I found myself inadvertently imposing on others. For example, I became skeptical of a participant after our initial conversations during the study's recruitment phase. After an encounter where the participant mentioned that there was an "autism section" at their church, I reflexively journaled the following:

> I was surprised to see how strongly and negatively I felt internally about the "autism section" comment. My mind automatically thought, "don't they know about disability studies?! About preventing patterns of discrimination and institutionalization?! Especially in church?!" Their comment even tempted me to potentially disregard this person as a participant. But reflecting on this now, I see how closed off I was in that moment. And how without this process of reflecting back, I would likely carry that closed kind of mind with me into our formal interview. I don't want to do that. And I need to extend grace—just like hundreds of people have extended grace to me as I've learned how to speak truthfully and faithfully about disability. And how I've received grace as I've tried to collaborate with disabled people to create meaningful church spaces with them.

In another set of notes written after the completion of my first two interviews, I reflected:

> My participants seemed to become visibly anxious when I asked them more general questions about baptism—such as "what happens when someone is baptized?" Their excitement decreased and many of them avoided eye contact. One person actually said something like "I'm not really good at theology." I panicked a bit inside, thinking we'd just lost a great rapport after exploring more open-ended questions. I felt guilty for unintendingly placing theological pressure on participants, especially because it seemed like some people with intellectual disabilities and their parents felt pressure about giving me the "right answer." So I found that giving a reminder at the beginning of the interview about there being "no wrong or right answers," and emphasizing

this again throughout the interview made people feel more at ease (evidenced in facial expressions and relaxation of their body posture throughout the interview process). I'll continue to offer this reassurance to help sustain rapport throughout future interviews and also to clarify the intent of these interviews in the first place—to share stories, not to tell me a "correct" theological proclamation about baptism.

These notes clearly illustrated areas where I needed grace: for myself, my participants, and the research process as a whole.

My processes of reflexive journaling and prayer also supported me in attuning more closely to my own biases throughout the research process, allowing me to make explicit my own influence upon research activities. For example, in the earliest parts of my research, practicing reflexive note-taking after each interview helped me uncover how parts of my tone, demeanor, and body language influenced the interview process.[46] Cultivating an awareness of research cocreation through the process of reflexive journaling helped me to not only make needed adjustments to my approach to interviews, but also to recognize the goods of reciprocity involved in the research process. These practices of self-reflexivity informed my data analysis process, continually reminding me to resist the temptation to significantly reinterpret, or perhaps more bluntly, to colonize the stories shared by my research participants. Instead, my practices of self-reflexivity helped me to see how my own story of Christian life intersected and stood distinct from the stories of my research partners. As Willie James Jennings argues, "baptism is nothing less than a convergence of life narratives, Jesus' and our own."[47]

STORIES OF BAPTISM: KEY FINDINGS

In the second half of this chapter, I provide an entryway into key themes and stories from my research partners' accounts of baptism. While in future chapters we will consider how the baptismal practices and theologies emerging from the human experience of disability can expand, critique, and offer new perspectives on identity and belonging in Christian communities, my goal here is to introduce my research partners through sharing overlapping parts of their reflections. We will begin with an exploration of how my research partners described and defined baptism and next turn to stories and excerpts from the interviews that illustrate the three core baptismal themes emerging from the research: community, Jesus, and participation. We will next look at insights from my research participants that draw together their baptismal experiences with Christian Scripture, some key attitudes surrounding baptism, as well as key tensions within the stories of baptism across research partners. Finally, we will conclude by considering some limitations of this study.

Accessible Summary

Providing an accessible research summary is one best practice when conducting research in partnership with disabled people, as well as other populations who may benefit from heightened access to study findings.[48] The following paragraphs provide an accessible summary of this book's research project.

> Sarah talked with people about baptism. Some people Sarah talked to have intellectual disabilities. Some people were parts of families, like moms, dads, brothers, and sisters. Some people were pastors and priests. Some people were from church. Sarah talked to people from many different churches. These people told Sarah stories about baptism.
>
> People said that baptism is about Jesus. In the Bible, Jesus was baptized by his cousin named John. When we are baptized, we are connected to Jesus. When other people are baptized, they are connected to Jesus. This happens to babies, kids, and older people.
>
> People said that baptism connects us to other people. Baptism puts us in a family. Being baptized is becoming family with people at church. We become family with people in our churches. We also become family with people at different churches in different places—all around the world! All different kinds of people are baptized.
>
> People said that being baptized is important. When we are baptized it can make us happy. When we see other people baptized it can make us happy. Baptism is being a part of a big and important thing. Baptism is a big and important thing that connects us to other people and to God.

Field Notes

The field notes I took as a participant observer testified to a great diversity of liturgies and access points to worship participation across my participants' communities of faith. The breadth of worship contexts among my research partners serves as a testament to the cohesion of particular baptismal themes across an ecumenical diversity of practices and stylistic preferences. As I discussed above, I primarily engaged field note data as a practice of self-reflexivity throughout my research. The detailed field notes I kept regarding my experience within the faith communities of my participants helped me appreciate some of the contexts influencing the study's interviews as well as participants' particular insights.

DESCRIBING BAPTISM

"I think baptism is primarily the act of God through the church in which God is proclaiming the truth of a person. The truth of God and therefore the truth of a person. And that this is, for whatever reason, the way God has given to us to draw people into that story in a corporate mode of worship and celebration."—Pastor John

Seeking to create maximal openness in exploring stories of baptism across the different ecumenical traditions of my research partners, I did not offer a formal definition of baptism during our research interviews. Instead, I invited my research partners to reflect on their own stories of baptism, what baptism meant to them, and how baptism might be broadly understood within their own experience of Christian community. Three key foci for describing baptism emerged from participants across both credobaptist and paedobaptist traditions. We will now explore these three key descriptions of baptism—a Jesus-centered and participatory welcome into community.

Baptism Is Jesus Centered

A rootedness in Jesus was a key description of baptism among all categories of research participants, occurring in nearly half the interviews. My research partners named both being a part of Jesus' body and a baptismal identity rooted in Jesus as particularly important within their experience of Christian discipleship. Examples include:

"Baptism is about following Jesus."—James

"Baptism is God in Jesus."—Henry

"People are made part of the body of Christ . . . baptism is being received into the body of Christ."—Steve

"I believe in being baptized I was fully adopted in the body of Christ."—Pastor Paula

"Baptism is a participation and a welcome into who Jesus is." —Randy

"I became a new man in Jesus Christ."—David

"Baptism is through—is like Jesus Christ, our Lord—he is with you and is with me."—Al

"I think we all got saved a long time ago. We got fully incorporated in Jesus' baptism."—Pastor John

"Baptism marks a turning point in someone's life. A transformation turning point. They're transformed from being turned to self to turning now to Christ."—Pastor Daniel

Participants also shared about baptism as a way of actively participating in Jesus' death and resurrection. Their descriptions reflected both symbolic and deeply embodied memories of the baptismal experience. Jesus' death and resurrection evoked central themes of renewal and sharing in Jesus' resurrection life. Participants with intellectual disabilities gave particularly striking first-person accounts of being buried and rising with Jesus at their baptisms.

"Baptism shows that Jesus was buried, and that he rose again from the dead. I was buried just like Jesus was. I was buried like Jesus. I was buried like Jesus and rose again. Rose up from the dead."—Danny

"And I rise like Jesus did."—James

"For me, baptism is symbolism of the burial and resurrection of Jesus, being made new."—Elisabeth

"Baptism is going to be a visible expression of an inward grace . . . it's a symbolic act . . . it really has to do with a witness. It's a way of bearing witness of this person, that they are giving physical and visible witness of the gospel. It goes to Romans 6. It is about sharing in Christ's death and sharing in Christ's resurrection. In fact, sometimes I will talk about this in the baptismal pool . . . and tell people that going into the water is a way of symbolizing and showing—or sharing in the death of Christ and coming up out of the water is symbolizing and giving a visible expression to our sharing in Christ's resurrection. And so we are sharing in what Christ has done for us."—Pastor Soren

"Baptism is to be immersed three times in the water of baptism through which we are made part of Jesus' death that we may experience the resurrection . . . you are baptized in the name of the Father, the Son and the Holy Spirit. You are put under the water . . . which is a reminder that you are so immersed that you can't breathe—that's death. But you are raised up. That's life."
—Steve

"They are dying to themselves and rising in Christ through the waters of baptism and are welcomed into the community . . . the community consists of Christ's body."—Hope

Baptism Draws Us into Community

The importance of community in stories about baptism also arose across all research partners: people with intellectual disabilities, their loved ones, and their clergy. Participants considered baptism a public practice of welcome into Christian life. For many participants, baptism as a public practice also proclaimed commitments of support, acceptance, and even belonging within their local churches.

"Baptism is a proclamation of our salvation and what that means. It's not for the candidate only, but it's for the whole community."
—Pastor Daniel

"Baptism is a decision that's important and it's important that it's public—saying it publicly to your congregation plus having the congregation support you in that decision . . . in baptism we enter a community of support. We are accepted for who we are."—Andrew

"To me, baptism is a way for the Christian community to welcome a new member . . . it is the way of the church community to welcome new family members. I do approve of the trend during my lifetime of making baptisms public . . . now it's moved out into the larger congregation, which if it's a way of welcoming new members, that's as it should be. And in The Episcopal Church, the words are something like, 'let us welcome the newly baptized.'"—Robert

"There is something in the act of worship, the public confirmation [in baptism] of something that matters."—Pastor John

"God has shown me [through relationships with parishioners and friends with intellectual disabilities] that God's baptismal theology is really for all of God's persons, all of God's children."—Pastor Ambrose

"Baptism means that for us as people of the church, we're here to connect with you through a hand given in the Holy Spirit."—Ava

Several participants also understood baptism as relating to a sense of communal identity. My research partners shared stories of baptism rich with language of "family." Their accounts of baptismal identity often emerged from baptism as a part of the Christian vocation to love one's neighbors.

"Baptism to me is, it's like joining the fold. Like everybody's in, regardless of who you are, what you believe, what you like—we're all in with God . . . Baptism sets you up in a community of people who are going to be your tribe."—Mary

"What baptism has meant for me is a commitment that my family made, that they didn't take lightly . . . this faith community is making a commitment to this person, to this baby, usually. And you as a family, you as their parents are making a commitment to bring this child up to love Jesus. And I feel so discouraged sometimes when someone moves churches, or the family isn't committed . . . and then we just have to remember it's like God's faithfulness that keeps us in . . . we belong to God. We belong to this faith community. And we belong to the church, maybe capital 'C' Church. Larger than just the little 'c' church that we're in. We belong to God. We belong to the Church. We belong to our family."—Randy

"I love to watch the mom's and dad's face during baptism—it's just joyful. It's just joyful . . . it's a moment of commitment to your child . . . and it's not just the family but the other people that are there—they are giving a commitment to that child also. Which is a lovely thing, because it's not just your own family. It's all these folks, and they are saying that they take ownership of this and they'll be there. They'll be your village."—Barbara

"Bob is a delight and a joy and a reminder in our baptism that we are to respect the dignity of every human being. And I believe that the way that we welcome Bob is the way that God welcomes us . . . as part of our church family, we are called to love one another the way that God loves us. And that love is part of our baptism."
—Pastor Paula

Baptism as Participatory

Reflections on baptismal participation constituted the third shared theme that emerged in descriptions of baptism among my research partners. Several clergy and lay leader participants affirmed participation in baptism as meaningfully connected to Jesus, as well as connected to practices of Holy Communion within their individual church communities.

"Baptism is a participation and a remembering too. I guess we're participating in an act that Jesus also participated in. And in doing that, we're remembering something that Jesus did."—Randy

"I think in a real way, we are participating in something that is already true . . . what we do is really a joyous participation in what God has emphatically and completely done in Christ."—Pastor John

"[Baptism] is an active, and I would even say conscious participation—in, you know, in the Triune God. This is sacramental reality. Right here. Right now."—Pastor Ambrose

"You know, I often tell my congregation as we celebrate the Eucharist, and as we baptize: we are participating in an unbroken stream with all Christians across time. You know, it seems so simplistic or whatever. But, I mean, we've done this for two thousand years straight. Isn't that awesome?"—Pastor Daniel

"I think a lot of our life of faith is one of participation. And one of remembering. And the Eucharist is a participation in the suffering and death—a participation and remembrance in the suffering and death of Jesus. And the liturgical calendar is a participation and remembering of the way of Jesus' life. And it is in the participation in this way that folks have ordered their life for many thousands of years."—Randy

"Baptism is fully realized through the reception of the body and blood of Christ in the Eucharist. So, there's a close connection between baptism, being received into the body of Christ, and the participation in that body through Eucharistic celebration."—Steve

For some participants from credobaptist traditions, specific reflections on participation in decision-making constituted a central part of their understanding of baptism:

"Baptism is the representation of the decision you've made to follow Christ . . . Baptists certainly don't believe that, you know, immersion or baptism is what makes one a believer. It's a decision that you make. But it is the visual representation, to me, of that decision."—Eric

"Baptism is a choice."—Andrew

"In Holy Baptism—they choose to have a heart and they get baptized then."—Al

Key Narratives: Community, Jesus, and the Materiality of Baptism

In addition to my research partners' emphases on Jesus, community, and participation in their descriptions of baptism, several overarching narratives arose as central to the participants' frameworks around their stories about baptism. These themes overlapped considerably with the participants' primary descriptions of baptism, such as the theme of community, illustrated by Lea's sharing here:

"Baptism is about the church saying that we are not going to be doing this by yourself. That we are a community of people together who are going to be witnesses in the world together and we're going to support you as an individual while you do that. And it's also . . . about God's call to us to be in community. Even in stories in the Bible where people start out in some sort of isolation . . . human beings are always called back into community. And so I think that the nature of God is togetherness. And baptism is a reflection of that."

Jesus was another primary thematic emphasis across different participant reflections. Experiences of Jesus in baptism included affirmations about the cross and God's work in baptism to connect the baptized to the body of Jesus.

"I felt like Jesus came into my soul."—Danny

"Jesus died on the cross for us."—Bunny

"[Symbolized in baptism] through the blood of Jesus and his death on the cross, our sins are completely washed away and as if they were never there."—Elisabeth

"This bodily act that Jesus did and also received is something we still do and it's unifying."—Randy

"I think baptism allows the church to feel that it is not in the declining headlines that we hear about. That in that one moment of baptism, we celebrate life and death and resurrection. And we celebrate incorporating a new member into the fuller body, the wider body."—Pastor Paula

The materiality and embodied nature of baptism arose as another common theme throughout participant stories, including connections between baptism and the Lord's Supper, as well as reflections on baptism and the body. Within these participant reflections, the baptismal waters played an especially meaningful role.

"Baptism is a reminder and confirmation that we are bodily. And that we are not just souls. So there's water. And there's people. And we touch the water in some way. And so that is . . . a reminder that we were created—that God created us human with bodies."—Randy

"There is that point in the liturgy where we hear the story of water. How in creation we began with water. Through water Israel moved from being slaves into freedom. And in water, Jesus Christ was baptized. And in baptism, we share in the life, death and resurrection of Jesus Christ."—Pastor Paula

"These [the baptismal waters] are the waters of the Red Sea, these are the waters of the Jordan. These are the waters of Mother Mary's womb. I mean, it's right here. Right now. Bam. It's amazing."—Pastor Ambrose

The theme of baptismal waters also surfaced in participant interviews in connection with their own embodied experiences of receiving or administering baptism. Many of these accounts highlighted how bodily limitations influenced experiences of encountering the baptismal waters.

"And at the beach, the man helped me into my baptism in the water."—David

"For Danny it was rather logistically challenging because his mobility was so limited. And, you know, it's like babies. There are two types of babies. There are some who know how to be held and there are some that are just like bags of sand. And Danny is a bag of sand. He didn't know how to help you help him. And so we had to make extra preparations to get him into the waters of baptism . . .

"We ended up having four or five deacons and strong bodies to help hoist him into the water. And I do remember very vividly how tenderly they spoke to him . . . I wish people could sort of overhear the gentle whispers and affirmations as they picked him up and reassured him they wouldn't drop him . . . I don't want to belabor it, but . . . the team effort that was required. The thing that touched me was hearing these men . . . many of whom are not very emotive or emotional or tender—being extremely gentle and affirming and caring of Danny, just very quietly telling him he's 'going to be okay,' 'we've got you,' those kinds of things . . . the narrative that came to mind and I've never been able to shake is the group of friends who cut a hole in the roof and dropped their paralyzed friend into to Jesus' lap. That was the image. You could just sort of lift that story out of the Gospel and change the names. And that's what Danny's baptism was like . . .

"I asked him, 'Are you ready?' Danny said, 'Yeah. I'm ready.' And I tried to take him back and he stiffened up like a board and would not go down. I said, 'Okay. We're going to try this again.' Waited a minute. I said, 'you want to try again?' He said, 'yeah. We'll try again.' And the second I kind of put pressure on him he just reflexively stiffened up and did not want to go back or under. None of that. Twice was enough.

"I said, 'Danny, I'm going to put some water on your head now.' And I did that three times. In the name of the Father, the Son, and the Holy Spirit. He smiled at me, toothless grin. And the church applauds."—Pastor Daniel

"There were certainly some conversations around logistics. Shaina [pseudonym, not a study participant] was the only one who's a wheelchair user who we've baptized. And Shaina was able to coach us and think through how we would do this. We did a full run-through with Shaina without the water, but had the tub and practiced how do we get her out of the chair and how do we get her into this tub. And that was quite an experience. It was a bit harrowing."—Pastor John

"So I just said to her quietly, 'Renee [pseudonym, woman with an intellectual disability, not a research participant], can I pour some water over your head?' And she said, 'Yes.' And so I said, 'Renee, having heard your profession of faith in Jesus Christ our Lord and in obedience to his commands, I baptize you, my sister. In the name of the Father.' And I put a handful of water on her head. 'In the name of the Son.' I put water on her head. 'And in the name of the Holy Spirit.' And I put water over her head.

"And she was happy. She was so happy that she got baptized. And for the first time I can remember that church erupted in applause for a baptism. They were not a totally high liturgical church that would never clap. But they weren't the kind of church that clapped at everything. And I had never recalled them clapping at a baptism. But that sort of unleashed for the church a different mentality . . . and after that, quite often at baptisms, they would clap when you baptized somebody. That was their contemporary way of saying amen. So be it. This is as it should be."
—Pastor Soren

"We get Eli [pseudonym, man with an intellectual disability, not a research participant] into the water. And we baptize him.

"Well, you know, he comes up out of the water. And I was kind of expecting to give him a big bear hug. I was like, 'Hey, I'm so happy for you. You did awesome.' Just joy, right?

"But he turned away from me and he turned toward the altar table. And everyone's just silent in the room. And he bends at the waist to the altar table and says, 'Amen.'"—Pastor Ambrose[49]

Participants also shared deeply emotive reflections, both in content and expression, about their embodied experiences of baptism.

"That water felt really good."—Danny

"I liked the pastor to dunk me."—Bunny

"Pastor Soren put me in the water and he called me a beloved son . . . he dunked me in the water."—James

"We sure are made of the most basic elements and those are incorporated into the baptism rite, the rite of baptism. Water and light and oil and flesh and holding and, you know, getting bathed. It's very incarnational . . .

"I've experienced most of my life through touch. That's just kind of who I am in that way, and so having the water present is really—I think it's just an amazing kind of connection . . ."—Anna

"The thing that's good about The Episcopal Church is . . . that we go through the baptismal service and that we get sprinkled as a reminder . . . If we didn't have that reminder, I would miss it. The first time I went through that, I thought this is the craziest thing. It was just funny. And sometimes it still can be funny. But it is meaningful. This is what we do. This is like when you go to the altar [for Eucharist], it's just that experience over and over again.

"And for Bob, he thinks baptismal reaffirmation is great. The priest always sprinkles the water right on him . . . it seems to be about three or four times a year that we do it. Enough that Bob is familiar with it. He knows he is going to get water sprinkled on him."—Barbara

Biblical Connections to Baptism

My research partners offered many reflections on different biblical stories that shaped their baptismal imaginations, practices, and theologies. Five distinct Bible passages emerged as significant for multiple participants, with the most common being Jesus' baptism in the four canonical Gospels.

> "I think that it just makes it such a personal connection that Jesus was baptized. And that was the transition of his life in a major way, and his connection with God, if you look at it in terms of the Trinity. And the Spirit was present that day, so I think that baptism kind of wraps that all up."—Anna

> "Jesus was baptized in the river—he was baptized God's son." —Ava

> "It's about Jesus being baptized by his cousin . . . it was on his shoulder and said to him, you're my beloved son in who I am well pleased."—James

> "We read the story of Jesus' baptism in the river . . . the fact that God spoke when Jesus was baptized. And that's something very significant. That the creator of all the universe spoke: that this is my son. I mean, that's powerful when you think about it. Sometimes when you hear the same story over and over, maybe it loses some of its power. But when you start to really think about that the God of the universe and the Maker and the Creator of all things, that He would speak so loudly."—Parke

Four additional passages from Scripture also resonated across participant interviews. Pastors John, Daniel, and Soren, as well as lay leader Steve, reflected on the importance of Pauline writings on baptism, especially Paul's account of baptismal participation in Romans 5–6. Pastors Daniel and Soren, as well as Lea and Eric, spoke about the meaningfulness of the baptism of the Ethiopian eunuch in Acts 8. Ava, Elisabeth, and Pastor Soren engaged the story of the Pentecost in Acts 2 as important in their own framings of baptism. Finally, Pastors Alicia and John reflected on the importance of Matthew 28 and Jesus' command to make disciples of all the nations, baptizing them in the name of the Father, the Son, and the Holy Spirit.

Meaningful Baptismal Practices

A host of meaningful baptismal practices emerged in my research interviews. The four most frequently mentioned practices were baptismal preparation, baptismal reaffirmation or remembrance, giving baptismal testimony, and the practice of Holy Communion as it connects with baptismal living. Research partners from both paedobaptist and credobaptist traditions shared perspectives on each of these four practices. Some participants' reflections demonstrated an integration of multiple practices, such as Barbara's story of how participating in the Eucharist served as a means of baptismal remembrance:

> "The thing that I think is special about The Episcopal Church is that you come to the altar every Sunday, that you are reminded of baptism every Sunday . . . if you've been miffed at someone at church and you're on your knees at the altar rail. Ours is circular. So we see everybody. It is always a form of remembrance."

Among other research partners, Christian identity was at the meaning-making center of their stories of baptismal practices. Pastor John reflected on baptismal remembrance as a primary activity of affirming one's baptismal identity:

> "We don't talk about remembrance of baptism as the memory of you being baptized. But the remembrance that you have that you were baptized. That you've been cleaned. That you have had this truth told over you countless times as we baptize . . . the remembrance of baptism is a remembrance of every baptism which we've ever been given a gift to participate in. It's the iterative declaration of who God is and therefore who we are."

This refrain of true identity offered by Pastor John—using language of "who we are" or "who I am"—also surfaced in research conversations with James and Al. James reflected to me that in discussing baptism with his pastor, "I was just asking Pastor Soren to be who I am." Al also shared his story of baptismal preparation by reflecting on an identity of baptismal becoming: "I told my Dad, yes. I would like to get baptized. It's truly in God that I become—I become who I am." Pastor Paula also reflected on baptismal practices as related to identity:

> "I think for The Episcopal Church, baptism is so much a part of who we are in our identity . . . a beautiful thing is when you have someone state their name—my name is Paula—and then say, 'I'm a beloved child of God' . . . that's what we get through our baptism . . . it's that we know that we are beloved."

Randy offered another key reflection on the practice of baptismal testimony and its intersection with baptismal identity. Engaging Pastor John's notion of baptism as "wordless preaching," Randy shared with me: "What Pastor John said was baptism is a way for you to preach to the church. To say without words that you belong to God. And to remind others that they belong to God."

APPARENT TENSIONS

Despite deep resonances across research partners from a variety of disability identities and denominational affiliations, several tensions arose within the research stories. In my analysis, I was particularly struck by the following questions at the heart of these research tensions: Is baptism primarily about volitional and verbal proclamation, decision, and understanding? Or is it ultimately about nonverbal, mysterious expression of what God has already done? Alternatively, should both of these factors be present as contemporary Christians with and without disabilities celebrate baptism? Let us turn first to the narrative tension regarding the nature of baptismal participation, including what actions are considered necessary for the sacrament or ordinance to be faithfully engaged.

Understanding vs. Unknowing

What aspects of baptism constituted the necessary elements of this practice as articulated by my research partners? Human decision, understanding, and commitment? Individual or communal action? Divine action? Wordless participation? Some combination? This cluster of questions highlights some of the greatest tensions when comparing baptismal stories of my research participants. Pastor

Soren, a pastor at St. Matthew's Baptist Church, described the scriptural foundation for practices of baptism that include central elements of human decision, understanding, and confession:

> "It has traditionally been very important for us that the norm of Scripture, not every single Scripture, but the norm of Scripture is that baptism follows confession of faith . . . that's why we do not baptize infants . . . so the chronology of the act is an important element of the Baptist tradition. And it's really based on confession of faith. A voluntary, non-coerced profession, or confession, of faith."

Other participants in confessional baptism traditions continued in this same theme:

> "We wanted to make sure Al wanted the baptism done. And he understood it and was clear."—Andrew

> "I think that when you look at baptism as a whole, it's the first time that God outwardly said that Jesus was His son and He was well-pleased with him . . . at that point in time, Jesus begins his ministry and follows what God wants him to do. And I think that that's what baptism represents for us is that at that point in time in our lives, after we have accepted Jesus as our Savior and we follow through with baptism, that's the point in time where we begin our ministry as believers and follow Christ's example on a day-to-day basis."—Elisabeth

> "I think the key for me is that baptism go with the decision. I think that's a very important representation that when you're old enough, whatever that age is, or when you get to the point of accepting Christ, then you are realizing what baptism means. I'm not putting down other denominations or faith traditions—but to me it's by far the greatest representation and probably for somebody experiencing baptism immersion after they have accepted Christ, it means more, far more to them than say if you were sprinkled very young . . . Baptists certainly don't believe that immersion or baptism is what makes one a believer. It's a decision that you make."—Eric

In contrast, other participants described baptism as a practice of the church primarily characterized by mysterious participation in the work of God. Hope, an Episcopal lay leader, shared the following reflection with me:

> "What happens in baptism and lots of other theological ponderings... I wanted to be able to approach them with a rational brain at a younger age... The idea was maybe that you would need to understand what was happening in baptism in order to be baptized. And I remember reading a particular book that I found in the stacks at my local university. And I can't remember the name of it now. But it really altered all of that to my understanding that, well, nobody really understands baptism... it's not really like we can wrap our minds around and about it. We can manipulate intellectual ideas so that they represent the most comfortable way possible... but that made me think that it certainly doesn't matter what level of cognitive ability you have in order to be baptized here. It's much more that you are going through a transformation that God and we are all enacting at once."—Hope

> "A sacrament is the mysterious blending of the already and the not yet in an instant. Where what is already true is actualized, if that's possible. But it was true before it was actualized... And so it was kind of within that framework that the question—the question of would I baptize a person who couldn't confess Jesus? And I thought surely we must be able to, because it's true. Like Jesus' life, death, resurrection, ascension and intercession incorporates that person. How dare we not baptize them? And then it was an easy job from that to, well, of course we can baptize infants... somewhere in that trajectory I came under the conviction that none of us really know what we're talking about anyway. We're fundamentally entering into mystery here. And so to attach some intellectual prerequisite to the sacrament is silliness." —Pastor John

Interestingly, however, participants from credobaptist traditions reflected on the power and even necessity of mystery and wordless proclamation within their baptismal practices. Responding to a question about what happens when someone is baptized, Ava illustrated a blurring of the tensions sketched above:

"I feel like they're not surely knowing what that means. But we tell the people this means you're majorly connected to God spiritually in the mystery of the Holy Trinity."

In addition, Pastor Daniel from St. Matthew's Baptist Church affirmed baptism as a wordless mode of preaching—not directly contingent on volitional or verbal action on the part of the baptized:

"At baptism services I'll say, 'Most folks are not going to remember what I preached about today—but they will never forget what they see you preach in your actions today.' You know, the very kind of core of our faith is that in being buried with Jesus we are raised with him to a life like his. And I say, 'You are preaching this in what you do today.' So, in a sense it's a proclamation of our salvation and what that means. It's a recitation of it and it's not for a candidate now, but it's for the whole community."

This account of wordless preaching resonated with Pastor John's description of practicing baptismal preparation within his United Methodist context:

"During baptismal preparation I talked about baptism as a sermon and a story ... I said a sermon is a way that we talk about how good God is. And how much God loves us. And baptism is one of the sermons that we preach in the church. And it tells a story about how good God is and how much God loves us. And how we belong. And I told them that it tells the story of who they really are."

Attitudes

A second significant tension in the research arose in baptismal stories related to differing attitudes among Christian faith communities regarding people with intellectual disabilities. While many participants in the research described beautiful experiences of unconditional welcome, some research partners told me about times when a past community, or even their current community, had cultivated an atmosphere of unwelcome or even hostility for themselves or a loved one with an intellectual disability. Hikari shared with me out of her own experience: "she [a former lay leader] made it clear that I was inferior to everyone else and did her best to get me off the acolyte list." In another interview, Barbara, a parent to an adult child with an intellectual disability, recalled an encounter with her pastor's wife when her son Bob was three years old: "The pastor's wife asked me, 'what are you going to do with Bob next year?' I responded, 'I don't know. We will probably keep him in Sunday nursery school for a bit.' Then the pastor's wife firmly responded . . . 'well, Bob can't come to church anymore.'"

In contrast, baptismal communities with attitudes marked by an embrace of "imperfection" as well as "acceptance" fostered a communal sense of genuine belonging. Andrew described the church where his son Al was baptized as follows: "Total support. When Al was baptized . . . everybody embraced it. I don't think there was any hesitation at all, from anybody. It was really quite wonderful." Despite Hikari's experience of exclusion in her faith community, a lay leader at her church shared the following:

> "Hikari's presence is, I'm sure, a gift to our whole community. She really has been to me . . . She's had all these gifts and now she's flowering in some other ones . . . This isn't about perfection. It's about inclusion and about experience together. And it doesn't have to be a perfect thing . . . all of us count the same here. And it was like you don't have to prove who you are to anybody. We all count the same."—Anna

In addition to Andrew, other research participants who are parents of adult children with intellectual disabilities reflected on their church communities as spaces of deep belonging both for themselves and their children:

> "I feel grateful to Holy Angels for being so accepting of Hikari. I mean, these people have just scooped her up and loved her and would do anything for her . . . I feel like if I left her on a basket on the doorstep, she'd be taken care of here."—Lea

> "We would never move from here because of St. Mary's. We would never . . . because for Bob, that's home. It totally is . . . he has big parties. We have big celebrations for his birthdays. We have forty people here from church. And they're always from church. Or we have the church at the bowling alley. It's the entire

church. You know, everything has always been the church for him."—Barbara

For Mary, Hikari's sister, attitudes of acceptance, despite imperfections, found a direct relationship to baptism:

> "Baptism is a visible symbol of being brought into that tribe and a part of the tribe. It's like an 'I got you' moment. You don't need to worry about things because, you know, this community of people, you little baby or you big person, you don't need to worry about what it is that you're going to be struggling with, because we've got you."

A final story from Barbara points to the centrality of the attitude of clergy in creating an environment of welcome and belonging for people with intellectual disabilities:

> "Bob was just really noisy during church. And he wouldn't do what he was supposed to do or whatever. He was too old to be in the nursery. But he was not behaving; he was on the floor kicking the folding chairs all during the service. And so Jim thought we should not return to church for . . . well, at that point it was ever. Because Bob was so disruptive to other people who were there worshiping.
>
> "I had to go in and talk to the priest, who was a lovely woman, because I had some commitments for that year that I had made. And so I went to talk to her and tell her I wasn't going to be able to do them. She listened to me. And then she said, 'Barbara, do you think that God's just for you?' And I was like, 'Uh, no.' And she said, 'Of course you don't. God's for Bob. And you have to promise me that you'll be here every Sunday with Bob. We're going to work this out.' She said, 'If he's kicking the chairs then he's kicking the chairs. That's just fine. I want him here. Every Sunday.'"

STUDY LIMITATIONS

Like all research projects, this study included several limitations. For instance, my research partners were all recruited from a particular geographical area (the state of North Carolina). Additionally, while the participants represented several Christian denominations, recruiting further participants to increase the denominational diversity could have impacted the study's findings.

With regard to the study's methodology, I see three primary limitations. First, I conducted this study as a solo researcher.[50] Though this approach proved advantageous in its flexibility, both during data collection as well as during my analysis,[51] diversified researcher (and research partner) participation in data analysis and interpretation could strengthen and clarify the study's findings.[52] Second, while I tailored the study's design and methodology to include the robust participation of people with intellectual disabilities during data gathering, my geographical and financial limitations did not allow for ongoing participation among my disabled participants in the analysis process. Both initial and ongoing guidance from disabled participants is the standard within inclusive research methodologies, particularly among people who experience intellectual disability.[53] Third, while people with profound intellectual disabilities could not participate in verbal interviewing for this project, they were present for interviews of their caregivers as well as during the participant observation stages of this research. In future studies, I will strive to more intentionally engage person-centered planning as it intersects with thematic inquiry—exemplified in the theological research of Swinton, Mowat, and Baines[54]—in order to more specifically investigate the impact of the witness of people with more significant disabilities on baptismal theology and practice.

RESEARCH REFLECTIONS: A SUMMATIVE DISCUSSION

During the planning stages of this study, as well as in my early processes of self-reflexive analytic journaling, I initially set out to analyze the overlapping and diverging narrative emphases among different kinds of partners who participated in the research process (people with intellectual disabilities, loved ones, and clergy leaders). I also anticipated analyzing the data along differences emerging from research participants in paedobaptist contexts and those in churches practicing confessional baptism. I hypothesized that analysis of the interview data, as well as my field notes from participant observation, would support and elucidate these differences in my findings. Surprisingly, I found that churches across several axes of diversity demonstrated a strong core of shared themes related to baptism and disability: participation, community, and Jesus. Despite theological and denominational differences in baptismal practices and theologies, a surprising unity of practices and themes arose, from narrative emphases to scriptural resonances.

The theological focus of my research at times evoked responses that I did not fully anticipate. For example, participants demonstrated intermittent signs of anxiety when I asked more theological questions about baptism. Some research partners expressed that they didn't want to answer questions "the wrong way" in the presence of a researcher and theologian. I encouraged participants that I was not seeking a particular answer, but rather desired to hear the stories that came to their minds—stories of beauty and joy, but also stories of challenge and doubt. In addition to this surprising need for reassurance, I initially anticipated that I would need to reframe questions about the intersections of biblical passages with participants' experiences of baptism. However, my interview question about baptism and biblical stories consistently evoked animated sharing within participant interviews—more so than any other question during the research process. I found myself surprised at how engaged participants became when sharing about the Gospel accounts of Jesus' baptism, as well as the excitement of participants who reflected on Paul's affirmations about baptism in his New Testament Epistles. The rich themes associated with the most-cited Scripture passages among participants—participation in Jesus' death and resurrection, the public nature of Jesus' own baptism, and baptismal proclamations of belonging, welcome, and belovedness—strongly resonated with the core themes of baptism advanced among my research partners with intellectual disabilities: participation, Jesus centeredness, and community.

The tensions I identified above, both in attitudes ranging from discriminatory to welcoming, as well as baptism as a volitional point of decision versus an unknowable divine action, mark important areas for further investigation. Future research could explore the potential comparisons and contrasts when baptismal stories are shared among individuals and communities apart from a strong connection to the experience of intellectual disability. Might the same tensions arise? Additionally, future studies could more directly probe questions about inconsistencies between expressed baptismal theologies and practices (for example, asking a pastor in a credobaptist tradition if they would baptize a nonspeaking individual with a significant intellectual disability that made symbolic communication inaccessible).

In summary, the research introduced in this chapter highlights the importance of baptismal affirmations of Christian identity, as well as engagement in baptismal practices, in sustaining belonging for people with intellectual disabilities across a variety of Christian traditions and local contexts. Despite marked differences in theologies, church membership, and denomination, the research stories offered by my participants gesture toward hope that baptismal practices offer a central framework for identifying and supporting the discipleship of people with intellectual disabilities. Across the great diversity of Christian traditions, God in Jesus Christ breaks in through the witness of baptism—the uniting of God's children with Christ in his death and resurrection life—with the Holy Spirit empowering all the baptized for a life of discipleship. Stories informed by the human experience of disability can elucidate this reality and call us to repent for the times when we have refused this baptismal life of renewal, and also to reimagine how our communities practice discipleship and honor the identities and vocations of all the baptized, both those with and without disabilities.

CONCLUSION

Engaging qualitative research, particularly among people with intellectual disabilities and those with lives closely connected to them, surfaces new and important considerations for theologies of disability. This study's exploration of ecclesial belonging and participation through the lens of baptism highlighted the importance of participation, community, and the life of Jesus as central to practicing community alongside people with intellectual disabilities. Interestingly, interviews and field note data yielded little remark on the specific themes of friendship, God's image, and inclusion—themes that as we saw in the previous chapter, tend to dominate scholarly accounts of disability in the fields of Christian theology and ethics.

The present research thus opens up new categories for reflection on the witness of people with intellectual disabilities in Christian ecclesial communities. In other words, engaging a baptismal hermeneutic among Christians with intellectual disabilities raises important challenges, critiques, and expansions of core themes and methods in contemporary disability theology.

The energy around biblical stories related to baptism among my research partners suggests further exploration of Christian Scripture as a source for fruitful expansion of current theological arguments concerning intellectual disability. As evidenced in this study, participants' engagement with the Bible highlighted key areas of synthesis between ecclesial practices and environments of belonging. In response to these key areas of baptismal nourishment identified by research participants, we will shift in the next two chapters to carefully explore how New Testament accounts of baptism might provide new insights for contemporary disability theology, particularly related to questions of Christian identity among people with and without intellectual disabilities.

Toward an end of reimagining communities marked by radical belonging and attentive to the Holy Spirit's work of empowering all the baptized in newness of life, we will turn our attention in the next chapter to my research partners' specific reflections on biblical accounts of baptism both in the canonical Gospels as well as Paul's Epistles. Drawing upon the interpretive categories for baptismal identity suggested by my research participants, I raise new questions at the intersections of disability, identity, and discipleship in conversation with biblical scholarship on baptism in the New Testament.

3

The Bible and Baptism

In their reflections on baptism and disability, my research partners highlighted how Christian Scripture supported both their baptismal identities as well as ecclesial spaces marked by belonging. Throughout this chapter, we will explore how biblical stories of baptism resonate in the lives of Christians formed by experiences of intellectual disability. Weaving together perspectives from both scholars and my research partners, I will argue that a disability-informed reading of the Bible offers a unique perspective on baptismal belonging. Exploring the role of Christian Scripture related to baptism in the lives of Christians formed by disability will also continue to demonstrate how theological reflection done in partnership raises new questions and categories for reflection within Christian community.

Guided by the three core interpretive categories for baptismal life shared among my research participants—Christocentricity, participation, and community—we will first investigate the canonical Gospels' accounts of Jesus' baptism as they relate to the lives of disabled Christians. Next, we will investigate how these three key themes find further expansion within Paul's writings on baptism within his New Testament Epistles. In connection with my participants' reflections on baptismal identity, intellectual disability, and Christian Scripture, I will illustrate how Paul's baptismal theology in Romans 6 offers a supportive foundation for the formation of disability-inclusive Christian communities. My research participants' perspectives will help us solidify how Paul's baptismal hermeneutic not only supports the inclusion of people with intellectual disabilities in Christian communities, but also underscores their active and indispensable participation in the ongoing sanctification of the baptized body: walking together in newness of life (Romans 6:4).

THE FOUNDATIONS OF JESUS' BAPTISM IN THE JORDAN

> Then Jesus came from Galilee to John at the Jordan, to be baptized by him. John would have prevented him, saying, "I need to be baptized by you, and do you come to me?" But Jesus answered him, "Let it be so now; for it is proper for us in this way to fulfill all righteousness." Then he consented. And when Jesus had been baptized, just as he came up from the water, suddenly the heavens were opened to him and he saw the Spirit of God descending like a dove and alighting on him. And a voice from heaven said, "This is my Son, the Beloved, with whom I am well pleased." (Matt 3:13–17)[1]

Stories of Jesus' baptism in the Jordan River arise "out of an old story drenched in Old Testament precedents, images, and language."[2] Strong themes of repentance and forgiveness of sin anchor Jesus' baptism in Jewish language of confession, repentance, and anointing.[3] Possible antecedents to John the Baptist's baptism of Jesus include Jewish rituals of cleansing and bathing, Jewish initiation of proselytes, and foundational Old Testament texts such as Isaiah 1:16–17 and Ezekiel 36:25–28.[4] Jesus' baptism also resonates with additional "watery" Old Testament narratives; for example, Martin Luther's "Flood Prayer" traces the continuity of Jesus' baptism with the flood in Genesis, particularly the deliverance of Noah and his family from these floodwaters (Genesis 6:9–9:17), as well as Israel's escape from bondage through the waters of the Red Sea (Exodus 14).[5]

From this rich foundation, Christians throughout the history of the church have responded to the witness of Jesus' baptism in shaping their theological commitments and lived practices. As the Gospel accounts of Jesus' baptism did for Christian disciples throughout the centuries, so they resonated among the research participants for this book, across a diversity of Christian denominational traditions. For example, Anna shared: "I think that it just makes it such a personal connection that Jesus was baptized. And that was the transition of his life in a major way, and his connection with God, if you look at it in terms of the Trinity. And the Spirit was present that day, so I think that baptism kind of wraps that all up." In the following subsections, we will explore the connections between the biblical stories of Jesus' baptism and the experiences of my research partners within the baptized body.

JESUS' BAPTISM AND COMMUNITIES OF BELONGING

The Gospel stories of Jesus' baptism in the Jordan River held central importance within the lives of many research participants, particularly in affirming their experience of belovedness within Christian community. During our interview, James put it this way: "baptism is really about . . . you're a beloved child." Later, James expressed it saying: "since I got baptized, I become a beloved son." James' parents affirmed his love for the biblical story of Jesus' baptism, especially God's proclamation of Jesus' belovedness. This centrality of belovedness in the Gospel accounts of Jesus' baptism also resonated with Pastor Daniel: "the baptism of Jesus sort of narrates who we are at the core, in our belovedness."[6] As James and Pastor Daniel illustrated in our conversations, this baptismal birth into a new life of belovedness offers a pattern for ecclesial life. Just as God the Father names Jesus "my beloved son" at his baptism by John the Baptist in the Jordan River, so James and Pastor Daniel shared convictions that the church's practices of baptism ought to align with commitments to name and uphold the belovedness of all the baptized—both people with and without disabilities. Parke also emphasized the significance of God's proclamation of Jesus' belovedness in the biblical stories of Jesus' baptism: "The creator of all the universe spoke: that this is my Son. That's powerful when you think about it." My research partners' focus on individual and communal belovedness rooted in Jesus' baptism echo long-standing Christian notions of Jesus' baptism as a womb or a site of new life marked by belovedness and adoption by Christ.[7]

For other research participants, this baptismal theme of belovedness connected closely to the realities of repentance and forgiveness of sin within the biblical stories of Jesus' baptism. During our research interview, Elisabeth connected Jesus' baptism to the forgiveness and "washing away" of sin. Reflecting on her own baptism at the age of 12, she shared: "coming up out of the baptismal pool I knew I was a new creature in Christ." Christ's own baptism in the Jordan, marked by repentance and new life, provided my research participants a way to affirm the new life present in all the baptized. Instead of connecting repentance with cognitive capacities, suggesting that people with intellectual disabilities might only participate in belovedness and not repentance, my research partners looked to Jesus' baptism as a witness that baptized communities must involve both practices of repentance and affirmations of belovedness for all disciples—both disabled and nondisabled.

As recounted in the Gospel stories, the public nature of Jesus' baptism and the Trinitarian affirmation of Jesus as God's beloved Son, anointed for ministry in the Holy Spirit,[8] provide a pattern for the transformed life of baptismal communities. As Hope told me, describing her Episcopal parish: "it certainly doesn't matter what level of cognitive ability you have in order to be baptized here. It's much more that you are going through a transformation that God and we are all enacting at once." As Hope affirmed, the public and transformational nature of baptismal life is rooted both in God's action and ecclesial grounding. Put differently, the community of the baptized body provides the context where this ongoing transformation, through the work of the Holy Spirit, is recognized, encouraged, and supported. Rather than imagining a kind of public transformation enabled by human effort, Hope and other research partners emphasized the action of God in supporting this shared baptismal life of transformation. Lea also affirmed this theocentric baptismal transformation emphasized in the witness of Jesus' baptism: "it's about God's call to us to be in community. It's about the church saying—you're not going to be doing this by yourself. In the Bible . . . human beings are always called back into community. And so I think that the nature of God is togetherness. And baptism is a reflection of that." Finally, Ava, a young adult with an intellectual disability, beautifully reflected on these themes of transformation during our conversation about accounts of Jesus' baptism. Reflecting on these biblical stories, Ava shared with me that baptism "means you're being cleansed by the Holy Spirit to God . . . this means you're majorly connected to God spiritually in the mystery of the Holy Trinity."

Biblical stories of Jesus' baptism also held strong connections with the baptismal identities of this book's research participants. Three research partners with intellectual disabilities described the connections between Jesus' baptism and their own sense of identity as follows:

> "Baptism shows that Jesus was buried, and that he rose again from the dead. I was buried just like Jesus was. I was buried like Jesus. I was buried like Jesus and rose again. Rose up from the dead."—Danny
>
> "I became a new man in Jesus Christ."—David
>
> "And I rise like Jesus did."—James

Just as Jesus' baptism by John in the Jordan River set the scene for God's revealing of Christ as "the long-awaited One," so too baptism made clear the identity of my disabled research partners—those, like all the baptized, who have been joined to Jesus.[9] My research participants' reflections on baptismal identity connected to the story of Jesus' baptism in the Jordan, with a particular emphasis on the embodied symbolism of Jesus' baptismal rising from the Jordan River, resulting in newness of life.

The interplay of communal transformation, Christian identity, and new life described among my research partners characterizes Winner's interpretation of the Gospel accounts of Jesus' baptism:

> Jesus' baptism models what every subsequent baptism should achieve: the both/and of affirming the baptizand's locality and particularity, and extracting him from it. In Jesus' baptism, as in our own, both the extraction and the affirmation are in service of incorporating the baptized person into the body of Christ. The extraction is in the service of my being incorporated because if I am not taken out of the thing I am in, I cannot be placed somewhere new. And the affirmation is in service of my being incorporated into the body of Christ because if all my particularities were *erased* (rather than affirmed), then I could not be incorporated into Christ (or into anything else)—because I would no longer be myself...[10]

The experiences of my research partners provide an embodied witness of this "both/and" of baptismal identity described by Winner. Through an active embrace of Christians with intellectual disabilities, rather than an erasure of disability identity, participants in the research for this book demonstrate a discipleship that embraces both an individualized identity marked by newness in Christ and incorporation into the ever-transforming communal body of the church.

My research partners' reflections on Jesus' baptism demonstrate how people with intellectual disabilities, as active participants in the life of the baptized body, contribute to the formation of ecclesial imagination that affirms resonances between Jesus' baptism and the lives of discipleship among all the baptized. Their reflections importantly underscore the notion that this vision of discipleship does not necessitate, as New Testament scholar Grant Macaskill puts it, "one's capacity to perform a certain kind of identity . . . and neither is it something that needs to be perceived in order to be real. It is something that is constituted outside of our own consciousness by our union with Christ."[11] In other words, theological reflections from a disabled perspective highlight the reality of identity rooted in Jesus for all the baptized, not only those who might actively express it. Just as God the Father named Jesus "a beloved son" in his baptism in the Jordan River, so too God names all those baptized in the church today as God's beloved, without requirement of particular human capacity or aptitude. My research partners' connections with the Gospel stories of Jesus' baptism suggest that living into a scripturally informed Christian identity does not require a particular "disability ministry" or a specialized appreciation of arguments from the field of disability theology. Instead, baptismal communities who approach God's word together and take it seriously for the lives of all the baptized, not only those with capacities for higher level reading and interpretation, demonstrate the profound outworking of a baptismally shaped imagination.

In the next section, we will continue to build on participant reflections, moving from biblical accounts of Jesus' baptism to Paul's baptismal writings. In this shift, we will continue to examine how experiences of disability within Christian community illuminate the role of baptism for supporting communities of belonging.

PAUL'S THEOLOGY OF THE BAPTIZED BODY

Resonating with the Christocentric nature of baptism affirmed among my research partners and explored in the previous chapter, liturgical theologian Bryan Spinks argues that in Pauline accounts of baptism, Jesus serves as "the eyepiece of the kaleidoscope . . . all other concepts and images are focused through him."[12] Through my participants' interpretive perspectives on baptism as not only Jesus centered, but also communal and participatory, we will next consider how Paul's baptismal reflections[13] in his New Testament Epistles can critically form baptismal communities marked by rich belonging for people with disabilities.

Participation: Death to Sin and Life "Under Grace"

> What then are we to say? Should we continue in sin in order that grace may abound? By no means! How can we who died to sin go on living in it? Do you not know that all of us who have been baptized into Christ Jesus were baptized into his death? Therefore we have been buried with him by baptism into death, so that, just as Christ was raised from the dead by the glory of the Father, so we too might walk in newness of life.
>
> For if we have been united with him in a death like his, we will certainly be united with him in a resurrection like his. We know that our old self was crucified with him so that the body of sin might be destroyed, and we might no longer be enslaved to sin. For whoever has died is freed from sin. But if we have died with Christ, we believe that we will also live with him. We know that Christ, being raised from the dead, will never die again; death no longer has dominion over him. The death he died, he died to sin, once for all; but the life he lives, he lives to God. So you also must consider yourselves dead to sin and alive to God in Christ Jesus.
>
> Therefore, do not let sin exercise dominion in your mortal bodies, to make you obey their passions. No longer present your members to sin as instruments of wickedness, but present yourselves to God as those who have been brought from death to life, and present your members to God as instruments of righteousness. For sin will have no dominion over you, since you are not under law but under grace. (Rom 6:1–14)

Paul's powerful theological account of baptism in Romans 6:1–14[14] resonated most frequently with my participants' experiences of baptismal belonging within their local communities. This passage from Romans hinges on participation in Jesus' death through the praxis of baptism: a dramatic, embodied witness of deliverance in Jesus from the realm of sin.[15] Throughout the passage, Paul frames participation in baptism as a central proclamation of Christian faith—witnessing to the salvific event of Jesus' incarnation, crucifixion, and resurrection. Similarly to my research partners' reflections on the Gospel accounts of Jesus' baptism, Romans 6 encapsulated for them a theological foundation for their baptismal identities as those incorporated into Jesus and empowered by the Holy Spirit for new life.

Paul's language of participation in Romans 6 conveys a radical baptismal message: Christian life is marked by a break with sin that undeniably shapes Christian identity and praxis.[16] In his research interview, Pastor Daniel put it this way: "Pauline statements in one way or another say baptism is participating in the work of God and Christ. Dying and rising. It speaks to your past, your present, your future." As Pastor Daniel highlights, a Pauline understanding of baptism, with its keen focus on incorporation in Christ's death in defiance of the realm of sin and death, concludes that in the mystery of baptism, Christians participate in Christ's salvific death.[17] Ava described a communal sense of awe within her own ecclesial community at this mysterious and transformative reality of baptismal participation: "I feel like they're not surely knowing what that means!"

Several responses from clergy research participants engaged the reality that this union with Jesus rests at the heart of baptismal participation. Pastor John, reflecting on baptisms at his congregation, Christ Church, shared that participation in baptism underscores that "we're interconnected. Because you can't baptize yourself." This reflection from Pastor John resonates with Rowan Williams' description of baptismal participation: "baptism brings you into the neighbourhood of other Christians; and there is no way of being a Christian without being in the neighbourhood of other Christians."[18] In the local community of Christ Church, members testify to this dependence upon each other, as well as their dependence upon the death and resurrection of Jesus, within the words and gestures of their baptismal liturgies. Reflecting on the dependency at the heart of Paul's baptismal logic in Romans 6, as it is embodied at Christ Church, Pastor John shared the following reflection with me during our research interview: "I think everything that is true of us happens in Christ . . . we can slip quite unintentionally into a Pelagian understanding of things where what we do really matters . . . and I would say what we do is really a joyous participation in what God, emphatically and completely, has done in Christ."[19] Pastor John's reflections emphasize that a mysterious, baptismal participation in Christ's action, rather than participation conditioned by human effort alone, is central to the transformation that Paul suggests happens to Christians in the waters of baptism.[20]

Pastor Paula articulated that participation in Jesus through baptism continues in a community's ongoing life of discipleship—living into "the good news of God and Christ corporately." The baptized body, through the indwelling of the Holy Spirit, lives out a communal vocation of discipleship that witnesses to their calling to walk in newness of life, not as a pursuit of their own merit and competencies, but rooted in radical dependence on Jesus. As we will see in the next chapter, Paul's vision of a baptismal identity of new creation, an identity wholly dependent on Jesus, holds implications that challenge ecclesial imaginations committed to elevating the possession of particular intellectual capacities among certain members of the baptized body. For Paul, the continual effects of baptismal participation are rooted in none other than the power of Jesus over the realm of sin and death. This power sustains the life of the baptized body by the indwelling of the Holy Spirit.[21]

The above insights from my research participants, attuned to questions of disability, find resonance within wider scholarly interpretations of Paul's account of baptismal participation in Romans 6.[22] Biblical scholar Rudolf Schnackenburg offers an important description of the radicalness of baptismal incorporation: "through baptism we have been united in the closest fashion with the event of Christ's dying and burial, and thereby attained to death (for sin)."[23] Leander Keck notes the power of sin's dominion and enslaving control and that it cannot be overcome by human commitment, and so can only be broken, according to Paul, through participation in Christ's death and resurrection.[24] Thus, freedom comes through the fullness of one's life being bound to Christ—a union enacted in the church's practice of baptism. In the mystery of baptism, those who are baptized participate in Jesus' salvific death and are incorporated into a community who lives out this participatory shift from sin and death to a grace-oriented newness of life. Paul's participatory description of baptism in Romans 6 (particularly verse 4) emphasizes that participation in new life cannot function apart from Christ—thus the stark inconsistency between a life of participation in sin, and a baptized life where believers, together and through the power of Jesus, participate in newness of life with hope of the final resurrection.[25]

In his work on autism and ecclesial communities, Macaskill describes baptismal participation as resonant with Paul's overall theological project—a vision of Christian life where discipleship is always "experienced through our constitutional weakness . . . our experience of salvation is not disembodied, but is lived within the context of the frailty of our flesh, which is both morally and physically needy."[26] Pastor Daniel's account of the baptism of Danny, an older adult with an intellectual disability, at St. Matthew's Baptist Church, offers a narrative that exemplifies Macaskill's account of dependency as central to Paul's overall theology, as well as his understanding of baptismal participation. During our interview, Pastor Daniel beautifully described the story as follows:

> For Danny it was rather logistically challenging because his mobility was so limited. And, you know, it's like babies. There are two types of babies. There are some who know how to be held and there are some that are just like bags of sand. And Danny is a bag of sand. He didn't know how to help you help him. And so we had to make extra preparations to get him into the waters of baptism . . .
>
> We ended up having four or five deacons and strong bodies to help hoist him into the water. And I do remember very vividly how tenderly they spoke to him . . . I wish people could sort of overhear the gentle whispers and affirmations as they picked him up and reassured him they wouldn't drop him . . . I don't want to belabor it, but . . . the team effort that was required.
>
> The thing that touched me was hearing these men . . . many of whom are not very emotive or emotional or tender—being extremely gentle and affirming and caring of Danny, just very

quietly telling him he's "going to be okay," "we've got you," those kinds of things . . . the narrative that came to mind and I've never been able to shake is the group of friends who cut a hole in the roof and dropped their paralyzed friend into to Jesus' lap. That was the image. You could just sort of lift that story out of the Gospel and change the names. And that's what Danny's baptism was like.

The community who baptized Danny encapsulates Paul's account of baptismal participation marked by dependency—"not a convocation of those who are privileged, elite and separate, but of those who have accepted what it means to be in the heart of a needy, contaminated, messy world."[27] Yet as Danny experienced it, this participation was wholly dependent upon, and parallel to, the life of Jesus: "I was buried just like Jesus was. I was buried like Jesus. I was buried like Jesus and rose again. Rose up from the dead." It is this Jesus-centered account of baptism in Paul's writings, considered from the perspective of disabled experience, that we turn to next.

The Centrality of Jesus in Paul's Baptismal Logic

As we have affirmed above, in concert with biblical scholars and the research participants for this project, Paul's participatory account of baptism is inextricably connected with the death and resurrection of Jesus.[28] Paul's Jesus-centered focus on baptism in Romans 6 challenges commitments among local church communities that display primary allegiance to human ritual or sentimentality in their baptismal practices. Baptism is more than an initiatory practice or a ceremonious rite of passage—it is an immersion into what Paul characterizes as the universe-altering Christ-event: Jesus' death, resurrection, and Parousia.[29]

Expanding upon the connections between Jesus' baptism and their own baptismal identities, research participants also emphasized their own sense of Christian identity as connected to Jesus' death and resurrection—the central animating power of Paul's baptismal logic in Romans 6. James shared with me about his baptism as an ongoing site of formation for knowing Jesus. James enjoys watching a video recording of his baptismal service, a practice he has taken up at least once a week for over fifteen years. James told me, "when I want to learn about Jesus, I watch my movie again."

In a different research interview, Steve reflected on the meaning of baptism within communities of disabled and nondisabled Christians, offering a description in parallel with Paul's centering of Jesus' death and resurrection: "baptism is to be immersed three times in the water of baptism through which we are made part of Jesus' death that we may experience the resurrection . . . you're put under the water in the third time down, which is a reminder that you are to be so immersed as you can't breathe, so that's death. But you are raised up. That's life."

Steve's definition of baptism as being "made part of Jesus' death that we may experience the resurrection . . . that's life" resonates with the identity-shifting consequences of baptism into Jesus' body captured by Paul within Romans 6. This transformation of identity plays out carefully in verses 6–11 of Romans 6: the old humanity (the "Adamic self") of Romans 5 is no longer definitive of human creatures following baptism. Instead, Paul's perspective of newness assumes that those who participate in baptismal solidarity with Jesus find their identity no longer defined by Adam, but instead by Jesus.[30] The identity of the newly baptized, derived from Jesus, offers a witness of new life in the midst of a world entangled with sin and death.[31] In this way, baptismal communities inhabit a double-sided identity: being dead to sin while also being alive for God.[32] Hope reflected on this reality during her interview, expressing "those baptized are dying to themselves and rising in Christ through the waters of baptism. They're being born to new life. And us around them claim that person as a baptized member of the church. And promise to support that person and their life in Christ." The church's practice of baptism proclaims the identity of baptizands as new creatures in Christ. And, as Hope suggests, the church as a baptized body welcomes the newly baptized into a community of support and witness—a community marked by Jesus' life in the midst of the realm of death.

But a tension remains: despite the radical shift in identity attained in baptism through the salvific work of Christ, on this side of the eschaton, Christians remain in the world, where the realm of sin is alive and active. Though the consequences of unity with Christ's death in baptism is that the Christian will attain full union with Jesus in the final resurrection,[33] this is an anticipatory reality. In this way, the unity of the baptized with Jesus' death grants an already but not yet reality—the baptized are empowered to walk in newness of life under Jesus' reign of grace but are also those oriented toward the hope of the final resurrection.[34] At Christ Church, Pastor John reflected on how practices of baptism affirm this tension for congregants both with and without disabilities: baptism is a communal act of confession that helps us name things "that need to die." As Christians long for the final resurrection, practicing baptism both solidifies hope, while also calling Christians to confession and repentance within the realm of sin. For Pastor John and his community, Christians with intellectual disabilities are not exempt from participating in confession and repentance—as those who are baptized into the already but not yet of Jesus' new creation, disabled Christians too join the nondisabled members of Jesus' body in the current realm of flesh.[35]

While a transformative identity shift occurs in baptism, human creatures continue to groan for the fullness of the coming new creation. Paul's Jesus-centered baptismal logic affirms that death is not the final word (Romans 6:7–8). The practice of baptism offers "a junction to life"—a unity with Jesus that empowers the baptized to live for God in the current age.[36] Jesus permeates not only the ritual moment of baptism for Paul, but also focuses the whole of the post-baptismal life of discipleship. The unity of the baptized with Jesus results in an identity redefinition oriented toward Jesus and performed communally in lifelong discipleship—being alive for Jesus.[37] From a disability perspective, this inseparability of all the baptized with Jesus invites the church not to erase disability identities and access needs, but to recognize that disability coexists with an identity of death to sin and rising with Jesus. Paul's baptismal theology invites us to imagine how we support the Jesus-soaked baptismal identity of all people, including those who may not explicitly articulate this aspect of who they are. Christians with intellectual disabilities do not face theological barriers to this full baptismal union with Christ. Rather, it is ecclesial imaginations about Christian identity and discipleship that hold the power to distort Jesus' work in and through disabled Christians because of their baptismal unity with Christ. As we will explore in the next section, Paul's vision of the baptized community pushes us toward an imagination that robustly welcomes all into belonging in Jesus.

Community: Belonging in the Baptized Body

Paul's baptismal logic in Romans 6 envisions a community of holiness in which a postbaptismal discipleship is cultivated and sustained by the Holy Spirit. As explored above, this discipleship is rooted in new life springing from a Christological unity between the baptized community and Jesus. Unity with Christ in baptism both entails a break from sin, as well as a communally expressed new life of discipleship. This Christological grounding of the baptized body provides a communal orientation[38] toward ongoing transformation, marked by fruitful discipleship that anticipates the coming of God's good future. As Paul exhorts the church in Rome to "present yourselves to God as those who have been brought from death to life," (Romans 6:13), so too contemporary churches sense this call to follow Jesus in loving practices marked by abundant life. Research participants with intellectual disabilities and their loved ones expressed to me the centrality of this kind of baptismal community in their own experiences. Barbara described her church community, saying "that's our home. That's our family. Bob has unconditional love there." Paul's framing of the church as an inclusive community rooted in baptism calls forth spaces of loving belonging such as that experienced by Barbara, her husband Jim, and their son Bob.

In contrast to Paul's contemporaries at the time his New Testament Epistles were composed, communal formation instead of individualized moral development receives greater emphasis.[39] Paul's distinctive baptismal vision supposes a community of the baptized, marked by transformation and anticipation, and strengthened through God's active work in the community, including a commitment to practicing baptism.[40] For Paul, radical inclusiveness marks the baptismal community: "do you not know that *all of us* who have been baptized into Christ Jesus were baptized into his death?" (Romans 6:3). This communal framing of baptism invites deep inclusion of all the baptized across their many particularities. Human differences (including advantages and positive characteristics) are displaced for a radical inclusion of all people into the person who constitutes the community of the baptized body: Jesus Christ.

Jesus-centered communities of transformative discipleship honor the baptismal identity of all people—including those with intellectual disabilities. This communal discipleship in Paul's baptismal thought challenges contemporary churches to not only include and foster belonging among disabled people in their midst, but also become careful observers, companions, and listeners who wait for, learn from, and cherish the ways of following Jesus among people with disability identities. During her research interview, Anna reflected on this kind of community at her home parish of Holy Angels Episcopal Church. She expressed how the church affirmed the baptismal identity of disabled (and nondisabled) church members by discerning together how each baptized person's presence offered a gift to "the whole community." Anna specifically spoke about the presence and ministry of Hikari, a young adult with an intellectual disability in her parish. Sharing about the abundance of Hikari's gifts, and how their continued unfolding offered a strong witness, Anna reflected: "Hikari has all of these gifts . . . she could just change your life." Anna's witness to Hikari's gifts highlights how disability experience can enliven imagination about Paul's notion of communal baptismal transformation: an ecclesial responsibility to embrace full partnership in discipleship with individuals with intellectual disabilities, as well as other groups of Christians often marginalized by the church. Anna's reflections on Hikari's witness resonate with New Testament scholar Samuli Siikavirta's understanding of Paul's description of Christian community in Romans 6: baptized members of Jesus' body who together seek freedom from sin through living into their shared belonging to Christ.[41] As Keck puts it, Paul's list of "stark contrasts" in Romans 6 calls Christians to "be what they became in baptism:"[42] Jesus-centered communities of mutual discipleship.

CONCLUSION

Throughout our exploration of biblical stories of baptism in this chapter, we have seen the research partners for this book embody how the biblical witness comes to bear on their lives in Christian community. Theological insights from Scripture come together with ecclesial practices, enabling my research participants' communities to embrace a baptismal discipleship marked by newness of life among both disabled and nondisabled Christians. In these communal exercises of discipleship, disability is not an experience to overcome, but a vital part of ongoing transformation in the baptized body. Additionally, disability experiences among members of Jesus' baptized body who participated in this book's research highlight for us embodied examples of the kind of ecclesial belonging encouraged in Paul's vision of baptismal discipleship.

Baptism as an initiating site of transformation underscores its potency as a Christian practice of renewal in the Holy Spirit. In Paul's writings, he expresses baptism as the beginning of God's creative work as the reality of "new creation." In the next chapter, in continued conversation with research participants and biblical scholars, we will consider how Paul's understanding of baptismal life as "new creation" raises important new questions for theological proposals about disability. As we will also explore, a disability theology of new creation highlights how reimagining baptismal identity can form ecclesial communities in patterns of belonging that fully embrace the presence of disabled members of Jesus' baptized body.

4

A New Creation

Paul and Baptismal Identity

Encountered through the disability perspective shared among the research participants for this book, Paul's Jesus-centered, participatory, and communal theology of baptism raises important considerations for Christian identity. As the integrative account of biblical scholars and research partners in the last chapter suggested, Paul's baptismal vision of Christian life holds robust space for the belonging of individuals with a wide variety of disability experiences. In this chapter, building upon the insights from research participants and Pauline scholars, I will articulate more clearly Paul's vision for Christian identity in the baptized body—those "in Christ."

While anachronistic to insist that Paul's baptismal description of Christian identity explicitly considered people with intellectual disabilities, I will argue that Paul's narration of a baptismally rooted Christian identity demonstrates a deep concern for the flourishing of people across many forms of difference.[1] In this way, Paul's baptismal understanding of Christian identity offers both a theological framework for supporting ecclesial communities of belonging, as well as underscores practices that can shape how Christian communities reimagine the human experience of disability.

We will begin this chapter by briefly identifying Paul's construction of the relational "self," guided by the work of Pauline scholar Susan Grove Eastman. Next, building on this relational notion of the self in Paul's writings, I will illustrate the foundational influence of baptism on his theological framework for Christian identity.

Turning to Paul's account of "New Creation" in 2 Corinthians 5, we will next explore this particular Pauline articulation of Christian identity, including its relevance for considering the experiences of disabled Christians. Finally, engaging with my research partners' theological reflections on baptism, we will discover additional resonances between Paul's articulation of new creation identity and disability experiences.

THE "SELF" IN PAUL

"For Paul the self is always a self-in-relation-to-others."[2] Susan Eastman's interpretation of Paul's concept of the "self" challenges accounts of Pauline identity that prioritize individualization. Other scholarship on Paul's notion of the self, such as Samuli Siikavirta's work on baptism, interprets cognitive capacities as central for Paul's account of how Christians embrace their identity as those baptized in Christ.[3] For Siikavirta, mental processes such as knowing, reasoning, and remembering play a crucial role in recognizing the transformative work of the Holy Spirit in Christian life.[4] His account of the Pauline self underscores that the unity of Christians with Jesus' death and resurrection in baptism calls forth a cognitive reckoning that ought to transform Christians' minds, occupy their thoughts, and direct their imaginations.[5]

In contrast to Siikavirta's cognitively focused and individualized interpretation of Christian identity in Paul, Eastman's account of the Pauline self as deeply relational creates robust space for the inclusion of people "in extremis"—people with dementia, autistic persons, and those with intellectual disabilities.[6] Not only does her resistance to an individualized account of identity help to create a theologically and conceptually expansive anthropology, but it also provides a foundation for resourcing the practices of care exercised among communities of belonging. Toward the end of our research interview, Hope expressed the difference that this kind of relational view of Christian identity within the community of the church makes: "we're all part of this. We need each other. The one who is baptizing and the one who is being baptized and the community that supports them is all one." Hikari shared a similar reflection on the foundational core of relationships in the church: "the part about church that I really truly love is the community. I think the church should be the people. Not the building, not any of the artifacts, but the people." Hope and Hikari's reflections highlight the interdependent and communal notions of Eastman's relational interpretation of Paul's understanding of human selves.[7]

Liberation from modern commitments to individualized and hypercognitive constitutions of identity allows Christians to reclaim Jesus as the source and continuity of who they are. Eastman expresses this reality as follows:

> Divine continuity and human discontinuity mean that death and resurrection, not development or maturation, are the watchwords of Christian existence. The result is a distinctive picture of the self over time: the embodied individual finds his or her vital existence only in and through the gifts and calling exercised in the body of Christ, which are 'new every morning' and not innate or gradually developing.[8]

In other words, Paul's description of the reality of life in Christ depends not on practices of cognitive refinement, or any kind of individualized developmental timeline, to enable faithful discipleship. Instead, Paul's vision of who Christians are rests in communities of belonging rooted in Jesus' death and resurrection. Reflecting on Paul's writing in Galatians 2, Eastman puts it this way: "God's action in Christ is the only sure foundation for the life of faith, which is lived out in the common life of believers. That divine action takes place in and through the crucifixion and resurrection life of Jesus." For Eastman, this divine action "gains traction in human lives through a mutually participatory union between Christ and those 'in Christ.'"[9]

The church's baptismal practices offer an embodiment of this participatory union of Jesus and those "in Christ." Baptism provides a sign and symbol of selves-in-relation within the body of Jesus. In the next section of this chapter, we will take a closer look at how Paul's construction of Christian identity finds deep resonance with his baptismal theology. As I will argue, baptism offers a key framework for Christians to witness to their participatory dependence upon Jesus. And it is within the community of Jesus' baptized body where Christians find the fullest embodiment and expression of their new lives in Christ.

BAPTISMAL IDENTITY IN PAUL

Attending to Paul's theology of baptism as it intersects with Christian identity will be our key task in the following pages. We will explore these intersections through the interwoven and inseparable baptismal themes of participation, community, and Christocentricity offered by my research partners. Beyond a simple formula that helps us imagine and live into Christian identity as relational rather than individualized, Paul's account of the baptismal contours of Christian identity highlights the subversive nature of discipleship within the body of Jesus. Just as the incarnate Jesus took on "full immersion in fleshly experience," so Christians too are immersed in the waters of baptism to emerge as those wholly changed by unity with Jesus throughout the whole of their life of discipleship.[10]

People who Belong to Jesus: The Participatory and Communal Contours of Baptismal Identity

Participation in baptism witnesses to the reconstituting work of God that marks the identities of all Christians. Baptismal participation in Jesus' death and resurrection reconstitutes identity within what John Barclay names as Jesus' "counter-reign" of grace.[11] Baptism proclaims that Jesus' gift of new life is noncontingent on human merit or obedience. Instead, the Triune God meets human creatures within "an avalanche of sin (Romans 5:12–21) . . . not by enhancing or supplementing their natural capacities but in an act of burial and new life: the old life is brought to an end and an impossible new life—life out of death—begins."[12] This impossible new life of Christian discipleship, in Paul's theological framework of baptism, emerges out of Jesus' burial and rising and not individualized human capacity—cognitive or otherwise.

As we explored in the previous chapter, Paul establishes baptism as the distinctive proclamatory enactment of Christian identity. This identity requires dependent participation within the life of Jesus. Thus, Christians undergo a "recentering" of their identities in baptism. In encountering the baptismal waters, a sign of drowned and then resurrected life, Christian communities testify to their lives as "wholly dependent on the life of Another, the One who is risen from the dead . . . (Romans 6:4; cf. 7:6)."[13] Paul's vision of baptismal participation as a proclamation of dependent identity deconstructs the notion that possessing particular cognitive skills underlay what it truly means to be a Christian. A baptismal identity characterized by a life of dependency on the risen Christ pushes conversations about selfhood away from capacity and individualization, opening up a space to consider all baptized believers, both disabled and nondisabled, as those who are radically dependent upon the Triune God for their new life, constituted in Christian community. This is good news, perhaps especially for those who experience intellectual disability in contemporary Western contexts, including the church, that too often hold fast to a competing vision of identity that pushes disabled people to the periphery. Instead of an identity that coalesces around exalting particular human capacities, Rowan Williams reminds us that in Paul's theological framework for baptism, "joining the Christian community is associated with the idea of going down into the darkness of Jesus' suffering and death, being 'swamped' by the reality of what Jesus endured."[14]

As I alluded to above, baptismal identity roots Christians in a subversive reality that wholly depends upon Jesus. In a Pauline construction of the self, human beings are not merely "isolated individuals in need of moving from their solitary existence to a shared life with others." Instead, in Eastman's reading of Paul, those "in Christ" do not simply escape a relational web entangled with death "into a different realm of power." Rather, the human realm of the flesh is "invaded" by Jesus, "who both assimilates to humanity's bondage and then subverts it through crucifixion and resurrection."[15] This reading of Paul highlights Jesus' invasion of the baptized community. Jesus accompanies baptized communities by participating with them in the struggle to walk in newness of life within the earthly realm of the flesh.

This account of participation in Jesus' death and resurrection offers a stark reminder of the ongoing complexity and struggle of baptismal living. As Grant Macaskill argues, reflecting on ecclesial communities where autistic people flourish and lead, "simply belonging to the people of God does not exempt us from the possibility that we will act viciously, with the best of religious intentions. Nothing should make us expect that churches will be safe spaces for the vulnerable; they will only become so through the Spirit's war with the flesh."[16] During my research interview with Hikari, she shared a painful story from her church experience, even though the community had largely been supportive of her presence as a disabled Christian. After serving as a service assistant for many years, a fellow church member suggested that Hikari's disability identity ought to disqualify her from this activity in liturgical leadership. Hikari recounted, "she made it clear that I was inferior to everyone else and did her best to get me off the acolyte list." Hikari illustrates here part of Macaskill's core argument—simply baptizing people with disabilities and verbally declaring that they belong within church communities does not constitute the end of the story. Instead, as Macaskill suggests, Christian communities must become places that together attend to and participate in the Holy Spirit's empowering movement for justice and belonging, throughout the whole of their lives together. Put simply, having disabled Christians present in church communities, even in contexts where they actively participate and lead, is not enough. Communities of belonging do not emerge because people with disabilities participate in ecclesial practices alongside nondisabled people. The baptismal participation in Jesus' death and resurrection at the core of Paul's notion of Christian identity requires communities to take seriously the daily practical consequences of participating in a way of life fully dependent upon Jesus—committing to a pattern of communal life that daily repents of and dies to the ways of the flesh. It is this community that repents and attends to the Spirit together that defines Paul's account of the baptized body.

So what does Paul specifically suggest characterizes these baptismal communities who participate in and depend upon Jesus? Paul's chief concept of baptismal identity as communally bound lies in the body.[17] Importantly, Paul's emphasis on Christian community as the body is not metaphorical alone. Paul engages the body on multiple planes, including engraftment into the very body of Jesus, as well as the importance of participation in embodied practices such as baptism. New Testament scholar Ernst Käsemann specifically emphasizes the role of bodily participation in baptism as the channel through which human creatures are joined to Jesus' one body, and thus constituted as a people with a necessarily communal identity: we are one body in Christ because by one Spirit we were baptized into one body.[18]

Paul's use of the body supports his claims about the shared communal identity of all baptized people. For example, as Paul explores in 1 Corinthians 12, the body requires each of its constitutive parts to function as a whole—even the parts regarded as weak and least honorable (1 Corinthians 12:21–26). Käsemann argues that this passage underscores the "non-isolable existence"[19] of all those who are baptized. Consequently, baptism, the site where human creatures are incorporated into Jesus' body and bound to one another, calls the church to discern the work of the Holy Spirit among all the baptized as the Spirit empowers each member of Jesus' body to witness to God's ongoing work in the world. This responsibility of the baptized body remains steady: no matter what a person's gifts might look like, part of communal Christian identity requires us to discern and support all members of Jesus' body.

The multiplicity of gifts among the multiplicity of selves that constitute the baptized body underscores the necessity of human difference for Paul and his account of Christian identity. Käsemann writes about the beauty and necessity of variety within the body of Jesus, suggesting that it is "the priesthood of all believers which manifests the reality of the body of Christ."[20] This priesthood of all believers entails the acknowledgement of the gifts of all selves in Jesus' body as necessary for constituting life together—a unified life of baptismal discipleship and transformation. In strong contrast to centering an individualized valuing of diverse members of the body, Paul's communal view of baptismal identity in Christ opens space for people who embody any range of decipherable capacities, with special attention to how these gifts are identified and supported within the context of community discernment and care.

Following her interpretation of Paul's anthropological logic, Eastman suggests that ecclesial communities embody their baptismal identities through transformation that occurs within "networks."[21]

For Eastman, "insofar as change happens, it happens through the characteristics of communal interaction that mediate Christ."[22] Eastman's reading of Paul here helps reframe the difficulties that often occur within churches where leaders or other members cannot seem to discern the work of the Spirit within the life of another member of the body—whether a person with an intellectual disability or someone else. Resonant with the relational self within Paul's writings, Eastman invites us to understand baptismal gifts and vocations as contextualized within communities of care. Just as important as discerning the gifts and work of the Spirit within members of Jesus' body, and perhaps even more important, is discerning the Spirit's work in webs of care throughout ecclesial communities and beyond. In this way, baptismal identity finds its embodiment in communal practices of love, empowered by the Holy Spirit. And the vocation of the baptized body is to name these relationships as vital to a shared identity in Christ.

Embodying baptismal identity through discerning the work of the Holy Spirit, both in individual members and networks of mutual care, emerges out of the church's unity in Jesus. For Paul, according to Romans 6, this unity finds its paradigmatic expression in communities that practice baptismal sharing in Jesus' death and new life.[23] As biblical scholar Richard Carlson argues, baptism for Paul is the event which inaugurates "people of radically different backgrounds . . . into the unifying reality of the body of Christ. Paul presents this common baptismal inauguration as the work of the Spirit rather than as the work of individual Christians themselves."[24] Carlson's argument paints Paul's baptismal theology as thoroughly pneumatological and communal, rather than strictly individualistic. Paul's particular writings on baptism in 1 Corinthians 12 (verses 13 and 27) highlight this Spirit-cultivated unity that marks Christian identity: "For in the one Spirit we were all baptized into one body—Jews or Greeks, slaves or free—and we were all made to drink of one Spirit." . . . "Now you are the body of Christ and individually members of it."

For Paul, this initiation and incorporation of the baptized into Christ does not end in a one-time identity shift. Rather, Paul's theology of baptism expects a baptismal community marked by ongoing transformation in the Holy Spirit. This transformation emerges from unity with Jesus. As Macaskill suggests, "God's dealings" with individuals in the baptized body are never separated from God's work in the community as a whole—"the lambs are part of the flock, regardless of their state of cognitive development."[25] Baptismal identity as unity with Jesus also includes unity with other Christians. In baptism, and other Christian practices, members of the baptized body are woven together, becoming "members of one another" as Paul writes in Romans 12.

Navigating this identity of being woven together with others in the body of Jesus requires ongoing ways to recognize each other and participate in life together, a process Paul calls "discerning the body" (1 Corinthians 11:29). This discernment of shared baptismal identity comes in part through recognizing that Christians are made members of one another through the strange gift of the Holy Spirit in baptism (1 Corinthians 12:12–13)—a gift that shapes the trajectory of their entire lives, more than any other human condition, capacity, or commonality.[26] In 1 Corinthians 12, Paul communicates that through the Spirit, all the baptized members of Jesus' body are to be known as "an active giver or conduit of divine love, a giving that is not reducible to any person's supposed physiological or intellectual deficiencies."[27] As theologian Brian Brock goes on to argue, in the context of 1 Corinthians 12, Paul argues that "the Spirit alone chooses which gifts will be dispensed by any given part of the body. No human management of leadership is needed to make the body of Christ efficient."[28] With regard to discerning the gifts of disabled Christians in the baptized body, Brock challenges assessments of vocation, gifts, and presence among people with disabilities that are situated as inferior to those of nondisabled Christians.[29] Paul's writings about the baptized body, especially in 1 Corinthians 12, remind ecclesial communities that the Spirit alone dispenses gifts. Baptized communities in turn ought to anticipate the Spirit's work in each member of the body, as well as throughout the process of each baptizand becoming members of one another.

While unity "in Christ" constitutes Christian communities, Paul does not presume that this constitution involves the flattening of distinctiveness between human creatures' various identities such as disability, race, and gender. As Paul writes in 1 Corinthians 12:20, "there are many parts, yet one body." Christian identity for Paul envisions communities marked by unity "in Christ" *across difference*—not the removal of distinction among the many parts of the baptized body. In fact, difference is necessary for the baptized body—if all those baptized in Christ were identical, the need for unity across difference in Christ would be unnecessary.[30] Put differently, particularities of human identity, such as social status, intellectual capacity, or age, become normative features of being together in Jesus' body.[31] The normative status of diversity in Paul's vision of new life in Christ rejects communal commitments or practices that support the erasure of particularities, including those categorized as undesirable by the dominant milieu. Instead, the unique identities of each of the baptized are woven into the fabric of Jesus' body. As Lauren Winner puts it, reflecting on Paul's theology of identity in Galatians 3, these particularities of each baptizand become "superinscribed"—they "remain legible" even through the drastic transformation of identity that happens in baptism.[32]

Participating in Jesus' death through baptism provides another perspective on Paul's understanding of Christian identity as both retaining particular characteristics and experiencing a communal unity in Jesus. In Galatians 2:20, Paul claims that in baptism we are "crucified with Christ." Eastman suggests that in this baptismal enactment of crucifixion of the individualized self, egos become "unmoored from any prior sources of identity, worth, and direction . . . henceforth all access to such sources of identity passes through union with Christ on the cross."[33] Thus, Paul's baptismal vision of Christian identity relies on a community of mutual dependence where distinctives among individual members of the body are not erased, but instead brought into Jesus. In Jesus' body, Christians become conditioned to perceive the identities of their fellow disciples as those who are also deep within Jesus' body—evaluating their identity and vocation through Christ crucified. In the following section, we will further explore this transformation of perception within the baptized body—a transformation inherent in those identified as "new creation" in Christ.

NEW CREATION IDENTITY

Paul's construction of Christian identity as new creation in 2 Corinthians chapter 5 provides a particular narration of identity that crystallizes the primacy of participation, Jesus, and community for thinking faithfully about the identities of all the baptized as full disciples. Verses 16–21 of the passage read:

> From now on, therefore, we regard no one from a human point of view; even though we once knew Christ from a human point of view, we know him no longer in that way. So if anyone is in Christ, there is a new creation: everything old has passed away; see, everything has become new! All this is from God, who reconciled us to himself through Christ, and has given us the ministry of reconciliation; that is, in Christ God was reconciling the world to himself, not counting their trespasses against them, and entrusting the message of reconciliation to us. So we are ambassadors for Christ, since God is making his appeal through us; we entreat you on behalf of Christ, be reconciled to God. For our sake he made him to be sin who knew no sin, so that in him we might become the righteousness of God.

Paul writes to the Corinthians that allegiances to external characteristics, perceptible to lenses conditioned by the realm of the flesh, do not establish a foundation for identity in Christ. Put differently, culturally and socially lucrative aspects of human identity no longer provide a primary perspective on our neighbors: "judgment is no longer to be made on the basis of a person's visible advantages."[34] In striking contrast to suggesting the constitution of human persons on the basis of externally perceptible embodied capacities, Paul's new creation identity invites Christians into solidarity with Jesus—a way of life that repents of worldly evaluations and avenues to privilege and advantage.[35] Instead, the identity of each person initiated into Christ's body at their baptism becomes the orienting perspective from which Paul encourages us to perceive their identity.

Throughout my research interviews with Christians experiencing intellectual disabilities, as well as their pastors, loved ones, and fellow church members, this theme of renewed perception of identity frequently surfaced. Entering into a life marked by new creation identity was a hallmark for James, a young adult with an intellectual disability who described that upon his baptism, "there was a new life for me." His mother, Elisabeth, also described baptism as a process of "being made new" (an identical phrase echoed by Andrew, another parent who participated in this research). Elisabeth emphasized to me that baptism symbolizes Christians "being a new creature in Christ." David, another participant with an intellectual disability, echoed Paul's Christocentric description of new creation identity in his proclamation about baptismal identity: "I become a new man in Jesus Christ." This newness, however, did not constitute the removal or disregard of disability identities among research participants. Instead, the new creation identity proclaimed in baptism was accompanied by "acceptance for who we are" as Andrew, Al's father, described it. My research partners received baptism as a proclamation of new life—a new life fully consonant with disability identity—yet a new life that invites others to perceive the lives of disabled Christians through a Jesus-centered hermeneutic.

New Testament scholar J. Louis Martyn famously described this radical shift in perspective as "the turn of the ages."[36] Martyn's turn of the ages refers to the context in which the Corinthians lived, an in-between reality of those baptized into Jesus' death and body but those still awaiting the fullness of new creation in the final resurrection.[37] Inhabiting this in-between space continues within Christian communities today, and serves as a reminder that Christians live within, and not before nor after, Jesus' cross. Cruciform identity, therefore, rather than identity formed from evaluation based on socially constructed hierarchies of human persons, becomes the mode of Christian perception. Eastman puts it this way: "Paul no longer sees others or himself on the basis of outward appearances . . . but rather through the prism of the death and resurrection of Jesus."[38] Practices of baptism become sites where Christian communities practice perception through this Christocentric prism, anticipating "a new beginning of God's creative work" in the lives of each newly baptized member.[39] At the turn of the ages, through Christ's cross and resurrection, Christians in the baptized body are drawn into a sphere of participation flowing from Christ's exchange with human plight in the body of sin (2 Corinthians 5:21, Galatians 3:13–14, Philippians 2:6–11, and Romans 8:3–4).

Resonant with Galatians 3:28, Pauline scholar Margaret Thrall suggests that those living in the in between of baptism and the new creation of the final resurrection are called to proclaim the equality of all human creatures in the unfolding but not yet of God's good future.[40] The message of reconciliation in 2 Corinthians 5:21 stands as a "soteriological credo,"[41] a point of confession to remind the baptized body of their common soteriological status, possible only through ongoing participation in the incarnate Christ who was made sin for the sake of all humanity, regardless of disability status or other external characteristic. God as "both the initiator and goal of reconciliation"[42] establishes an even playing field for the outworking of the gospel in the body of Christ: an embodied participation of God's diverse children in the life of the church and the world. Overall, the message of reconciliation depends not on human possession of particular capacities, but rather, rests "wholly on divine initiative"[43] that proclaims "the very call and invitation of God"[44] through communal participation in Christ.

Baptismal practices provide one central site where God proclaims a new identity for Christians. In and through baptismal practices, Christian communities are formed to perceive themselves and the newly baptized as those identified as God's new creations. The kind of imagination invited forth by this new creation perception supports Paul's claims that all members of Jesus' body are indispensable. Paul's Christocentric identity of new creation primes Christians to anticipate what creative and renewing work the Holy Spirit might be up to in the lives of the baptized, both individually, and as a community of mutual care. This view of Christian identity is deeply anticipatory, in contrast to other perspectives on identity that might foreground deficit or loss. For Paul, the implications of this new creation life in Jesus are played out only in and through Christ, in the context of the communal baptized body. In this way, the Pauline framework of new creation holds deep implications for Christian perspectives on disability.

New Creation Identity and Disability

Paul's Christological and baptismal account of new creation identity opens space for reflection on the diverse gifts that all people in Christ offer to the church. Paul illustrates this reality in his own context in 2 Corinthians, redefining his "apostolic work" not through boasting of "external advantages,"[45] but only through the power of new creation life in Christ. Paul rejects fleshly lenses as those that can accurately perceive apostolic legitimacy. Instead, anyone in Christ becomes part of the community of Jesus' baptized body where the Holy Spirit works toward transformative newness of life. In this way, Paul's sketching of the new creation challenges communities who do not actively work toward the embrace of all the baptized, including people with intellectual disabilities as well as others often marginalized in the baptized body—people with severe and persistent mental illness, children with emotional challenges, homeless neighbors, and elders living with dementia, to name a few.

In his reflections on 2 Corinthians 5 from an autistic hermeneutic, Macaskill applies a disability critique to contemporary Christian communities who tend to only ascribe value to those who are "socially impressive." Not only does the church easily underscore the value and gifts of these individuals, but,

> These are the people the church celebrates, and its structures and practices are often built around this celebration: significant space is typically carved out for the delivery of an act of oratory, framed by music led by charismatic performers, followed by social times in which we can enact our precious normality.[46]

In this way of understanding Christian identity, those who lack a socially impressive status become outliers in ecclesial leadership, worship, and even discipleship. When societal conceptions of normative characteristics displace Jesus as the center of Christian identity, attending to and joyfully anticipating God's work of new creation in all the baptized becomes thwarted.

Anna spoke to me about this difficulty in our research interview. She expressed to me a tension within her own experience of raising a nondisabled child in her church community of people with and without disabilities. Anna described her own child as part of a group of "super high achievers: academically, in sports, winning scholarships, and all that stuff." Anna reflected to me that the church newsletter included celebrations of these achievements—things she described as "cultural successes." Notably absent in these types of announcements were the doings of young people with intellectual disabilities within Anna's church community. Anna lamented, "I really struggled sometimes about how our church held people up. There are some people that don't have these cultural successes . . . and I wonder what that feels like to see those all celebrated, and you're sitting there and there's none of that going on for you." Anna's lament illustrates the painful gap of an unrealized embrace of the transformative power of the Spirit in shaping Christian perception. While the realm of the flesh conditions communities to celebrate "cultural successes," a new creation perspective invites identification of God's work of new creation alive in each of the baptized, as well as an embrace of communal care practices that perceive others as unconditionally beloved in Christ, not only as the sum of their achievements.

Anna highlights for us that the church's barometer for celebration can often root its calibration in societal successes. Without alternative ways of imagining who Christians are, and without connections to core practices of how Christians ought to imagine, celebrate, and worship together, ecclesial communities will continue to fall short of joining with the Holy Spirit to discern God's work of new creation in the baptized body, including members of the body with intellectual disabilities. And because Paul's account of baptismal new creation identity does not erase disability, Christians might eagerly consider how disability identity is amplified through the ongoing work of the Spirit. The absence of disabled Christians in Anna's story of church celebration calls communities into repentance about perceiving and celebrating neighbors. A disability reading of new creation identity asks Christian communities to take seriously the work of the Spirit in the lives of disabled people as both those called to give and receive love in the baptized body.

Perceiving others through the perspective of new creation, rooted in the life and death of Jesus, opens a way to accept and celebrate difference between the diverse members of Jesus' body. As Paul argues in 2 Corinthians 5, Jesus abolishes the hostilities of fleshly perspectives that sustain patterns of homogenous belonging in ecclesial communities. My research partners spoke of the witness of disabled Christians in their own communities as revealing the hostility of ecclesial affinities for perfectionism. Pastor Soren described his experience in previous congregations around a need to "be exact in doing things, decently and in order." Anna also described this sense of faith communities outside of her current Episcopal context—"people would assume things have to be done in a very precise way." Anna observed how this posture, especially toward disabled Christians, fed assumptions that church members with disabilities did not desire participation in church activities, and resulted in nondisabled leaders "closing things off" to disabled parishioners.

Anna reflected on a different way of embodying worship and Christian life together at Holy Angels Episcopal Church—fostering an approach that "isn't about perfection—it's about inclusion and experience together." At St. Matthew's Baptist Church, Pastor Soren similarly described members with intellectual disabilities increasing the church's openness to "things that, you know, just aren't perfect." For Anna and Pastor Soren, worship that included leadership among disabled members invited their communities to repent of the idolatry of perfection. Claiming a shared new creation identity in Jesus displaced the need for perfection as a primary driver of church leadership and practice.

In Anna and Pastor Soren's churches, parishioners with disabilities troubled the prioritization of worship practices associated with dominant norms of perfection. As a result, an embrace of human limitation in following Jesus, and of imperfection within worship, invited greater recognition and exercise of gifts among all present. Anna shared, "one of the things I do love about this congregation is we're not into perfection . . . I think we handle really well when something doesn't go right." Anna recognized how this embrace of imperfect participation allows the community to anticipate and receive the gifts of people with and without disabilities, focusing their attention instead on taking care of one another. Once Anna recognized this commitment at Holy Angels, she came more fully into offering her own gifts as a nondisabled person in the church's music ministry. In the economy of new creation, Christian communities embrace a shared identity in Christ that helps them prioritize attending to the Spirit's call to repentance and celebration, rather than first attending to maintaining a veneer of perfection.

If Christian communities affirm alongside Paul that the new creation life of each baptized person is indispensable to proclaiming God's inaugurated yet not fully realized new creation, churches must find ways to accompany, learn from, and support the new creation witness of people with intellectual disabilities. These kinds of accompaniment, learning, and support require a baseline commitment of being with others despite the strain of difference, through prayerful, ordinary, and sustained fellowship. Informal practices such as eating together, accompanying one another on typical errands or to appointments, or being together in the context of a prayer or worship service, provide some of the best ways to begin to perceive Christians with intellectual disabilities not from a "human point of view," but rather recognize their shared baptismal identity "in Christ." For Pastor John, this work is rooted in 2 Corinthians 5—Christians who seek to perceive others and follow Jesus together from the perspective of new creation can find encouragement and strength through "participating in what is already true—Jesus' death and resurrection."

Paul's relational and baptismal hermeneutic of new creation identity centers on becoming who we truly are in Christ. This narration of Christian identity robustly welcomes disabled identities and experiences—it is unmoored from intellectual capacity and instead rooted in Jesus. In baptism, my research participant James said, "I was just asking to *be who I am.*" Al shared a similar perspective on his new identity in baptism: "It's truly in God that I become—*I become who I am.*" Becoming "who we truly are" in baptism—those in Christ—brings forth a new creation identity shared with all the baptized across a range of disability identities. Rather than centering the hostilities of social identity hierarchies, Paul's shift to the primacy of the Christ event in shaping communal imagination invites all believers into practices that anticipate the Spirit's active transformation in the here and now. Becoming the baptized body testifies to a shared unity across difference in Jesus. And in this community of baptismal unity, the members of Jesus' body become together who they truly are: witnesses to a new creation life only possible through the power of Jesus' resurrection. This life together of new creation is expressed in mutual love.

CONCLUSION

The baptized body lives, moves, and has its being through communal dependence on Jesus. As we have explored throughout this chapter, Paul's account of baptismal identity as new creation highlights that baptism does not provide a mechanism to "supersize" one's Christian status through the bestowal of new capacities. Rather, Paul highlights radical dependence on Jesus' resurrection life to underscore communal Christian identity and frame understandings of the Spirit's work of transformation within baptized communities. This reality of new creation challenges contemporary ecclesial communities to reimagine their own commitments surrounding Christian identity, as well as their practices that may currently inhibit belonging among members of Jesus' body with disability identities.

As I have articulated throughout my theological method and arguments so far, doing theology in partnership with Christians with intellectual disabilities raises new questions and critical perspectives for the practices of Christian communities. In the remaining chapters, in partnership with my research collaborators, we will turn to how biblical frameworks for baptism and baptismal identity come to life in the practices of ecclesial communities.

In chapter 5, we will consider how baptismal services themselves offer opportunities for both repentance and celebration with regard to renarrating disability and Christian identity. Baptismal liturgies hold the potential to shape Christian imagination toward belonging, while also offering concrete avenues for active participation among both disabled and nondisabled Christians. How do contemporary baptismal liturgies affirm, challenge, or expand the realities of new creation we have explored in this chapter? Put differently, how have baptismal liturgies either enriched or inhibited the participation of Christians with intellectual disabilities in the church's life of discipleship and worship? We turn to these questions next.

5

Baptismal Liturgy and Disability

As we explored over the past two chapters, biblical accounts of belonging to Jesus in baptism provide important foundations for Christian communities committed to theologies and lived practices critically attentive to disability. From the perspectives of both my research partners and Pauline literature, participation in baptism serves as a proclamation and initiation of a communal Christian life, marked by ongoing transformation in the Holy Spirit. In this shared life of transformation, Christian ecclesial communities assume responsibility for embodying a life of discipleship marked by belonging and love for all members. In addition to interpreting biblical stories of baptism as a way of attending to the discipleship of disabled Christians, research participants for this book also noted how baptismal services helped expand and form their imagination about Christian identity and disability.

In this chapter, we will consider how liturgies of baptism interface with the witness of Christians with intellectual disabilities. As we will explore, baptismal liturgies can both restrict and reenliven how Christian communities attend to disability experiences and embody their communal baptismal identities in Jesus. After an introductory section about the formational role of worship and liturgy in Christian life, we will examine one contemporary liturgical framework for baptism: The Episcopal Church's rite of Holy Baptism from the 1979 *Book of Common Prayer*. In light of reflections on the meaning of baptism from my research partners with intellectual disabilities, we will identify resonant key themes in this particular baptismal liturgy. In addition, we will attend to disability-informed critiques of some features of the baptismal liturgy. Responding to these critiques in the final section of this chapter, I will guide us through a constructive response that synthesizes the thought of Dietrich Bonhoeffer on baptism with insights from this book's research participants on baptismal discipleship marked by participation, community, and Jesus centeredness. Both within and beyond the liturgy of The Episcopal Church, we will consider how Christian liturgies of baptism might serve as faithful companions to the baptized body in welcoming, supporting, and learning from the lives of Christians with intellectual disabilities.

WHY LITURGY?

Our practices of worshiping God shape our imagination about who belongs in the baptized body. And the liturgies that pattern Christian worship teach us which bodies belong. Worship calls forth embodied participation that can bear witness to a community's implicit beliefs about who God is, who human beings are, and how to live as the baptized body. Stanley Hauerwas and Samuel Wells argue that liturgy "is the most significant way in which Christianity takes flesh."[1]

This formative power of Christian worship was captured within research participants' reflections on their experiences of baptismal liturgies and services. Speaking out of the "just joyful" character of baptisms in her home church, Barbara shared that the baptismal liturgy supported her church community in "taking ownership" of each baptized member—committing to "being there" and "being their village." At her church home, Lea described how services of baptism include the sign of the cross being traced on the forehead of the newly baptized person, followed by a public proclamation of their belonging to Jesus, "sealed in the Holy Spirit." For Lea, these "moments of joy" call the church to remember the identity of all the baptized and the community's commitment to love and care for them.

The emphasis on communal responsibility identified by Barbara and Lea illustrates how liturgical participation, particularly around the baptismal rite, invites communities to abandon overly individualized structures of belief and confession, and instead enact the reality of interdependence inside of Jesus' body. Baptism is the event where singular bodies are joined to the baptized body and are thus welcomed into the life of ongoing sanctification through the witness and exercise of gifts through the power of the Holy Spirit. The communal emphasis of baptismal services across Christian faith traditions sets up what liturgical theologian Kimberly Belcher understands as a participatory and sacramental framework for Christian identity, over and against Christian identity as something intimately intertwined with higher cognition.[2]

Baptism, as the paradigmatic sign and seal of Christian identity as unity with Christ, is enacted through the liturgy: sprinkling, dipping, or immersion within water, marking with the sign of the cross, or anointing with the oil of chrism. In these acts, the liturgy models embodied participation in identity formation. While words are certainly important and formative in the Christian liturgical life (as we will emphasize and explore in the coming pages), shared nonverbal practices around the font also generate knowledge about communal identity and belonging to the church and to Jesus.[3] In this way, baptism serves as a bold and public witness that anyone who a church baptizes, including those with intellectual disabilities, is wholly welcomed into Jesus' body.[4] In the next section, we will attend to key themes of this welcome present in The Episcopal Church's liturgy for baptism.

THE RITE OF HOLY BAPTISM IN THE *BOOK OF COMMON PRAYER*

With nearly half the research participants for this book hailing from the Episcopal tradition, we will next explore their liturgical framework for baptism in the *Book of Common Prayer* as an example of identifying core themes and critiques from a disability hermeneutic. The *Book of Common Prayer*, originally composed in 1549 by Archbishop Thomas Cranmer,[5] was the first written prayer book in the Anglican tradition. Since then, the prayer book has developed into various forms across different geographical provinces of the worldwide Anglican Communion, including the edition we will focus on in this chapter—The Episcopal Church's 1979 *Book of Common Prayer* (BCP).[6] In contrast to pervasive emphases on individualized piety among many Protestant Christians in the twentieth century, the church leaders tasked with revising the 1979 BCP sought to reshape the rite of Holy Baptism with a distinctive commitment to community.[7] This reshaping included adding "The Baptismal Covenant" to the baptismal liturgy, comprised of an interrogatory form[8] of the Apostle's Creed, followed by five questions addressed to not only the baptismal candidates and their sponsors, but all those gathered in the worshiping body.[9] As we will further appreciate in the following sections, the communal nature of the baptismal rite and Christian identity were further infused throughout the liturgy's key themes.

Key Themes in the 1979 BCP Rite

The baptismal liturgy in the 1979 prayer book provides both a linguistically and theologically compelling rite. In the following section, I will argue in conversation with my research partners that the rite's two key themes of renouncing sin and transformation encompass not only theologically foundational expressions of baptismal doctrine, but also hold particular relevance for Christian communities intentionally attending to the experiences of people with disabilities.

Sin, Evil, and Renunciation

During our interview as she described what happens in baptism, Ava, a young adult with an intellectual disability, emphasized the centrality of turning away from sin, sharing: "baptism means being cleansed from the Holy Spirit to God." David and Bunny, two other participants with intellectual disabilities, also drew my attention to the connection between baptism and God's power over sin. In describing baptism, Bunny stated "it's because when Jesus died on the cross for us," while David shared, "God sent his Son and the cross for our sins. And on the cross he did that for us."

These themes of redemption, cleansing, and being washed of sin that arose throughout the research interviews have a parallel emphasis within the BCP's baptismal liturgy where those baptized are incorporated into Jesus' body. In fact, the theme of sin emerges almost immediately in the BCP's rite of Holy Baptism, seen in the following questions:[10]

Question Do you renounce Satan and the spiritual forces of wickedness that rebel against God?
Answer I renounce them.

Question	Do you renounce the evil powers of this world which corrupt and destroy the creatures of God?
Answer	I renounce them.
Question	Do you renounce all sinful desires that draw you from the love of God?
Answer	I renounce them.

Continuing into the Baptismal Covenant, the theme of attending to sin and evil in order to renounce them with the help of God continues:

Celebrant	Will you persevere in resisting evil, and, whenever you fall into sin, repent and return to the Lord?
People	I will, with God's help.

And again, as the baptized community prepares to witness the initiation of a new member, the power of Jesus to free the baptized from the power of sin is emphasized in both the "Thanksgiving over the Water"[11] and the blessing of the baptismal waters, as this excerpt highlights:[12]

> ... Now sanctify this water, we pray you, by the power of your Holy Spirit, that those who here are cleansed from sin and born again may continue for ever in the risen life of Jesus Christ our Savior.

In the contemporary ecclesial scene where many individuals actively avoid associating sin and disability—either in resistance to perpetuating damaging hermeneutics of disability as a punishment for sin,[13] or conceptualizing people with disabilities as somehow sinless "holy innocents"[14]—the baptismal liturgy foregrounds the bondage to sin among all humans in systemic and communal ways. Likewise, the liturgical rite also emphasizes God's power to cleanse God's people from sin, and invites communal participation in shared renunciation, with God's help, to actively address the effects of sin and evil in the present realm of the flesh. Disabled Christians within the baptized body are integral to this commitment to renunciation, and as we will explore further now, the transformation of ecclesial communities seeking to inhabit their Spirit-empowered baptismal vocation to discipleship.

Transformation: The Active Verbs of the Baptismal Rite

During conversations with research participants, stories of what happens in baptism often centered on new beginnings, new life, new birth, or being born again. James and David, both young adults with intellectual disabilities, shared with me that "baptism was a new life for me" and "I was made a new man in Jesus Christ [in baptism]," respectively. Reflecting further on witnessing the baptisms of others, David told me "I feel like it makes you new." These theological reflections on baptism highlighted transformation into new life among Christians with and without intellectual disabilities. Following cleansing from and renunciation of sin and evil, services of baptism hold the promise of new life in Jesus—both realized in the here and now and hoped for in the future.

The rite of Holy Baptism features repeated verbs that underscore the centrality of transformation in God within the Christian practice of baptism. These verbs of transformation not only suggest individualized change among the newly baptized, but also place an impetus upon the gathered community, drawing the whole of the baptized body into sustained practices that cultivate a life of baptismal transformation.[15] This mutual commitment to transformation is exemplified in the "bidding" to the congregation toward the beginning of the BCP baptismal liturgy:[16]

Celebrant Will you who witness these vows do all in your power to support these persons in their life in Christ?
People We will.

This serious commitment to do "all in your power" to support the newly baptized, without exception, presents ecclesial communities with a striking challenge. Imagine how differently church communities might order their priorities, commitments, and action around doing all in their power to support each member's life in Christ? Here, liturgical language invites the baptized body into unreserved support for not only those who possess particular capacities and characteristics that align them with the dominant milieu. Instead, the language of promise with regard to support through transformation lays bare the theological thrust of practicing baptism: with

God's help, churches must find ways to directly and wholeheartedly support the baptismal vocations and identities of people with intellectual disabilities.

Interestingly, the locus of agency for this holy work of baptismal transformation shifts throughout the baptismal liturgy, moving between individual and communal action, as well as between human and divine agency. For example, the three affirmations[17] following the opening renunciations of the baptismal rite read:

> **Question** Do you turn to Jesus Christ and accept him as your Savior?
> **Answer** I do.
> **Question** Do you put your whole trust in his grace and love?
> **Answer** I do.
> **Question** Do you promise to follow and obey him as your Lord?
> **Answer** I do.

These active verbs, "turning," "putting," and "promising," carry a sense of individualized agency, accentuated by the singular address of the questions and the "I" answer provided by either the baptismal candidate or their sponsor(s). However, as the liturgy unfolds, communal agency and divine agency emerge as the primary frameworks for baptismal transformation. We see this first in the rite's rendering of the Apostle's Creed, that holds together individual affirmations voiced communally. The questions of the Baptismal Covenant that immediately follow include key verbs related to baptismal transformation that find their realization only with divine assistance: "persevering," "repenting," "returning," "proclaiming," "serving," and "striving." The final two affirmations of the Baptismal Covenant read:[18]

> **Celebrant** Will you seek and serve Christ in all persons, loving your neighbor as yourself?
> **People** I will, with God's help.
> **Celebrant** Will you strive for justice and peace among all people, and respect the dignity of every human being?
> **People** I will, with God's help.

As the liturgy proceeds to the Prayers for the Candidates,[19] the intensity and directness of both divine and communal agency heightens. In the Prayers, the active work of transformation shifts to God, who hears the communal prayers offered by the baptized body. Within each petition, the liturgical leader identifies the source of transformation in the work of God, and in response the gathered respond communally with the refrain "Lord, hear our prayer." Through this section of the liturgy, those in the baptized body together acknowledge the necessity of God's agency in sustaining their lives of baptismal transformation. Finally, after proclaiming God's transformative work within the baptized community and reaffirming baptismal commitments, the liturgy supports the gathered church in a proclamation of transformative welcome:[20]

> We receive you into the household of God. Confess the faith of Christ crucified, proclaim his resurrection, and share with us in his eternal priesthood.

As with the core theme of sin and repentance, the liturgical thread of transformation supposes inclusion of baptized people across a wide diversity of identities. In other words, the liturgical language does not hold caveats or exceptions about any particular exclusivity with regard to baptismal transformation. However, as I will point out in the following section, other aspects of the BCP's rite of Holy Baptism likely condition ecclesial communities to question the full applicability of these core theological themes of the liturgy to the lives of disabled Christians.

CRITIQUES OF THE LITURGY: A DISABILITY PERSPECTIVE

Though key themes in the BCP's baptismal liturgy boast avenues for ritual and theological inclusion among people with intellectual disabilities, other aspects of the rite emphasize individuality or possessing certain capacities—aspects of the liturgy that hold potential to cast a negative valence on the lives of Christians with intellectual disabilities. Further, these individualized and capacity-focused features of the rite may fuel imaginations about Christian identity and discipleship that align with anthropological commitments of modernity, instead of Paul's deeply relational and communal framework for new creation Christian identity. One key example of this reality in the liturgy is the BCP's characterization of baptismal candidates: either those "who can speak for themselves" or "infants and younger children" for whom "the parents and godparents . . . speak on behalf."[21] This dichotomy in liturgical language creates a clear issue for noninfant candidates, who for a variety of reasons, including some experiences of intellectual disability, cannot "speak for themselves." Though many laud the BCP's liturgical flexibility in structuring a single rite for participation among people across ages, disability disrupts the binary of who should and should not be expected to speak for themselves.

This binary between candidates who are infants or young children and candidates who can speak for themselves also highlights tensions around assumptions about agency within the baptismal liturgy. Within the linguistic structure of the BCP's rite, candidates who speak for themselves make promises from an individual posture, raising potential conflicts with the more communal narration of sin and transformation within the baptismal liturgy as a whole. These tensions between individualized and communal aspects of the liturgy highlight the potential for slippage into affirming the baptismal candidate as the locus of agency for baptismal transformation, rather than the Triune God.

These liturgical tensions provide a site where the baptized body might reevaluate and reimagine liturgies with robust avenues for all baptismal candidates, regardless of age and disability identity, to participate more fully. The reality of human disability invites an expansion of rubrics for liturgical participation—helping communities to disentangle their set paths of engagement from strict needs around discrete human capacities. Perhaps revised words, accompanied by new or revised wordless centers of action, are needed throughout the liturgy—those that center the mutual, interdependent, and communal life of discipleship, sustained by the Holy Spirit within the body of Christ.

Centering the liturgical expression and interpretations of liturgy offered by disabled Christians offers another interesting path forward. Take, for example, the prayer that the BCP commends immediately following baptism in the name of the Father, Son, and Holy Spirit:[22]

> Heavenly Father, we thank you that by water and the Holy Spirit you have bestowed upon *these* your servants the forgiveness of sin, and have raised *them* to the new life of grace. Sustain *them*, O Lord, in your Holy Spirit. Give *them* an inquiring and discerning heart, the courage to will and to persevere, a spirit to know and to love you, and the gift of joy and wonder in all your works. *Amen.*

While this postbaptismal prayer emphasizes divine action, my own disability-conscious reading of its content raised concern with regard to its centering of discrete cognitive capacities, such as the processes of "inquiring" and "discerning." However, Hikari shared with me that she receives this prayer as a gift for both herself as a disabled Christian, as well as for others in the church seeking to live into a baptismal community inclusive of people who experience disability. Hikari shared with me, "I really like the mind that the church wants you to have. A questioning mind. Which means they want you to ask questions." Hikari and I began to talk about this prayer as a gift to churches—how asking questions around disability identity and ways to promote disability justice might serve as key aspects of discernment and growth in the knowledge of who God is and the kind of community God invites Christians to pursue. In reflecting upon this research conversation with Hikari, I was also challenged to reconceive of this prayer as an invitation to attend to the witness of disciples with disabilities who might call forth different kinds of discernment and knowing within the church. Hikari's experience of the liturgy challenged me to move beyond a superficial identification of potentially ableist language, and instead, come to appreciate her own experience of how this part of the baptismal rite in The Episcopal Church might call forth greater interdependency and disability awareness. In this spirit of seeking new interpretations, we will next turn to the work of a theologian deeply attuned to the intersections of baptism and discipleship within ecclesial communities, to further discern how baptismal liturgies (including and beyond the BCP) might provide sites that accentuate the Spirit's active work in all the baptized, including Christians with intellectual disabilities.

ADDRESSING LITURGICAL CRITIQUES: BONHOEFFER AND DISABILITY

Theologian Dietrich Bonhoeffer provides a salient conversation partner, whose writings draw upon the human experience of disability and attend to the central role of baptism within Christian worship and communal life. Helpfully, Bonhoeffer's theological construction of human creatures includes clear attention to embodied limitations while also explicitly resisting temptations to abstract or idealize individuals with disabilities.[23] As theologian Michael Mawson argues, Bonhoeffer's Christocentric view of the baptized community, those who recognize each other "as God's gift and grace only through the intervention and mediation of Christ," embraces rather than resists human limitation in the work of communal life together.[24] This recognition and the subsequent living out of Christian community requires, in Mawson's interpretation of Bonhoeffer, committing to sustained relationships with other members of Jesus' body across difference (including members with intellectual disabilities), acknowledging human inability to fully "recognize and respond to others in the ways that we should," and finally, responding to this inability by sustained small acts that attend to neighbors and better their concrete situation in the here and now.[25] Bonhoeffer captures this Christian calling in the following way:

> The full life in Christ, in the church-community is granted to every Christian through being baptized into the body of Christ ... To allow other baptized Christians to participate in worship but to refuse to have community with them in everyday life, and to abuse them and treat them with contempt, is to become guilty against the body of Christ itself. To acknowledge that other baptized Christians have received the gifts of salvation, and then to deny them the provisions necessary for this earthly life, or to leave them unknowingly in affliction and distress, is to make a mockery of the gift of salvation and to behave like a liar ... baptism into the body of Christ changes not only a person's personal status with regard to salvation, but also their relationships throughout all of life.[26]

In the following sections, we will attend to how Bonhoeffer's perspective on the far-reaching consequences of unity with Christ in baptism might shape not only liturgical participation, but also the whole of life together in the baptized body—including the disabled members of Jesus.

Contending with Sin in the Baptismal Rite

As we explored above, the BCP's emphasis on renunciation of sin highlights key theological affirmations about the rite of baptism and ongoing baptismal transformation in the life of Jesus' body. The liturgy's framework for renunciation, however, also raises serious questions for Christians with intellectual disabilities. How might Christians with cognitive limitations, especially those least able to "understand" the seriousness of renouncing sin, faithfully participate in the baptismal liturgy? And, as Bonhoeffer emphasizes above, how might they join the wider Christian community in ongoing practices of repentance and renunciation?

As I alluded to above, suggesting that disabled Christians are exempt from the power of sin creates a dangerous disjuncture from the necessity of God's power to rescue human creatures and empower them with a new creation identity in Jesus. Strangely, this theological move can result in dehumanizing Christians with disabilities, exempting them from participation in key aspects of Christian discipleship and also in funding impoverished theological accounts of who they are as creatures before God.[27] In *Discipleship*, Bonhoeffer explores the implications of Jesus' actions in baptism for the lives of *all* human creatures caught in the realm of the flesh, writing,

> [Baptism] implies a break. Christ invades the realm of Satan and lays hold of those who belong to him, thereby creating his church-community . . . In baptism we die together with our old world . . . We die in Christ alone; we die through Christ and with Christ . . . True, in this death judgment is passed on the old self and its sin. But out of this judgment rises the new self which has died to the world and to sin. This death is thus not the final, angry rejection of the creature by its creator but rather the gracious acceptance of the creature by the creator.[28]

Echoing the Pauline language of new creation, Bonhoeffer roots the importance of the baptized body's newness of life in Jesus as a gracious rescue from the realm of sin. Exempting people with intellectual disabilities from this powerful theological narrative, including liturgical expressions of it, releases ecclesial communities from serious consideration of the place of disabled Christians, and by extension, those who are infants and young children, in the church's baptismal witness to God's power over sin.

For Bonhoeffer, baptismal enactments of dying to sin "must never be understood as a mechanical process" but as a reception of the Holy Spirit, "Christ Himself dwelling in the hearts of believers."[29] Bonhoeffer's emphasis on receiving the Holy Spirit in baptism resonated with my research conversation with Ava, who not only emphasized the ongoing work of the Spirit in the life of the baptized body ("baptism means for us as people of the church, we're here to connect with you through a hand given in the Holy Spirit") but also the important work of the Holy Spirit in baptism as transforming those who are baptized away from a life of sin. When I asked her what baptism meant, Ava responded, "it means that you're being cleansed by the Holy Spirit to God . . . redeeming yourself from sin and temptation." I found myself curious about Ava's strong emphasis on both sin and the Holy Spirit and asked her to tell me more about what happens in baptism. She responded: "I feel like they're [people being baptized] surely not knowing what baptism means. But we tell the people this means you're majorly connected to God spiritually in the mystery of the Holy Trinity."

Ava's characterization of the mystery at the heart of baptismal participation—"surely not knowing" how God rescues those baptized in Christ from the realm of sin—highlights the possibility that perhaps all human creatures, apart from age or disability identity, are those the BCP names as "unable to answer for themselves."[30] This individualization of responding to sin in the baptismal liturgy tempts Christians to see the locus of repentance and renunciation as individual members of Jesus' body, rather than all those gathered and mysteriously transformed through God's work of new creation. Writing in close dialogue with Bonhoeffer's understanding of the church's baptismal practices, theologian Tom Greggs argues that the "continuity of human reception of forgiveness does not stem, therefore, from any individual state of faith or existential individualism or subjective identity, but from the word of the gospel addressed to, heard in and proclaimed by the church."[31]

What might these accounts of baptism and sin have to say to the shape and form of baptismal liturgies, including that in the 1979 BCP? Ava's emphasis on the Holy Spirit's cleansing work and Bonhoeffer's stress on divine agency both critique the individualization of renouncing sin and instead call for language that more clearly highlights divine agency working through community. Although participation in discrete liturgical speech acts of renouncing sin may not be available to people with more significant experiences of intellectual disabilities, liturgies must make clear that these individuals are not exempted from how their communities take seriously the renunciation of sin. In addition to providing a communal framing of this reality through liturgy, preaching, and formation within church communities, liturgical bodies might also evidence a postbaptismal commitment to renunciation of sin through their practices of mutual care, including for those with disability identities, within the baptized body.

Focusing on a Jesus-Centered Community

Bonhoeffer defines baptism as a Christian practice focused intensely on the action of Jesus: "Baptism is not something we offer to God. It is, rather, something Jesus Christ offers to us . . . in baptism we become Christ's possession."[32] This Jesus-focused framework for baptism not only resonates with the Christocentric theological reflections on baptism among this project's research partners, but also challenges hyperindividualized aspects of baptismal liturgies, underscoring God's action in drawing the community of the baptized together within the body of Jesus.

As we surveyed in chapters 2 and 3, this book's research participants shared a focus on the centrality of Jesus' death and resurrection for their participation in baptismal services as well as their sense of communal baptismal identity. Across a diversity of liturgical traditions, unity with Jesus' crucifixion and resurrection in the act of baptism, rather than allegiance to a particular tradition's theological or liturgical distinctives, resonated most strongly for Christians with intellectual disabilities in addition to their loved ones and clergy. Danny, an older man with an intellectual disability, told me that baptism ". . . shows that Jesus was buried, and that he rose again from the dead . . . I was buried like Jesus and rose again. Rose up from the dead." Bonhoeffer affirms the centrality of Jesus that Danny expressed in his baptismal reflections, asserting, "the body of Christ is his church-community . . . to be in Christ means to be in the church-community."[33] Traditions that differentiate between baptismal candidates based upon their ability to offer an active response, and those communities who require an active response before one is even eligible for participation in baptism, receive a challenge from Bonhoeffer and Danny's perspectives. Heightened attention to revising or supplementing sections of liturgy that showcase individual spoken expression not only creates more accessible pathways for some disabled people becoming part of Jesus' body, but also reinforces to the community that unity with Christ sits at the heart of baptismal participation.

Reconsidering liturgical language focused on individualized response can also be made increasingly accessible when the realization of baptismal community in Jesus' body is emphasized. In the opening pages of *Discipleship*, Bonhoeffer stresses that "baptism without the discipline of community . . . [is like] grace without the living, incarnate Jesus Christ."[34] The centrality of community for both baptism and the constitution of baptismal identity offers a significant theological challenge to the individualized aspects of the BCP's baptismal liturgy. Reflecting on the importance of the public setting of baptismal services, Mary described the liturgy as supporting the reality of baptismal community: baptism reminds ecclesial communities "you are set up in a community of people who are going to be your tribe." For Mary, church community finds its roots in the practice of baptism—the occasion for public proclamation of the belonging of the baptized. Thus, for Mary, the church must take its baptismal promises with utmost seriousness—promises as the community of Jesus to emphasize that all the baptized belong—"no matter who they are."

Without the embodied participation of people with intellectual disabilities in baptismal liturgies, the fullness of community finds itself hollow. Churches that resist creating space for disabled Christians in baptismal liturgies neglect a full sense of communal hospitality and miss opportunities to offer teaching that addresses liturgical shortcomings as they relate to people experiencing disability. Providing avenues for embodied participation in baptismal liturgy among people of diverse disability identities can both emphasize key theological affirmations related to Jesus and community while also adjusting, or at the very least challenging, over-individualized aspects of liturgical rites.

Bonhoeffer portrays this Jesus-centered community of baptismal belonging and new life as follows:

> Through baptism we have become members of the body of Christ . . . the body of Jesus Christ is the ground of our faith and the source of its certainty; the body of Jesus Christ is the one and perfect gift through which we receive our salvation; the body of Jesus Christ is our new life. It is in the body of Jesus Christ that we are accepted by God from eternity.[35]

This kind of unbounded belonging underscores what truly matters for liturgical participation. Instead of scrutinizing an individual's ability to recite all aspects of the liturgical rite, a shift to wonder at the beauty of diverse bodies present within liturgies of baptism can help Christian communities recapture the heart of their liturgical work together—witnessing to the reality of God's in-breaking work of new creation in Jesus Christ. This transformation of the baptized body cannot neglect any of the baptized—as Robert summarized: "once you're welcomed in baptism, you're part of the community for good." Being incorporated into Jesus' body in baptism does not hinge on a particular recitation of a liturgical script. Rather, the baptismal rite ought to provide "a basis for deepening [baptismal] identity in the communal context of the church."[36] Greater attention to how the possibilities and constraints of particular forms of disabled participation in baptismal liturgies surface within ecclesial communities can help these communities unearth their own ableist assumptions and embedded liturgical commitments.

CONCLUSION

In the BCP's baptismal rite, the prayer for the newly baptized reads:

> Heavenly Father, we thank you that by water and the Holy Spirit you have bestowed upon *these* your servants the forgiveness of sin, and have raised *them* to the new life of grace. Sustain *them*, O Lord, in your Holy Spirit. Give *them* an inquiring and discerning heart, the courage to will and to persevere, a spirit to know and to love you, and the gift of joy and wonder in all your works. *Amen.*

The final petition in this prayer, that all the baptized may receive the gift of joy and wonder in God's work, provides a fitting conclusion for the explorations of this chapter. The proper response to the limitations of over-intellectualized and over-individualized liturgical participation lies in a cultivation of joy and wonder in the good gifts God provides in the context of community. When commitments to ableism in liturgical expression are unearthed, named, and addressed, baptismal liturgies can more fully invite ecclesial communities into embracing a sense of joy and wonder—a perspective from which they might newly perceive their siblings with intellectual disabilities.

But how might this perspective of baptismal joy lead church communities into a more robust embrace of the discipleship of all the baptized? In the two final chapters of this book, we will turn to an exploration of three concrete practices: baptismal preparation, baptismal testimony, and baptismal reaffirmation. These three pragmatic and pastoral means of enlivening the baptized body in a life of fuller discipleship arise out of stories from this project's research participants. I will situate these three practices not only in relationship to the human experience of disability, but illustrate in tandem with my research partners how these practices create space for deep belonging of disciples across a range of disability identities.

6

Practicing and Proclaiming Baptismal Identity

Continuing our exploration of baptism and baptismal identity from a disability perspective, this chapter marks a transition to three key practices that proclaim and sustain the community of the baptized body: baptismal preparation, baptismal testimony, and baptismal reaffirmation. Before attending to each of these specific practices in chapter 7, we will first draw upon wisdom from my research partners and theological scholars across the ecumenical spectrum to illustrate some key commitments and assumptions surrounding the place of baptismal practices within Christian life, especially as these practices might form Christian identity.

Expanding upon our survey of baptismal practices within the field of disability theology in chapter 1, I begin this chapter in conversation with practical and liturgical theologians to explore the following dimensions of baptismal practices: their identity-shaping power, their embodied richness, their place in the whole of Christian worship, and their promise for ecumenical unity. I next illustrate my understanding of the nature of baptismal practices as both interdependent and limited, followed by highlighting the importance of access concerns in relationship to Christian practice. In conclusion, I reflect on one framework for how these practices might "do their work" in ecclesial communities, drawing upon Gerald Arbuckle's notion of "refounding." Throughout the chapter, I will seek to offer an expanded framework for John Swinton's claim that baptism offers a liturgical space where people experiencing intellectual disabilities can receive public welcome into the body of Jesus in a way that provides "a unique place of discipleship and belonging that is carved out within God's hospitable community."[1]

EMBODIED PRACTICES AND IDENTITY

As highlighted in previous chapters, baptismal practices helped my research participants embody a participatory, communal, and Jesus-centered Christian identity—as both James and Al described it, "becoming who I am." Liturgical theologian Gordon Lathrop underscores the central importance of proclaiming Christian identity in baptismal practice, arguing that one's "station or rank" in life is not what ultimately defines oneself.[2] All the baptized come together before God in worship as a people constituted and sustained by the Holy Spirit, whose primary vocation is to embody their baptism—being a people who were once far apart yet now brought together in God. Put in the words of theologian Fred Edie, "the Christian baptismal vocation is to embody and practice the fullness of Christian identity. In other words, Christians are called to become who they are through baptism!"[3] The Presbyterian Church (U.S.A.) document "Invitation to Christ" raises a similar emphasis:

> Our baptismal identity in Jesus Christ unites us as the church: it is the foundation for our communal life and the ground of our ministry in the world. A renewed focus on baptismal identity and sacramental practice will enable us to live together with our differences and enjoy the unity that is Christ's gift to his church. The church may become better able to recognize this gift as we gather regularly and deliberately around the font . . .[4]

As these various Christian voices assert, echoing claims about Christian identity we explored in chapter 1 from scholars like Medi Anne Volpe and Gordon Mikoski, baptismal practices draw communities into further theological reflection, while at the same time, enlivening and reaffirming their Christian identities as those who belong in the body of Jesus. Pastor Daniel summarized this process of how baptism draws together theological reflection and embodied practice of community in his Baptist context, among both disabled and nondisabled members of his church:

God loved you and loved the world enough to take on a body like yours and to be baptized. Your baptism is an affirmation of your belovedness—of the belovedness that brought Jesus to us. You are never alone and we affirm that in our incarnational theology. God's always with us. Baptism is an initiation, a common shared kind of practice with our bodies that reminds us of our connection to one another . . . you're not alone because you are part of this family of God. We weren't made to be by ourselves. We're not by ourselves. We're part of community.

Theologian and disability scholar Rebecca Spurrier argues that baptism not only draws together theology and practice to form communal life among Christians, but urgently impresses "relational obligations" on members of the baptized body within their local church contexts.[5] The public nature of baptism across Christian traditions was emphasized in my research conversations with Andrew, Al, Eric, Hope, Pastor Alicia, Pastor Ambrose, Pastor Daniel, Pastor John, Pastor Soren, and Robert. Not only the public nature of baptism as an act of proclaiming Christian identity, but also the inclusion of promises made by the gathered body of worshipers to the newly baptized person, underscore the kind of relational obligation Spurrier suggests flows forth from the church's practices of baptism. Barbara shared a story of how these baptismal promises were reiterated and kept in a situation where she struggled to continue to bring her son, Bob, to church after a period of what she considered highly disruptive actions from Bob during the middle of church services. In conversation with her pastor about a discernment to step away from the church with Bob, Barbara heard in response "God is for Bob. And you have to promise me that you'll be here every Sunday with him. We're going to work this out . . . if he's kicking the chairs then he's kicking the chairs. That's just fine. I want him here. Every Sunday." For Barbara, these words embodied the relational obligations of this pastor to Bob as a baptized member of Jesus, affirming his identity as an indispensable part of the church by nature of belonging to Jesus. As we will further explore in chapter 7, specific baptismal practices of preparation, testimony, and reaffirmation support faith communities in attending to the Christian identity of all members of the baptized body and help form imaginations within local communities that embrace the work of the Holy Spirit across baptized people of various disability identities. Faithful participation in baptismal practices acknowledges ecclesial dependence on the work of God in Jesus to challenge, renew, and reenliven Christian communities in their baptismal identity of new creation arising from death.

THE EMBODIED RICHNESS OF BAPTISMAL PRACTICES

The proclamation of Christian identity through baptismal practices takes on a myriad of richly embodied forms. These multisensory ways of "robust ritualizing around the font"[6] include practices such as touching the baptismal waters, hearing the pouring of the baptismal water or someone's immersion within the waters, saying or listening to baptismal prayers and songs, smelling the postbaptismal application of anointing oil, reading or hearing Christian Scripture concerning baptism, and soaking in baptismally oriented preaching. Embodied participation in these various avenues of baptismal engagement reinforces Christian identity as a new creation, proclaimed in accessible and tactile ways far beyond words alone. Pastor Daniel joked with me during his research interview about how church members will likely never remember what he preaches about on Sundays when his church baptizes new members. But, he said slowly and deliberately, "folks will never forget what they see you preach in your actions today . . . the very core of our faith is in being buried with Jesus we are raised with him to a life like his." Randy reflected on this embodied proclamation of baptism at Christ Church, especially as Pastor John framed it for people with and without intellectual disabilities preparing for baptism. Randy expressed it like this: "baptism is a way for you to preach to the church. To say without words that you belong to God. And to remind others that they belong to God." This wordless witness of baptism, a witness we will explore further in the next chapter, offers an embodied declaration of the identity and vocation of all baptized people as those who belong to Jesus and witness the good news of belonging to Jesus. My research partners with intellectual disabilities offer a particular, embodied witness that brings alive theological commitments surrounding baptism, such as the following claim by Louis Weil:

Our fundamental engagement with the sacraments is not cerebral; it is visceral . . . because of our physical nature, all aspects of our lives engage us not only with our minds, but with the whole of that physical nature. We 'know' through our senses. This sensual knowing engages us in ways that are much deeper than words alone. As precious as words are, we engage our world with a special intensity through our senses, an engagement which is beyond words.[7]

As we will continue to explore, Christians with intellectual disabilities at the faith communities who made this book possible testify to the central importance of multisensory and wordless engagement of baptismal practices. Their lives embody a resistance to theological abstraction and challenge ecclesial communities to renew their worship practices.

BAPTISMAL PRACTICES AS A PART OF THE WHOLE

The practice of baptism itself, as well as related practices of baptismal preparation, testimony, and reaffirmation, do not encompass the complete tapestry of Christian worship practices. Instead, these baptismal elements of Christian life inhabit an "ecological relationship" with the other practices of the baptized body, including reading, interpreting, and preaching Scripture, celebrating Holy Communion, and attending to the rhythms of the liturgical year (what Edie has named "bath, book, table, and time").[8] As we saw within my research partners' reflections on Scripture and broader experiences of their ecclesial communities, baptismal practices exist within a mutually reinforcing relationship with the wider practices of Christian worship, formation, and service.

Many clergy research participants also offered stories depicting strong links between Holy Communion and baptism within their own communal lives of faith. Pastor Daniel described practicing baptism and Eucharist as essential "links with Christians across time . . . we are participating in an unbroken stream, and it seems so simplistic or whatever. But, we've done this for two thousand years straight. Isn't that awesome?" Pastor Paula reflected on both communion and baptism as sources of "who we are in our identity"—through these practices, Pastor Paula shared with me, "we know that we are beloved." Speaking about the importance of holding baptism within the fullness of liturgical participation, and making this participation open to people of many diverse disability identities, Pastor Ambrose reflected, "If a church has not invited someone to participate in the Eucharist, they're probably not going to invite them to participate in baptism either." Pastor Ambrose's comments here remind us of the importance of expanded imagination about who churches might expect as liturgical participants and disciples.

Other lay leader participants also shared stories about how baptism related to wider practices of Christian worship and discipleship in their local churches. Anna described the activities of worship at her Episcopal church as oriented around the altar—the altar draped with colors of the liturgical season, a baptismal font located adjacent to the altar, receiving Holy Communion around the altar, and the altar's close proximity to the lectern where Scripture is read and preached. Anna's sense of her church's attention to creating a place of belonging for people with and without intellectual disabilities was captured in her expression that people "belonged at the altar rail." Randy described baptism and Holy Communion as vital parts of "participating and remembering" within worship—"participating in an act that Jesus also participated in. And in doing that, we're remembering something that Jesus did." Randy described both baptism and the Lord's Supper as gifts Christians receive within worship—"Pastor John always says we don't take them. We receive them . . . I really like it. We never use the word take. Because they're a gift we're receiving."

These integrative visions of practicing baptism as both essential to and supportive of everyday discipleship push back against notions of baptism as a "spotlight" activity—a singular event without implications for the whole of a community of faith.[9] Instead, repeated celebrations of baptism and related baptismal practices, alongside other forms of Christian worship, offer a path of ongoing Christian formation for local churches. Liturgical theologian Maxwell Johnson frames it in this way:

> Baptism itself is the liturgical and sacrament center out of which we live; it is the watery Spirit-filled womb and tomb to which we are called to return time and time again to find a welcome place in our displaced lives . . . baptism places into the world a community

of displaced people, people on a pilgrimage who really belong nowhere except where they are led, a people sure of their identity as the Body of Christ, as those who always walk wet in the baptismal waters of their origin.[10]

This baptismally rooted framework for Christian community and worship helps to foster a baptismal spirituality within communities of faith.[11] As we have surveyed, attentiveness to this baptismal shape of Christian life holds important implications for Christian identity—as James and Al both put it—"becoming who we are."[12]

BAPTISM AND ECUMENISM: TOWARD A SHARED UNITY

As the stories of this book's research participants testify, baptismal practices hold great significance for Christians from a wide variety of particular traditions. Being baptized into the body of Jesus binds Christians of diverse denominations, baptismal theologies, and liturgical practices to one another through the power of the Holy Spirit. In *Baptism, Eucharist and Ministry* (also known as the "Lima Document,") the World Council of Churches seeks to shift the normativity of baptismal practices away from "individual confessional positions," and instead take up a generous spirit of ecumenism.[13] The Lima Document asserts the centrality of baptism in cultivating this spirit of unity across Christian communities: "the need to recover baptismal unity is at the heart of the ecumenical task as it is central for the realization of genuine partnership within the Christian community."[14] As portrayed in the central importance of stories of Jesus' baptism for research participants in this book, Christian baptismal unity finds its roots in the life, ministry, death, and resurrection of Jesus.[15] Various reports emerging from ecumenical dialogues, including the Roman Catholic Church and the Baptist World Alliance's "The Word of God in the Life of the Church,"[16] and "Baptism and Incorporation into the Body of Christ, the Church,"[17] from the 2012–2017 Trilateral Conversations between Mennonite, Roman Catholic, and Lutheran Christians, underscore the unifying power of baptism rooted in Jesus. A mutual recognition of the core theological proclamations of baptism—incorporation into Jesus' death and resurrection, transformation into newness of life through the Holy Spirit, faith in the context of the church, and forgiveness from sin—calls for baptismal partnerships across ecumenical communities, seeking to respect and not erase diverse theological, practical, and doctrinal differences.

Embracing ecumenical unity in baptism can, however, present churches with potential difficulties. While baptism, *in theory*, provides the basis of Christian unity, Weil questions why "Christian initiation seems all too often to take an insignificant place in the lived experience of many Christians? If our churches affirm that baptism is theologically significant, why does our baptismal practice often marginalize—or, at worst, trivialize—this fundamental rite of Christian incorporation?"[18] Weil's observations about the frequent insignificance of baptism in contemporary ecclesial life call for a reexamination of baptismal practices to support the preparation, proclamation, and reaffirmation of not only baptism in and of itself, but the ongoing formation of identity, discipleship, and vocation among all members of the baptized body. This kind of heightened attention to baptism resists homogenous belonging oriented around nonbaptismal identities and serves as a practice of accountability for Christians to live into their postbaptismal newness of life, through the power of the Holy Spirit. In the next chapter, through the experiences of my research partners, we will more fully explore how baptismal practices across the ecumenical spectrum underscore the fundamental place of belonging in Jesus' body for Christian identity and community.

"THIS ISN'T ABOUT PERFECTION"

One compelling approach for embracing practices that affirm baptismal identity and discipleship among disabled and nondisabled Christians alike lies in the imperfect interdependence marking participation in these various practices. In her interview, Anna described her church's embrace of people with intellectual disabilities and their involvement in ecclesial practices in this way: "This isn't about perfection. It's about inclusion and about experience together. And it doesn't have to be a perfect thing." Anna's frankness in her response initially surprised me, especially since some churches choose to attend to disciples with intellectual disabilities through organizing separate "disability ministries." In contrast, Anna's community of

Holy Angels Episcopal Church centers imperfection both as a mark of authentic community as well as a central feature of her community's inclusive liturgical practices. Anna's embrace of imperfection helps frame one witness of the baptized body: a community of baptismal identity enacted through imperfect yet mutually engaged baptismal practices among disabled and nondisabled Christians.

Pastor Soren reflected on the same reality at St. Matthew's Baptist Church, something he described as a "sense of casualness, a comfort level, with imperfections. A sense of being okay with things that just aren't perfect." Mary picked up on a similar theme, expressing that in baptism, Christians both with and without disabilities become part of community: "it's like an 'I got you' moment. You don't need to worry about things because this community of people, you know, you little baby or you big person, you don't need to worry about what it is that you're going to be struggling with, because we've got you."

Anna, Pastor Soren, and Mary's comments resonate with Spurrier's description of worship occurring "through limit"—"at the limits of our individual abilities, the art of the (communal) liturgy takes shape."[19] It is not despite but within limits that baptismal practices powerfully witness to the presence of Jesus and the transformation of communal life made possible through the Holy Spirit. Baptismal practices do not constitute a set of actions for nondisabled people to "do for" or "on behalf of" disabled people, nor are they the only practices that constitute a distinctive form of witness for people with intellectual disabilities. Instead, baptismal practices offer occasions of interdependence, partnership, and collaboration across human difference—places where the baptized body lives out its radically communal, participatory, and Jesus-rooted constitution.

In its limitedness and diversity, ecclesial participation of people with and without disabilities presents not a set of abstract theological propositions, but a dynamic, interdependent, and communal proclamation of the church community's fellowship of love. In this community, each member of the baptized body serves an indispensable role. Among some disciples, including some people with intellectual disabilities, baptismal living includes more traditional modes of theological study and the practice of verbal proclamation through ministries of preaching and teaching. And among some other disciples, including some people with intellectual disabilities, the fullness of a prophetic ministry does not necessarily, as Jill Harshaw argues, "consist in predictive language expressing new revelation but in embodied reminders of previously revealed truth which has been overlooked or underemphasized or is particularly pertinent to a current situation or need."[20] In our interview, Hope described it this way: "We're all part of this. We need each other. The one who is baptizing and the one who is being baptized and the community that supports it is all one. And that starts very early and it goes all the way through death." Hope later added, "and it certainly doesn't matter what level of cognitive ability you have . . . it's much more that you are going through a transformation that God and we are all enacting at once." Welcoming and embracing the limited gifts of Christian disciples—those with and without intellectual disabilities—provides sites where, as Mary described it, Christian communities can pay attention to "the little cracks" where "God can get in."

ATTENDING TO ACCESS

For churches seeking to embrace baptismal practices as a way of proclaiming the communal, participatory, and Jesus-centered identity of all disciples, including those with a range of disability identities, "tangible environmental changes" alongside "critical reflection on how environments reflect underlying, often unquestioned social assumptions about disability" are necessary.[21] Spurrier frames accessible liturgical practices as "sacred and essential, not just something that would be good to have if possible and feasible."[22] In the preceding chapters, we have already uncovered many assumptions that can restrict ecclesial participation for people with intellectual disabilities. In the book's final chapter, we will describe not only the lived experiences and theological contours of the baptismal practices of preparation, testimony, and reaffirmation; our exploration of research participant stories, those that value "embodied, personal accounts that emphasize the agency of people with disabilities,"[23] will also highlight the concrete aspects of baptismal practices that promote multimodal access. In these chapters, the stories of research partners will provide us with generative starting places to reflect on facilitating accessible participation in the full life of the church among all of God's children.

Facilitating accessible ecclesial environments requires communal effort. As Pastor Ambrose suggests, supporting "all of God's children" takes not only the action of a single disabled Christian or a nondisabled ally. Barbara described the realities of accepting, inclusive, and accessible community life at St. Mary's Episcopal Church for her son, Bob, as follows: "it's the entire church. Everything has always been the church." As liturgical theologian and clergyperson Susan Maire Smith also stresses, responsibility for facilitating environments of access should not fall to a single person, but rather be cultivated through compassionate collaborations.[24]

A FRAMEWORK FOR CHANGE

How might churches intentionally welcome and affirm the baptismal vocations of disabled Christians within ecclesial life? Gerald Arbuckle, a theologian and anthropologist, commends a process he names "refounding." In his framework of refounding, Arbuckle outlines a process of change to assist churches responding to pressing questions in their life together.[25] As we have explored throughout this book, the lives of Christians with intellectual disabilities present pressing questions around belonging, Christian identity, and baptismal participation across contemporary Christian churches.

The process of refounding focuses on bringing church members together around urgent needs at the heart of community life, even when addressing these needs might stir up disagreement.[26] This process assumes that previous practices and efforts have not sufficiently attended to the specific needs of a current church community, calling forth creativity and intentionality to embrace new practices and ways of life together. In this way, refounding as a change process centers opportunities for attention to local concerns, followed by communal practices of confession and repentance, leading to transformation. The specific practices we will attend to in the next chapter—baptismal preparation, testimony, and reaffirmation—provide communal, participatory, and Jesus-centered ways that embrace the experiences of disabled Christians. Exploring these practices in partnership between disabled and nondisabled disciples can provide clear avenues for communities to confess, repent, and grow together around needs related to the human experience of disability.

Attending to change at the level of a church community, Arbuckle stresses the necessary role of "refounding persons" to devote energy and leadership in response to pressing questions and wounds in particular ecclesial spaces. Processes of refounding flourish when small groups of individuals who perceive and experience "the gap between the Gospel and the contemporary world" (often manifested in prejudice, discrimination, and grave justice issues) lead churches in transformation.[27] These people, however, do not act alone to initiate change in church communities. Instead, much like in the stories of access and belonging shared by this book's research participants, small groups of people attentive to the discipleship of disabled Christians are often those to create coalitions of care and accountability that provide support throughout processes of intentional change. As we have explored in this chapter, the identity-shaping power of the work of God in baptism, the ecumenical unity undergirding baptismal proclamations of Christian identity in the body of Jesus, as well as the accessible, interdependent, and limited nature of participation in ecclesial practices, underscore the communal, Jesus-centered, and participatory processes of change in the church.

CONCLUSION

Toward the end of our research conversation, Steve and I talked about the place of baptismal remembrance and other baptismal practices in the landscape of Christian life. Steve reflected, "every time we baptize the priest comes through the congregation and sprinkles the water. And you remember your baptism. But I think it's partly hard to remember our baptisms because we're not threatened right now ... but we may be getting closer and closer to the time when just to survive as Christians we'll need to remember our baptism." Steve's reflections on the lack of threat perceived by many Christians in contemporary Western ecclesial contexts perhaps ring true. However, in the context of this book, we have identified and sought to resist the threat of homogenous belonging within churches, particularly how an account of Christian identity that prioritizes individualized and cognitive constructions of identity often sustains patterns of marginalization, rejection, and discrimination against Christians with intellectual disabilities.

Baptism and baptismal practices provide key sites to help church communities return to their identities in Jesus, through confession, renewal, and ongoing transformation in baptismal life. Multisensory baptismal practices provide avenues where all people, whether those we describe as living with profound intellectual disabilities or those who are nondisabled, testify to the basis of Christian identity and life together—Jesus Christ. Participation in these baptismal practices affirms and renews the life of discipleship among the whole baptized body—not only among the theologically educated, the socially mobile, or the liturgically savvy. An intentional and enlivened embrace of baptismal preparation, testimony, and reaffirmation opens the floodgates to people across the spectrum of human limitations, radically affirming their communal, participatory, and Jesus-centered identities. It is through these practices that communities of baptismal belonging might be for each other and for the world the baptized body of Jesus.

Let us now turn to the specific baptismal practices of preparation, testimony, and reaffirmation that gather Christians "in Jesus" and around the font; no longer bound to ecclesial imaginations that ignore disability, but communities who the Holy Spirit empowers to a baptismal vocation of remaining attentive to and celebrating each other's identities of new creation.

7

Practices of the Baptized Body

Preparation, Testimony, and Reaffirmation

Throughout the research interviews for this book, participants told stories of meaningful baptismal practices that continued to shape their own sense of baptismal vocation as well as the imaginations of their church communities. Beyond services of baptism, my research partners' practices fell into three broad categories: baptismal preparation, baptismal testimony, and baptismal reaffirmation. In this final chapter, drawing upon the theological wisdom and lived experiences of these research participants, we will explore these three practices of the baptized body. Throughout our exploration, I will highlight how these practices emerging from disabled experience can apply across ecumenical contexts, how they might reshape ecclesial imagination around Christian identity, and how they can inform contemporary churches as they attend to the work of the Holy Spirit in the lives of all members of Jesus' body, both disabled and nondisabled.

PRACTICES OF THE BAPTIZED BODY: PREPARATION

Practices of baptismal preparation provide one way to reenliven the life of the baptized body, emphasizing the Jesus-centered, communal, and participatory identity of Christian disciples, regardless of disability identity. Intentional engagement in practices of baptismal preparation helps church communities move away from overly passive, sentimental, and individualized practices of baptism that fail to grasp the radical affirmation of identity in Christ, whether in paedobaptist or credobaptist traditions. Baptismal preparation provides opportunities for communal formation that resist homogenous belonging by joining together intergenerational groups of people—those who are baptized and those yet to be baptized—to explore what this act of initiation into Jesus' body means for their life together.

The World Council of Churches understands practices of baptismal preparation to include "reading and teaching about the faith of the church ... experiences of hearing, learning, and doing ... intended to lead to conversion, appropriation of the faith in heart and mind, trust in the triune God, and baptism."[1] To imagine how these practices might be cultivated within a diversity of Christian traditions, we will turn to stories from this book's research participants in the following sections. First, we will explore how practices of baptismal preparation provide an occasion for joyful anticipation and how this might relate to new opportunities for Christian formation. Second, we will explore how practices of baptismal preparation serve as avenues of nurture, especially through the roles of baptismal sponsors and godparents. Finally, embracing the framework of Universal Design for Learning, we will consider how practices of preparation for baptism might be made increasingly accessible for participation across a wide range of disability identities and learning styles.

Anticipating Baptism: Embracing the Practice of Preparation

> "And I'm telling you that almost every night for two months ... Amanda would call me on my phone and she would say, 'When am I going to get baptized?' And I would tell her the date, we're going to baptize you then. And she would say, 'Okay.' But she just wanted to stay right on top of that. And every night, or almost every night, she would call me and ask about her baptism."—Pastor Soren

I could sense Amanda's excitement (a woman with an intellectual disability) in this story Pastor Soren recounted to me, even though it was nearly two decades since the date of her baptism. In Pastor Soren's telling of this story, I appreciated not only Amanda's individual enthusiasm in anticipating her baptism, but how her anticipation facilitated an anticipatory posture within St. Matthew's Baptist Church as a whole. Pastor Soren relayed how Amanda's anticipation of her baptism fostered anticipation in many others throughout the church, in a parallel fashion to other times of joyful anticipation in this church community. For example, Pastor Soren told me stories about a semiregular service at St. Matthew's where adults with intellectual disabilities involved in the church community would provide musical leadership during the Sunday service. Pastor Soren reflected, it was "sort of like Amanda anticipated her baptism . . . it gave the adults with intellectual disabilities something to look forward to. And they would sing with joy and beauty and gusto." The congregation at St. Matthew's appreciated that these individuals' musical talents were brought "as their gift to God. And so, it became a gift for everyone"—an event anticipated with joy. Anticipation did not revolve around musical accuracy or technical skill, but rather a "mutual edification" comprised in the giving and receiving of gifts in the setting of Sunday worship.

Practices of baptismal preparation that anticipate the full and joyful participation of people with intellectual disabilities, as well as all those preparing for baptism in the life of Christian communities, provide one such poignant site of what Pastor Soren names as "mutual edification." Preparatory activities, such as multiweek series of catechetical instruction, as well as repeated rehearsals of the baptismal service for pragmatic practice as well as experiential formation, provide powerful spaces for communal formation for the whole life of the church.

Randy described another experience of significant anticipation in relation to baptism. He recalled a series of conversations that he and Pastor John had with a small group of young adults with intellectual disabilities who were preparing to be baptized. Randy told me about a young man named Dennis who excitedly proclaimed after one of these conversations: "I cannot wait to be baptized!" Randy explained: "What Dennis was saying was I can't wait to say this to my church, that I belong to God and I belong to you . . . they all [Dennis, Ava, and others] just left that meeting just like sort of giddy and excited." Randy's story illustrates not only the key role of anticipation in baptismal preparation for cultivating an excitement surrounding baptism, but also the positive impact of sustained, intentional pastoral presence for groups of individuals preparing for their baptisms.

In addition to this small group for accountability and support in preparation for baptism, Randy also described a weekly Bible study that met among intergenerational adults with and without disabilities at Christ Church: "there was just so much formation that was happening . . . they talked about baptism a lot during the Bible study . . . and this discernment doesn't happen—often doesn't happen in like flashes or in like moments of clarity. It happens over time and in prayer." The extended, intentional practices of baptismal formation at Christ Church through small group support as well as in the context of a weekly Bible study focused on baptism attuned me to the particular practice of coming alongside those to be baptized, no matter what their limitations, and engaging them through communal formation. Christ Church witnesses to how shared lay and clergy leadership can create spaces of anticipation where both the already baptized and those to be baptized, with and without disability, can discern their Christian identities and vocations together.

Baptist scholar Stanley Fowler argues that churches ought to embrace a posture of wonder and expectation in regard to God's action in baptism.[2] Anticipating that God's graciousness will manifest in the lives of all the baptized provides a theological orientation for practices of baptismal preparation. Liturgical theologian Alexander Schmemann describes this anticipatory orientation to the work of God in the church as a "double rhythm of preparation and fulfillment."[3] Preparing to welcome the newly baptized into Jesus' body is the work not only of family members and close friends of those to be baptized—it is an anticipatory act where all church members ought to be encouraged to participate. As those in the baptized body prepare and anticipate welcoming the newly baptized, they too might enter a season of expectant discernment about their own baptismal vocation to ministry. Communal preparatory activities, where small, intergenerational groups of church members meet together for support, formal study, or fellowship, help individuals receive affirmation and challenge in regard to their formation as Christian disciples. In other words, baptismal preparation is not solely an individualized and speculative endeavor—it is an expectant activity shared together with other church members, a cycle that is constantly being refreshed as churches prepare to welcome the newly baptized in an act of God fulfilling God's promise to incorporate us into Jesus' body.

Schmemann emphasizes that this double rhythm of preparation and fulfillment does not hinge on understanding. Put differently, understanding is not the ultimate goal of baptismal preparation activities. In Schmemann's tradition of Orthodox Christianity, he encourages infants to participate in these rhythms and practices of preparation, acknowledging their inability to understand what will happen to them.[4] Growing in one's "understanding" of baptism and ministry may be a fruit for some Christians who take part in baptismal preparation activities. But Schmemann has a larger vision for anticipatory and intentional practices of baptismal preparation: these practices emphasize that apart from any requirement of understanding, when a child of God becomes a newly baptized member of Jesus' body, "the whole Church is changed, enriched, and fulfilled."[5]

Christina Lappa, a disability and special education scholar, piloted a baptismal education program for intergenerational adults with moderate and severe intellectual disabilities in the context of the Greek Orthodox Church. Lappa (and her research team's) scholarship illustrates an example of practicing baptismal preparation among those already baptized, in order to anticipate the baptismal joining of new members to Jesus' body. The researchers' innovative approach to baptismal preparation included experiential learning facilitated by a priest—weekly meetings where intergenerational participants with intellectual disabilities not only reviewed key catechetical questions and answers, but interacted with the font, water, olive oil, dolls, and pictorial cards to provide a multisensory learning experience.[6] The participants also ate together, enjoying traditional Greek Orthodox baptismal celebration foods (such as candied almonds).[7] Following the study, the participants were all found to sustain "basic knowledge about the Christian-Orthodox mystery of baptism and its symbolism"[8] as well as maintain a deeper and more meaningful connection with a local parish.[9]

Baptismal Preparation as a Practice of Nurture

> "The church is, among other things, the place where we grow in our awareness . . . of our belovedness and of our calling as disciples . . . baptism marks our discipleship. Go forth into all nations . . . making disciples, baptizing them . . . the church is the

kind of place where discipleship is nurtured and cultivated and shepherded."—Pastor Daniel

Pastor Daniel's reflections on the church as a community of nurture spurred my thinking about how practices of baptismal preparation serve to nurture discipleship among congregants. Finding particular ways to support people with intellectual disabilities in baptismal preparation practices provides one distinct form of nurture in church communities. In particular, churches might attend to specific learning and environmental needs among people with disabilities to enable their maximal participation in practices of baptismal preparation. Part of nurturing all people, including those with profound disabilities, requires sustained discernment and responsiveness to how individuals receive love and presence, and then extending these forms of love and presence to them throughout church practices.

The Lima Document emphasizes that all Christian traditions, regardless of baptismal theology, ought to assume a "responsible attitude towards Christian nurture."[10] These practices of care occur, as explored above, in both prebaptismal and postbaptismal contexts. The Lima Document exhorts practices of nurture that help each baptized person identify and express their gifts for ministry. These practices offer one opportunity for collaboration among various Christian churches in a shared geographical area, rooted in a common commitment to support the baptized life of all God's children.[11] For example, churches in a local region might collaboratively host small groups where people of different traditions and ages preparing for baptism (or preparing for baptismal renewal) might meet together for mutual support, discernment, and care.[12]

In our research conversation, Pastor Paula reflected about the powerful and bidirectional nurture present among those preparing for baptism and the church members given a special role in their nurture (in some traditions, those set apart as sponsors or godparents). Paula shared, "baptism happens to the child but it really also happens for those who surround the child. Because the promises that we make on behalf of the child, we also make for ourselves in our journey, in our faith development." Paula reflected on her experience of having "very active" godparents who cared for her, encouraging her Christian formation and supporting her throughout her childhood and into adulthood. Every year, on her baptismal anniversary, she and her godparents would prepare to celebrate by finding the candle from her baptism, talking about a renewal of baptismal promises to serve God and seek to uphold the dignity of all people, and share in how they would do these things together.

Also reflecting on baptismal preparation, Pastor Alicia described to me a shift among clergy in the Episcopal tradition, involving the taking on of greater responsibility for facilitating practices of baptismal nurture, especially since the 1979 revision of the *Book of Common Prayer*. She underscored a rising dissatisfaction among many of her clergy colleagues, particularly when interacting with godparents or adults preparing for baptism, who wish to eschew practices of baptismal preparation. Pastor Alicia expressed,

> "I think that's actually good that this is something that is frustrating to clergy . . . it would be better, obviously, if they were more enthusiastic about coming for millions of hours of baptismal preparation. But, I think that it suggests that baptismal preparation is important in and of itself, and is important in Christian formation. And that it's sad and frustrating when it doesn't happen."

Both clergy and lay leaders can play a crucial role in embodying practices of baptismal preparation as ways to enact the promises to care for the newly baptized throughout the whole of their Christian lives, rather than framing activities of baptismal preparation as rote requirements. As Pastor Daniel emphasized, preparing for baptism presents churches with the precious opportunity to proclaim the belovedness of each member.

Universal Design for Learning: An Access Paradigm for Baptismal Preparation

"Universal Design for Learning" (UDL) refers to principles that support transformative and meaningful learning through the accessible delivery of information, interactive learning modalities, diverse learning materials, and "multiple options for student design, delivery, and expression."[13] In seeking maximal avenues for participation among people with intellectual disabilities in the formative activities of baptismal preparation, and all those preparing for their baptism or the baptism of another, applying a framework of UDL offers one pragmatic approach to support the flourishing of Jesus' gathered body.

As we saw in the research study conducted by Lappa et al., the physical elements of baptism, including water, specific kinesthetic movements in a particular church's ordinance or rite, music, preaching, candles, special clothing, and anointing oil, can be engaged to help encourage formation through all the senses. Liturgical theologian Gordon Lathrop exhorts contemporary Christians to embrace baptismal practices with "intensity"—"let them be done with focused intensity, not ignored. But let them be used to speak the holiness of the triune God and so be made a source of meaning for our world."[14] This intensity not only applies to celebrations of baptism themselves, but also to preparatory practices. Again, this provides an opportunity for ecumenical unity and cooperation: local churches can learn from one another through exploring specific patterns of preparation at other congregations, gathering ideas and even shared practices of baptismal preparation, to enhance accessible ways into Christian baptismal formation.

Pastor Ambrose shared with me a striking story of engaging UDL in his work with a family preparing for their son's baptism:

> "We [Pastor Ambrose and Eli's parents] just chatted about baptism and Eli and the work that God was doing in Eli's life. And basically I sent them away with some homework. Eli's homework was to watch some YouTube videos of baptism, sprinkling, pouring and immersing. And see which ones he kind of connected with, because . . . in United Methodism we're supposed to at least offer all three modes and let the person choose for themselves. So, I said you go check on some baptism videos and see what you connect with. I didn't want to make any assumptions about what mode he would be willing to participate in or not. So, I said, go check it out, see what you think."

While remaining true to his tradition's rubrics for preparing to celebrate baptism, Pastor Ambrose also exhibited practical wisdom[15] for how to engage Eli, who did not communicate with spoken language, in a process of baptismal preparation. Pastor Ambrose later told me more about Eli and his family's preparation for baptism:

"In the United Methodist Church in the hymnal, there are a couple different baptism rites. And they are actually worded very interestingly. They're not necessarily worded as this one is for adults and this one is for kids. One of them is called the baptism ritual for those who can answer for themselves. And the other is the baptism ritual for those who can't answer or can't speak for themselves. I said to Eli's parents, that honestly as the pastor in this scenario, I'm going to follow y'alls lead. So, take a look at those rites. And come back and tell me which one we're doing. If you think, because you know Eli better than I do, take a look at the rites, take a look at the logic within the rites, and then talk to us about which one we're going to go with. So, they came back. They had read *By Water and the Spirit*,[16] which was awesome. We talked about that. Eli had so loved his YouTube research that he got in the bathtub and practiced immersing because that's what he decided on doing."

Eli's story illustrates the powerful avenues for participation that open up with accessible engagement of baptismal preparation materials. Though in this particular story, the materials were engaged by Eli and his family in their home context, other ecclesial settings might gather larger groups to participate in multisensory practices of baptismal preparation together, engaging and interacting with the baptismal waters, reading through the liturgy, repeatedly singing familiar songs about baptism, and hearing one or two familiar Scripture passages about baptism week after week. Together, some participants engage sight, and others hearing; those willing might participate in touch, and smell, and movement, alongside more "traditional" forms of didactic curriculum for catechesis. These kinds of practices for baptismal preparation draw in participants who cannot communicate with symbolic language or have learning differences, not by making sure they are merely in the room, but instead creatively offering multiple forms of engagement directly related to baptism, in the spirit of UDL.

Sister Mary Therese Harrington, S.H., highlights the importance of "the role of affectivity in catechesis and the need to develop a symbolic consciousness"[17] in practices of baptismal preparation. She argues for a vision of catechesis as formation beyond intellectual knowing. Engaging in practices that evoke feeling and the expressing of emotion (much like Eli's YouTube videos) provides one such example of affective Christian formation through practices of baptismal preparation.[18] This affectivity can and should be attended to carefully by leaders in baptismal preparation contexts, through offering multisensory modes of engagement for different learners in the process of baptismal preparation.[19] Harrington suggests that affectivity is always and already present, and therefore, the quality of it depends on the intentionality of leaders in baptismal preparation.[20]

In an effort to support maximal communal participation in practices of baptismal formation, Harrington recommends that individual sponsors (or support people) for each baptismal candidate attend baptismal preparation activities with them.[21] Though Harrington has in mind the baptism of adolescents and adults, rather than infants, her suggestion offers an important consideration for baptismal preparation within paedobaptist traditions, where godparents or other sponsors might participate in a multisensory experience to prepare for the baptism of their loved one (and renewing their own baptismal vows). In this way, Harrington and others throughout this section demonstrate how *all* people benefit from intentional accompaniment in their journeys of baptismal preparation. This model of facilitating a preparation partner for each baptismal candidate provides a pragmatic means of meeting the specific needs of each baptismal candidate, as well as a natural way to draw more people from the church community, across life experiences and generations, into the process of preparation.

The above stories and practical applications of baptismal preparation highlight opportunities to embrace celebratory anticipation, mutual nurture, and accessible formation for all present in a church community. As Schmemann and Lathrop commend, these practices of baptismal preparation can and ought to be integrated into a cyclical pattern of Christian life together. Gordon Mikoski frames this as follows: "Baptism in all its fullness can only come to realization through sustained and intentional processes of ecclesial pedagogy spread over the entire lifecycle."[22] Churches might consider a continuous offering of baptismal preparation classes, small groups, and experiential formation opportunities, encouraging participation of all those present in a congregation.[23] Practices of baptismal preparation thus become a communal and caring avenue for the renewal of baptismal promises to one another, and empowerment for exercising baptismal gifts for ministry, granted by the Holy Spirit, in both the church and world.

PRACTICES OF THE BAPTIZED BODY: TESTIMONY

Alongside practices of baptismal preparation, the practice of baptismal testimony, both in instances of discrete spoken testimony, as well as in cases of testimony proclaimed by the wordless living out of a baptismal vocation, creates new space for ecclesial participation among people with and without intellectual disabilities. The World Council of Churches' Lima Document urges both paedobaptist and credobaptist traditions to "embody God's own initiative in Christ and express a response of faith made within the believing community" as a hallmark baptismal practice.[24] Baptismal testimony, as I will illustrate in conversation with my research partners' stories in the following sections, provides a faithful way of proclaiming this response of faith. It calls communities to cultivate sustained practices of presence, listening, and attending to the witness of all people, including those with intellectual disabilities, in order that they might faithfully proclaim, together, the work of the Holy Spirit in enabling newness of life within the community, marked by a shared identity as God's new creation.

We will first consider practices of baptismal testimony as a source of renewal for Christian imagination around baptismal identity and vocation. Next, I will share examples from research partners about how baptismal testimony helped them and their communities to proclaim the work of Christ in baptism and the Holy Spirit's renewal of their communities through the living out of a baptismal vocation to discipleship. Next, we will explore the power of testimony inherent within baptismal liturgies themselves. And finally, I will highlight scholarship from the field of disability theology on vocation, suggesting how practices of baptismal testimony might amplify the baptismal vocation to discipleship among people with intellectual disabilities in contemporary Christian faith communities.

Baptismal Testimony as a Source of New Imagination

In my conversation with Anna, a lay leader at Holy Angels Episcopal Church, she wondered out loud how baptismal practices might make space for people with intellectual disabilities in church communities. As we explored previously in chapter 4, Anna expressed to me her concerns about churches celebrating the "cultural successes" of their members—things like high school graduations, job promotions, and personal achievements. In particular, Anna's concerns related to the lack of celebration for people with intellectual disabilities and others "that don't have these cultural successes . . . how do we recognize somebody that's maybe not having those kinds of hallmarks in their lives? How do we make sure that all are celebrated?"

I continue to carry the impact of Anna's questions with me. Anna's concerns illustrated for me one danger of an imagination about Christian identity rooted in values of contemporary Western liberal democracies—the restriction of ecclesial celebrations to successes marked by individualized productivity and achievement. I recalled memories from my own life amongst various communities of faith, thinking about how many people must have been excluded, and deeply wounded, by the repeated celebration of "cultural successes" in church—celebrations that displaced the primacy of baptismal identity at the heart of the church's life of following Jesus together.

Anna's deep longing for a faithful response fueled my exploration of practices of baptismal testimony as a faithful alternative to the church's highlighting of successes often unachievable among people with and without intellectual disabilities. As I ruminated with Anna's struggles, a number of potential practices of testimony struck me as profound ways to celebrate the vocation of discipleship among all the baptized—not just those with "cultural successes."

Testifying to Transformation

Across diverse theological traditions of baptism in the Christian church, incorporating practices of baptismal testimony can help communities to resist rote or overly sentimental practices of baptism that deemphasize the Holy Spirit's work of ongoing, communal transformation in the church. As churches seek to identify the work of the Holy Spirit in their midst, for challenge, confession, repentance, and transformation, discerning the "visible discipleship" among members of Jesus' baptized body is one crucial practice.[25] Baptismal testimony, a proclamation of the work of the Holy Spirit in empowering embodied discipleship among the baptized members of Jesus' body, provides one concrete practice to highlight the discipleship of people with intellectual disabilities, helping renew the church's anthropological imagination with particular regard to people whose lives are not typically celebrated.

At St. Matthew's Baptist Church, Pastor Soren reflected on the importance of testimony at each service of baptism. Pastor Soren described the composing of a testimony of faith as a key practice in baptismal preparation. Among disabled and nondisabled people preparing for baptism, Pastor Soren would have them communicate their testimony of discipleship to someone they knew and loved, whether writing it down, or expressing it to a loved one in words. On the occasion of the person's baptism, this loved one would read aloud their testimony of discipleship for the gathered community—a declaration witnessing to the power of God in shaping the person's life of Christian transformation. As Pastor Soren described it to me, this was one of the most powerful aspects of not only his church's baptismal practices, but their whole life together.

James, a young man with intellectual disabilities, talked to me about the process of preparing his own baptismal testimony as a deeply meaningful act: "I was preparing with my Mom. And she helped me to tell my testimony to my sister." The work of testimony for James came from an interdependent effort with his mother and sister, with their voices added to amplify James' witness to his life as a disciple of Jesus. James' father, Eric, reflected on the celebratory and communal aspects of James' baptismal testimony: "Well, for me it was just a very special moment . . . not only were we as a family celebrating it, but it was a church celebration too. They appreciated his testimony and it was just a great testimony to the church of the value of every person, which St. Matthew's has always valued anyway. It was just a celebration."

The communal celebration of James' baptism and the proclamation of his baptismal testimony, read by his sister, provides a striking example of how churches might lift up the witness of people with intellectual disabilities. James' testimony resonates with the World Council of Churches' affirmation of providing spaces "where candidates offer a personal testimony at the time of their baptism ... as a powerful sign of the working of the Holy Spirit in their lives, thus revealing God's power to convert and save."[26] However, James' example of this practice seems to resonate only within credobaptist traditions. In addition, James' story suggests that practices of testimony require some capacity for a verbal or written expression of faith. What about people with intellectual disabilities who do not communicate with spoken or written words? And what about Christians in paedobaptist traditions?

For example, imagine a person with profound limitations who does not communicate with words. They have been a part of a particular church community in the credobaptist tradition for decades. Though they have no words to request baptism or to testify to their journey of Christian discipleship, the ecclesial community receives this person's presence as indispensable to their life together. This kind of community might practice a communal writing of this individual's testimony of discipleship, perhaps as part of a process of communally discerned baptismal preparation. The practice of a church coming together to write a testimony of discipleship for someone who cannot express it in their own words strikes me as a profound way for the church to take seriously the belonging, gifts, and discipleship of people with profound expressions of disability.

This kind of communal attention to the wordless discipleship and ministry of nonspeakers, resulting in a practice of composing a baptismal testimony about the Holy Spirit's work of transformation and renewal through this individual and in the community as a whole, might also be cultivated within churches that align with a paedobaptist tradition. For example, churches might practice composing a baptismal testimony on the occasion of the baptism of an infant or small child (with or without a disability). Annually, on this person's baptismal anniversary, the church could commit to writing a renewed testimony of this person's baptismal vocation in their midst—how their life has shaped the church's practice of proclaiming the good news of Jesus. Writing this kind of annual testimony not only highlights the ongoing work of the Holy Spirit through individual members of the baptized body, but also serves as a sign of the community's commitment to sustain their promises to uphold each baptized person throughout their Christian life. In smaller ecclesial settings, these testimonies might be shared as an integral part of weekly worship, whereas larger congregations might find additional ways to amplify these testimonies, such as inclusion in handouts, newsletters, or special liturgies held on a biweekly or monthly basis.[27]

Cultivating a communal discipline of composing baptismal testimonies for all those who make up a local faith community provides churches with accountability to attend to the lives of faith among all the baptized. It also provides an occasion for a great celebration of the work of the Holy Spirit in enabling the ministry of all the baptized—a faithful alternative to church practices that focus primarily upon "cultural successes" of congregants. A practice of communally composing baptismal testimonies on the occasion of a person's baptismal anniversary also provides a key site of accountability—in order to faithfully write a testimony, people in a church must actually spend enough time together to perceive the work of the Holy Spirit! In this way, accountability to the practice of testifying to the baptismal identity and vocation of others requires close attunement to our neighbors in the baptized body. Ultimately, practices of baptismal testimony witness to God's faithfulness and grace manifest in the transformed lives of all the baptized.

The Embodied Testimony of the Liturgy

In faith communities from both paedobaptist and credobaptist traditions that I visited as part of the research for this book, celebrations of baptism themselves served as acts of testimony. As we reviewed in chapter 6, some participants including Pastor Daniel and Randy described baptisms as testimonies of "wordless preaching." Pastor John expressed it like this: "Baptism is one of the sermons that we preach in the church. And it tells a story about how good God is and how much God loves us. And how we belong. It tells the story of who we really are."

Mary shared with me about her powerful experiences witnessing the baptisms of others, receiving these moments as transformative testimonies:

> "To me it's just one of those moments where you can see God entering that person who's being baptized. Like I said, it's like a little crack so God can get in. Cracks you open a little bit. Whether you know it's happening or not. It's happening... I think it changes the person who's being baptized. And I think it also changes the people who are there supporting them, witnessing that."

Ava, a young woman with intellectual disabilities, shared a similar sentiment to Mary's during our interview in perceiving this transformation among babies baptized in her home church community: "It's shocking. I cry. I get emotional. It's just overwhelming seeing little babies do it [be baptized]—it's just amazing." Parke also shared her experience of witnessing baptisms among people with and without disabilities as follows: "When I see a baptism, I just think like wow, this person is going in the water like Jesus did. And now they are a member at our church. Jesus' forever. That's what I experience too, and I think, wow."

Writing from the context of communities who practice confessional baptism, Melissa Florer-Bixler encourages the adaptation of baptisms for credobaptist communities who seek to baptize individuals with significant intellectual disabilities, entering into an ongoing relationship of what she names as "baptismal covenanting." Drawing together testimonies from both the community of the person to be baptized, as well as the ritual celebration itself, Florer-Bixler argues,

> For a person unable to make a publicly discernable confession of faith, baptismal covenanting may include testimonies about her life, her growth and commitment to community over time, and the impact of her gifts on the life of the church. Churches may adapt liturgies to proclaim to the gathered body how the person has expressed their agency in the ways they are able, and to describe the process of learning 'the language' of that individual.[28]

Testimony at the time of baptism and through the celebration of the rite of baptism can help attune ecclesial communities to God's work in the lives of individuals to be baptized, whether infants or adults, and to the Spirit's transformative work in the Christian practice of baptism itself. These testimonies can help Christian communities cultivate renewed commitments to accompany one another, to attend to each other's gifts for ministry, and to testify to these gifts as sites of baptismal discipleship. This communal attention to the gifts of each particular member of the baptized body, those with and without disabilities, helps shape imagination about God's work in all the baptized in unexpected, creative, and refreshed ways. As practical theologian Ben Conner suggests, "somatic, spatial, kinesthetic, aesthetic, inter- and intrapersonal intelligences yield knowledge beyond the critical rational intellect. And, when we are attentive to the different ways that people learn and know, we will be more open to the many different modalities of Christian witness."[29] Baptismal testimony provides one occasion for attentiveness to the Spirit's ongoing work in diverse forms of Christian witness.

Testifying About Vocation

Practices of baptismal testimony also serve to affirm baptismal vocation among all of God's children. John Swinton puts it this way:

> Within Jesus' body diversity has become the new norm, and living faithfully in the midst of diversity is the expected way of being in the world. As people are baptized into the body of Christ, so they enter into a space of deep and radical belonging. Within the body of Christ, every body has a place, and every body is recognized as a disciple with a call from Jesus and a vocation that the church needs if it is truly to be the body of Jesus. Such vocations stretch our ecclesial imaginations in powerful and deeply healing ways. Doing nothing can be an act of discipleship. Being cared for can be a fulfillment of one's humanness. The truth of who we are is held and hidden in Christ . . . if the only norm is Jesus, then our task is to live well and to live faithfully with our differences. If difference cannot separate us from Jesus, then it should not separate us from one another.[30]

Church communities might renew their perception and reception of the baptismal vocations of all people through the holy space that Swinton names as "the sacrament of the present moment."[31] In this space of "soulful companioning," marked by slow and attentive accompaniment of others, Christians can begin to notice "things that they never could have noticed before and, in noticing them, to see and respond differently. To be with someone in the moment is to be open to surprise, new possibilities . . . ."[32] Schmemann describes this shift in perception as cultivating an openness to be surprised by the joyful inbreaking of God: "no matter what our vocation, calling or occupation is—glorious or humble, meaningful or insignificant by the standards of 'this world'—it acquires a meaning, becomes a joy and a source of joy, for we begin to perceive and to experience it not in itself but in God and as a sign of His Kingdom."[33] As ecclesial communities accompany followers of Jesus with disabilities, this space of slow and sustained discernment might occasion not only the composition and proclamation of a baptismal testimony, but also reveal the riches of the Spirit's work in the vocational life of all members in Jesus' body.[34]

What faithful examples can instruct us in testifying about the baptismal vocations of people with intellectual disabilities, including those with profound disabilities? For theologian and clergyperson Frances Young, her son Arthur (who lives with multiple, severe disabilities) offers a wordless testimony as his baptismal vocation of discipleship. Young reflects on Arthur's participation in the liturgy, through his silence, his rapture during music, and his vivid facial expressions.[35] In this liturgical context, Young illustrates how Arthur witnesses to the reality that we may receive grace from God without being aware. The baptismal vocation that Arthur expresses through his participation in the liturgy, for Young, is being loved—and an exercise of this vocation does not require words or intellectual assent.[36] In her memoirs and other theological writings, Young writes a testimony of Arthur's joyful vocation of wordless discipleship.

Swinton writes about the vocation of Stephen, a young adult with intellectual disabilities who attended the same church:

> If we take seriously Stephen's contribution to our understanding of the worshipping community we find that the perspective he brings opens up a whole new dimension on what worship is and what it means to be a worshipping community. In the music, in the dance, in the bread and in the wine he encounters a joy and

evokes a sense of celebration that surpasses rational understanding and deeply challenges a church that equates faith and knowledge of God solely with intellectual comprehension.[37]

Stephen's vocation evokes both joy as well as challenge for those who worship with him—inviting an examination and expansion of assumptions about imagined forms of Christian discipleship. In addition, theologian Brian Brock offers a poignant reflection on testifying to the baptismal vocation of those living with intellectual disabilities, including his son, Adam:

> As a baptized Christian, [Adam], too, needs a local church body that can carry him and listen for the Spirit's gifts through him and people like him. He is more than autistic, and the life of the church challenges the individualized and medicalized account of his life that assumes his most important need is for therapies that will solve his (individual) problems and deficiencies. What is lost in this approach is any envisioning and praising of communities that can recognize him as a conduit of the Spirit's gifts to the community, whether in a 'leadership' role or not.[38]

Practices of baptismal testimony equip churches with not only an avenue to carefully accompany all those baptized into Jesus' body, listening for the Spirit's gifts in their lives, but also a practice that forms communities in new patterns of discernment and imagination, oriented to the action of the Triune God in baptism and the ongoing baptismal life of the community. The work of proclaiming testimonies of baptismal vocation, discipleship, and Christian identity falls as a responsibility upon the baptized body as a whole. It is through practices of proclaiming the gifts for ministry of all the baptized that churches can come to more carefully attend to all who gather to worship God, more keenly listen and perceive the movement of the Spirit, and more readily proclaim the good news of radically transformed life in Jesus.

PRACTICES OF THE BAPTIZED BODY: REAFFIRMATION

> What incorporates us into the body of Christ, that is, into his death and resurrection, is the sacrament of baptism. Just as Christ died once and once only, so we are baptized and justified once and

for all. Both baptism and justification are unrepeatable events in the strictest sense. What can be repeated is only the recollection of what happened to us once and for all; it is, in fact, not only capable of, but in need of, daily repetition.[39]

In this final section on the practices of the baptized body, we will take up Dietrich Bonhoeffer's commendation—baptismal remembrance as a necessary practice for sustaining Christian discipleship. Across different Christian traditions, practices of baptismal reaffirmation[40] provide a central way to affirm baptismal belonging in Jesus as the core of Christian identity. In addition, these practices provide avenues for meaningful participation across disciples of varied ages, gifts, and disability identities.

Practices of baptismal reaffirmation resist the notion that baptism is a single and sentimentalized ecclesial occurrence. Communal baptismal reaffirmation is not simply remembering a particular baptismal event, but also God recalling and reaffirming to us our participation in Christ's death and resurrection.[41] In this closing section, we will begin by exploring stories from research partners that illustrate communal practices of baptismal reaffirmation empowering a sense of ecclesial belonging. Next, in conversation with interdisciplinary scholars, we will explore the importance of multisensory engagement in practices of baptismal reaffirmation, exploring practical and pastoral ideas for these practices. In conclusion, we will consider how baptismal reaffirmation can strengthen a sense of Christian identity and how these practices of renewing baptismal identity often call the church to confession, repentance, and a renewed imagination regarding the discipleship of people with intellectual disabilities.

Stories of Practicing Baptismal Belonging

Practices of reaffirming baptismal identity occur among both paedobaptist and credobaptist traditions. Throughout research interviews, a variety of participants spoke about the importance of reaffirmation practices in the life of their faith communities. Ava recounted to me, "We have a little small bowl so you can remember your baptism." Dipping her fingers in the baptismal waters at Sunday services was a practice of great importance for Ava—especially because she had so loved her baptism: "I kept telling Pastor John I want to do it again!

... if I could relive it again, that would be awesome. Just to have that feeling, knowing that you're with God and you're connected with God and the church." For Ava, a bowl of baptismal water provided one means of connection to the occasion of her baptism as an adult, a reaffirmation of her belonging in the church and to Jesus' body.

Others reflected on the importance of baptismal reaffirmation during rites of baptism for others in their community. Parke noted the liturgy in her Episcopal tradition as a key site of baptismal remembrance: "You know, in The Episcopal Church, we renew our baptismal vows every time someone is baptized. So it's a significant reminder of our own baptism when we see other people be baptized." Hope also reflected on the importance and joy of baptismal remembrance at the occasion of the baptism of new members of Jesus' body:

> Some kids were on their parent's shoulders so that everybody could see. That was a wonderful tradition. It made me feel really good. And it was a way of ... having children remember their own baptisms, which they wouldn't have as a memory ... essentially part of formation, letting them know that this was an important part of our church and why.

Pastor John, whose United Methodist congregation commonly baptizes both infants and adults, spoke about his church's practices like this:

> We frame remembrance of baptism for everyone at the beginning of a baptism service. Because we always do a congregational remembrance of baptism when we baptize. We say to everyone here who has been baptized, 'we're telling your story right now' ... we don't talk about remembrance of baptism as the memory of you being baptized. But the remembrance that you've been cleaned. That you have had this truth told over you countless times.

Pastor John's reflections on baptismal reaffirmation highlight the importance of communal acknowledgement and reaffirmation of the baptismal identity of all the gathered, as well as the centrality of the work of the Triune God in baptism and in ongoing sanctification in the life of the baptized body.

Barbara, a member at St. Mary's Episcopal Church, specifically reflected with me on liturgies of baptismal remembrance, and in particular, the practice of the priest sprinkling baptismal waters on everyone gathered for the liturgy. Barbara's son, Bob, who does not communicate with words, always enjoys this time of reaffirmation: "It seems about three or four times a year that we do it. Enough that Bob is familiar with it. He knows he is going to get water sprinkled on him!" Though at first Barbara found this practice somewhat strange, she talked with me about how meaningful it had become to her: "The first time I went through that, I thought this is the craziest thing. It was just funny. And sometimes it still can be funny. But it is meaningful . . . and for Bob, he thinks it's great [baptismal remembrance]. And they always sprinkle right on him."

Beyond Words: Baptismal Reaffirmation as Multisensory Formation

Ava, Parke, Hope, and Barbara's reflections on baptismal reaffirmation highlight the embodied and multisensory points of engagement in this practice—feeling the water, seeing the baptism of others, and hearing a familiar liturgy. These multimodal avenues for participation highlight God's power to recall our baptismal identities to us as individuals and to us as gathered communities. The wide-ranging opportunities for multisensory engagement in practices of baptismal reaffirmation make them particularly suited for resonance across a wide range of embodied experiences. Pastor Daniel spoke about this reality in the following way:

> Being in an ecumenical seminary really shaped my appreciation for seeing baptism not as an act that had to be performed 'just so.' But instead, as a kind of a centerpiece of visually, sensory, bodily, connected centerpiece of the witness of the church to what God has done through Jesus Christ and what the church is doing through Jesus Christ.

Sociologist David Goode, speaking out of experience as an ethnographer among children with profound disabilities who are born deaf and blind, highlights modes of engagement apart from symbolic language use, like many of the practices of baptismal reaffirmation highlighted above. Goode notes the possibility of "rich, complex, multifaceted, and maturing social relations ... without shared symbolic language," arguing "that language is not a necessary precondition for thought and reflection (although the quality or character of that reflection may not be available to us)."[42] Goode sees language as one of "many human faculties that allow us to experience and participate" within communities.[43] This potential for powerful formation across multisensory practices underscores the importance of frequent baptismal reaffirmation for the formation of the baptized body, especially among those who experience life outside of the use of symbolic language.

Providing an example of this rich, multi-sensory engagement in practices of baptismal reaffirmation, liturgical theologian Bryan Spinks challenges churches to maximize the primary symbol of baptism:

> The font is often so small as to preclude dipping an infant in the water. Often the baptistery area is dull and without ornamentation, or tucked with pews, or so small as to be unnoticeable. It is little wonder that baptism has been undervalued if its symbolism and place of celebration is muted.[44]

Spinks laments the underengagement of opportunities for embracing baptismal themes and practices across ecumenical contexts, encouraging churches to rediscover "the multi-layered significance of baptism."[45] Thus, not only the new birth imagery at Epiphany, and the paschal imagery at Easter, but also other emphases throughout the liturgical year with icons, banners, paintings, or projected images on baptistery walls.[46] One powerful yet simple practice is to ensure not only that the font is always in a prominent location, but also always has water in it. This could take shape by having the font at the entrance of the sanctuary for people to touch, see, and feel the waters as they enter into worship and as they leave worship, to encounter the world as witnesses to new life in Jesus.

The Lima Document also urges churches to rediscover the "vivid signs" of the gift of the Spirit in baptism as a means to "enrich the liturgy."[47] These "vivid signs" help congregations take up a frequent practice of baptismal reaffirmation.[48] Drawing on the fullness of the church's liturgical and sacramental life, the Lima Document affirms "the most obvious form of . . . reaffirmation is the celebration of the eucharist. The renewal of baptismal vows may also take place during such occasions as the annual celebration of the paschal mystery or during the baptism of others."[49] Church communities might consider positioning the font on the path to the communion table so that as the people come forward to participate in Holy Communion, they encounter an embodied reminder of the deep connections between the church's practices of baptism and communion.

Louis Weil, an Episcopal priest and liturgical theologian, commends an abundance of engagement with the physical materials of baptismal practices to support communal reaffirmation of baptismal identity. Weil offers a story of this abundance:

> I had a small pitcher filled with consecrated chrism, and I poured the oil upon the crown of the child's head and then took both hands and spread the oil over his head. As I poured the oil, some people who were there gasped: they were accustomed to a bit of oil in a pyx on a piece of cotton, of which perhaps a drop would be signed upon the head—hence, the gasp. But as I spread the oil, the fragrance of the balsam permeated the chapel. Not a word of explanation was needed: the entire community smelled the fragrance of Christ.[50]

The opportunities to abundantly awaken the senses of the baptized body, especially when regularly practiced within a community, affirm the primacy of belonging in Jesus' body among all the baptized, regardless of disability.[51]

Shaping Identity and Imagination

The potential for practices of baptismal remembrance to shape identity was most profoundly revealed to me in my conversations with James. James, who was baptized at St. Matthew's Baptist Church, has an audio-visual recording of his baptism, which he has watched frequently (at least one time a week) for nearly fifteen years. As a result, James saw his baptism as central to who he was. He reflected to me, after we had watched the video of his baptism together: "It makes me a very important person. When I want to learn about Jesus . . . I watch my movie again." James' participation in rewatching his baptism, an obvious practice of baptismal remembrance and reaffirmation, shaped his vision of identity as primarily rooted in baptism.

Creating a video or audio recording of a baptismal service may not prove appropriate or possible within all ecclesial contexts. More liturgical traditions may find resonances throughout the liturgical year and feast celebrations as important occasions to reaffirm baptismal identity. Liturgical theologian Maxwell Johnson expands upon this possibility, writing, "another way to expand our appreciation for the richness of baptismal imagery is to pay attention to the entire liturgical year itself as the hermeneutical key for ongoing liturgical catechesis, ongoing mystagogy in the meaning and significance of our initiation."[52] Later, Johnson continues, "the recovery of a baptismal spirituality calls us to the liturgical year itself as the ongoing celebration and continued formation in our baptismal identity."[53]

For churches who do not live primarily within the rhythms of the liturgical year, occasions such as homecoming celebrations, founders' days, or celebrations of the baptisms of others constitute occasions for reaffirming baptismal identity. Ideally, practices such as preaching, service, and formation would resonate with baptismal reaffirmation, reinforcing the deep theological wells of meaning surrounding baptismal identity and participation in the community of the baptized body.[54] Pastor John described the importance of encouraging active community participation in practices of baptismal remembrance in order to emphasize the core identity proclamation occurring in these practices:

> We also say, you know, pastors don't baptize. The church baptizes. We are baptizing. We are the body of Christ. We are the incarnate presence of Jesus in this moment, that is immersing these folks in the truth of their identity. And so we frame it as the church—God's work through the church . . . it's the iterative declaration of who God is and therefore who we are.

Practices of reaffirming baptism not only testify to a shared identity as it relates to the work and declaration of God, but also provide a means for calling the community to responsibility and repentance, particularly in relation to how churches respond to people with intellectual disabilities.⁵⁵ In this way, practices of baptismal reaffirmation provide what pastor and liturgical theologian Gordon Lathrop envisions as "a place of alternative imagination about the structures of the world," practices that "speak the meaning of Jesus Christ that all things may live."⁵⁶ Here, Lathrop gestures to how practices of baptismal reaffirmation reshape our imaginations about identity away from contemporary Western ideals of individualized autonomy and cognitive assent, helping to bring our attention back to the transformative resurrection life of Jesus that rests at the heart of the baptized body's identity.

During our research conversation, Andrew described to me the sense of communal responsibility welling up within him as he participated in his church's practices of baptismal reaffirmation:

> Most of the baptisms that I've seen at St. Barnabas are children. What I experienced is the choice of the body to embrace and to take responsibility for the child . . . it's quite wonderful. I mean . . . certainly I believe that the choice [for the baptismal candidate] can be important, but the choice can't be made unless the church embraces and supports and commits . . . so that means a lot to see that it happens. And to be reminded that that support and commitment of other people is critical, I would say for my own baptism.

Andrew's reflections on the importance of the communal responsibility evoked in practices of baptismal reaffirmation serve as a call to repentance within communities seeking to support the baptismal identities and vocations of people with intellectual disabilities. As individuals remember their own baptisms, might they survey their community and wonder who is missing from this affirmation? Where have promises of baptismal support been broken? Where have baptismal identities been exchanged for the facade of a homogenous community where discomforts associated with human differences have seemingly been erased? Where has the church failed to remember the baptism of people with intellectual disabilities, or even failed to baptize them at all? And in remembering the baptismal identity of all the gathered, might these practices of remembrance constitute an opportunity to seek out those who have yet to be gathered into the baptized body?

CONCLUSION

Frequent and multisensory practices of baptismal reaffirmation, baptismal testimony, and baptismal preparation remind church communities that belonging to Jesus constitutes their core identity. Through practices of remembrance, testimony, and preparation, acts where God recalls to Christians their communal participation in Christ's death and resurrection in the waters of baptism, Christians find themselves reaffirmed in their identities as God's new creation. These practices can serve as a primary source of reorientation and confession within the baptized body, calling for humility before the Triune God, confessing failures to affirm and support the baptismal identity of people with intellectual disabilities, and asking the Holy Spirit for guidance and newness of life in embracing the discipleship of all the baptized.

Conclusion

It was a sunny day, and as we sipped lemonade in the shade, I asked Ava what baptism shows us about being human. She squinted a bit and then began to slowly nod, sharing the following: "I think as a human being we can be steady, but still and gentle, knowing who you are, where you belong with Christ."

Ava's expression of baptismal identity—a gentle assurance of belonging with Jesus—seems a fitting summary of the work of this book. Engaging with Ava and other Christians with intellectual disabilities has shaped our exploration of baptism, including theological insights related to identity, Scripture, and belonging. Receiving the baptismal witness of disabled Christians challenges us to reexamine the adequacy of existing theological methodologies in the field of disability theology, in order to faithfully describe the rich integration of theology and practice manifest in my research partners' lives of discipleship. The stories of my research participants around the centrality of Jesus, community, and participation in baptism encourage us to newly explore Scripture, liturgy, and baptismal practices as gifts to ecclesial communities, that through the power of the Holy Spirit, lead to radical transformation of life. I hope that as a reader, you have begun to encounter these new explorations throughout the pages of this book.

Baptism is the church's ancient practice of making Christians, of initiation into the church, marking members of the body of Jesus. In baptism, the power of the Holy Spirit joins each of the baptized to Jesus, as they share in his death and resurrection. Those baptized are marked as Christ's own forever:[1] people gifted by the Holy Spirit with a communal vocation of discipleship in newness of life. Baptismal practices are ritual reminders of what Paul names as new creation: an identity rooted in Jesus, noncontingent on human skill and capacity, and primary over all particularities of gender, race, age, class, or disability.

All too often, baptism has become the site of marginalization or even rejection of people with intellectual disabilities within Christian communities, either by baptismal refusal or by refusing true belonging and support in communities of supposed postbaptismal nurture. As I have argued throughout this book, in conversation with disabled Christians, their clergy, and loved ones, baptismal practices offer significant ways for the church to welcome the belonging, participation, and gifts of all the baptized, including people with even the most profound expressions of disability. For church communities marked primarily by homogenous belonging, reconsidering baptismal theologies and practices offers avenues for ecclesial transformation.

As contemporary churches increasingly seek wisdom for ways to foster Jesus-centered belonging for people with intellectual disabilities, and new ways to embrace the gifts and discipleship of all in the baptized body, the theological approach of partnership embodied throughout this book provides theological, scriptural, and practical reflections for congregations seeking to enact disability justice work. Instead of addressing ecclesial questions of belonging through popular frameworks in existing disability theology literature, theologizing out of baptismal stories recounted by those in the disability community opens for us more integrative possibilities for the transformation of ecclesial imagination around identity and discipleship. The research partners for this project identified the participatory, Jesus-centered, and communal features of baptism as especially salient for drawing all in the baptized body together in communities of radical belonging. In particular, the baptismal practices of preparation, testimony, and reaffirmation are sites in which communities may be drawn more closely to one another and to the Triune God. These baptismal practices suppose and support a radical transformation of communal life, offering sites for challenge, repentance, and renewal among Christian communities.

This book encapsulates my imperfect yet courageous response to address the abstraction of theological propositions about disability from the lived practices of disabled Christians and the baptismal communities that receive and amplify their witnesses. Committing to a theological methodology of partnership, through inclusive qualitative research, I have begun the work of doing disability theology *together*—a work I hope continues in new and even more constructive ways in future scholarship. Theological ethnography equips the saints called to scholarly work for the life of the church with fertile ground for "witnessing witnesses to aid and multiply witnesses."[2] It is this call to witnessing witnesses, out of the site of wounds related to Christian belonging, that this work began, and I hope will continue to grow.

Writing disability theology for the church from a theological approach of partnership comprises the distinctive contribution of this book. The work of disabled theological witness cannot end until those like Hallie, who seek public initiation into Jesus' body and a community that will sustain their baptismal vocation, encounter Christian communities actively attentive to the Holy Spirit's work of new creation. By offering a disabled perspective on baptism—a core ecclesial practice that constitutes the body of Jesus—this volume also insists on disability as a critical experience that theologians, churches, and Christians can no longer push into abstract propositions or segregated disability ministries. As made clear throughout the pages of this book, the responsibility inherent in being brought together with all baptized Christians within the body of Jesus presses ecclesial communities to remain open to the Holy Spirit's work of renewal—through confession and repentance of sin, and through Spirit-empowered care and support of the baptismal identities of all of God's children. All the disability theology in the world cannot sufficiently change imaginations apart from the work of the Triune God in disrupting and reforming Christian imagination about unity with Jesus and all those drowned and resurrected to new life in Jesus' body. As I have argued, disabled Christians bring the press of this responsibility to our shared consciousness, inviting nondisabled and disabled Christians alike into a new kind of imagination and faithful practice.

The Holy Spirit empowers each member of Jesus' body to witness to God's ongoing work in the world. This book, the first of its kind, amplifies disabled witnesses through a theological methodology of togetherness. Through a methodology of inclusive and theological qualitative research, I not only described and identified key themes and categories of critical analysis arising from research partners with intellectual disabilities, but also embraced these themes and analytic categories as distinctive conversation partners alongside more traditional sources of theological and biblical reflection. In their disability-informed perspectives on God's work in Christian communities, my research participants highlight for us transformative new readings of New Testament baptismal stories, liturgical participation, and ongoing practices of baptismal life. In this way, *Becoming the Baptized Body* witnesses to the promise of faithfully responding to wounds and disability experiences within Christian communities as an act of uncovering new gifts and challenges in the baptismal vocation of following Jesus. This book provides a model for shaping future theological work supportive of the church's life of baptismal discipleship.

The work of this book at the intersection of disability and baptism opens new avenues for future inquiry across a variety of registers, including further theological engagement of inclusive qualitative research in partnership with disabled Christians. Additional sites for further research include ongoing critical disability engagement with Pauline literature, especially Paul's baptismal theology and his framework for new creation, renewed engagement with historical theological texts and archival resources documenting the experiences of Christians with intellectual disabilities, and attention to how a baptismal hermeneutic might continue to inform and expand existing arguments within the field of disability theology. The baptismal doings of Christians with intellectual disabilities also raise new questions for liturgical design and theology, as well as how distinct baptismal practices such as preparation, testimony, and reaffirmation might embody characteristics of nurture and access, to enlarge Christian witness and engagement in baptismal life.

Baptism is a site of critical transformation in the Holy Spirit within contemporary ecclesial communities. Baptismal theologies and practices embraced by disabled Christians invite the church into a Jesus-centered, communal, and participatory account of Christian identity. May the whole baptized body, empowered by the Holy Spirit, find new depths of belonging, discipleship, and new creation life, led by the witness of Christians with intellectual disabilities.

Notes

FOREWORD

1 The theoretical groundwork for Theological Ethnography can be found in John Swinton and Harriet Mowat, *Practical Theology and Qualitative Research*, 2nd ed. (London: SCM, 2016); Pete Ward, ed., *Perspectives on Ecclesiology and Ethnography* (Grand Rapids: Eerdmans, 2012); Peter Ward, "Ecclesiology and Ethnography with Humility: Going through Barth," *Studia Theologica* 72, no. 1 (2018); Paul D. Murray, "Searching the Living Truth of the Church in Practice: On the Transformative Task of Systematic Theology," *Modern Theology* 30, no. 2 (2014); Christian Scharen and Aana Marie Vigen, eds., *Ethnography as Christian Theology and Ethics* (New York: Continuum, 2011).

INTRODUCTION

1 All names in this book, including individuals and faith communities, have been changed to protect identity and preserve anonymity. Repeated names across this book represent the same person, community, or entity.
2 Mary McClintock Fulkerson, *Places of Redemption: Theology for a Worldly Church* (New York: Oxford University Press, 2007), 13–14.
3 Craig Dykstra, "Pastoral and Ecclesial Imagination," in *For Life Abundant: Practical Theology, Theological Education, and Christian Ministry*, ed. Dorothy C. Bass and Craig Dykstra (Grand Rapids: Eerdmans, 2008), 60.
4 Swinton and Mowat, *Practical Theology and Qualitative Research*, 4.
5 Recent studies include Erik W. Carter et al., "Congregational Participation of a National Sample of Adults with Intellectual and Developmental Disabilities." *Intellectual and Developmental Disabilities* 53, no. 6 (2015); Valerie Miller and Camille Skubik-Peplaski, "A Systemic Review of Supports for Participation in Faith Settings for People with Disabilities," *Inclusion* 8, no. 2 (2020); Jared H. Stewart-Ginsburg et al., "Sanctuaries, 'Special Needs,' and Service: Religious

Leader Perceptions on Including Children with Disability," *Journal of Disability & Religion* 24, no. 4 (2020); Andrew L. Whitehead, "Religion and Disability: Variation in Religious Service Attendance Rates for Children with Chronic Health Conditions," *Journal for the Scientific Study of Religion* 57, no. 2 (2018).

6 Willie James Jennings, *Acts: A Theological Commentary on the Bible*, Belief: A Theological Commentary on the Bible, unabridged ed. (Louisville, Ky.: Westminster John Knox, 2017), 139.

7 World Council of Churches, *Baptism, Eucharist and Ministry*, 25th anniv. ed. (Geneva, Switzerland: World Council of Churches, 1982), viii.

8 Craig R. Dykstra and Dorothy C. Bass, "A Theological Understanding of Christian Practices," in *Practicing Theology: Beliefs and Practices in Christian Life*, ed. Miroslav Volf and Dorothy C. Bass (Grand Rapids: Eerdmans, 2002), 31.

9 Ranna Parekh, "What Is Intellectual Disability?" American Psychiatric Association, last modified July 2017, accessed October 15, 2018, https://www.psychiatry.org/patients-families/intellectual-disability/what-is-intellectual-disability. Marc J. Tassé, "Defining Intellectual Disability: Finally We All Agree ... Almost," *Spotlight on Disability Newsletter*, 2016, http://www.apa.org/pi/disability/resources/publications/newsletter/2016/09/intellectual-disability.aspx.

10 The characterization of "profound" in relationship to intellectual disability refers to people with the most notable expressions of intellectual disability. I appreciate John Swinton's clear rendering of profound intellectual disability as "a group of human beings who are deemed to have limited communicational skills, restricted or sometimes no self-care skills, and significant intellectual or cognitive difficulties, or both. Such people reside in the world without language and concepts that many people use and that are often assumed, by some, to be necessary to understand the fundamentals of the Christian faith. Those living out their lives in such ways are people to whom the modern category of free, autonomous individual—someone whose life is marked by individual choice—could never be applied ..." (*Becoming Friends of Time: Disability, Timefullness, and Gentle Discipleship* [Waco, Tex.: Baylor University Press, 2016], 89).

11 Jill Harshaw, *God beyond Words: Christian Theology and the Spiritual Experiences of People with Profound Intellectual Disabilities* (London: Jessica Kingsley, 2016), 16–17.

12 Notable organizations of people with intellectual disabilities embracing this focus on empowerment (and basic rights) include People First (https://www.factmo.org/people-first/#PeopleFirst) and Self Advocates Becoming Empowered (https://www.sabeusa.org/).

13 For an excellent account of the history of the category of "intellectual disability," as well as careful attention to the power and privilege of naming certain people as those with intellectual disabilities, I commend Licia Carlson's *The Faces of Intellectual Disability: Philosophical Reflections* (Bloomington: Indiana University Press, 2009).

14 For further reading, see Lydia Brown, "The Significance of Semantics: Person-First Language: Why It Matters," https://www.autistichoya.com/2011/08/significance-of-semantics-person-first.html; William Evans, "'I Am Not a Dyslexic Person I'm a Person with Dyslexia': Identity Constructions of Dyslexia

among Students in Nurse Education," *Journal of Advanced Nursing* 70, no. 2 (2014): 360–72; Morton Ann Gernsbacher, "The Use of Person-First Language in Scholarly Writing May Accentuate Stigma," *Journal of Child Psychology and Psychiatry* 58 no. 7 (2017); 859–61; Anders Gustavsson, Catarina Nyberg, and Charles Westin, "Plurality and Continuity—Understanding Self-identity of Persons with Intellectual Disability," *Alter* 10, no. 4 (2016): 310–26; Beth Haller et al., "Media Labeling *versus* the US Disability Community Identity: A Study of Shifting Cultural Language," *Disability & Society* 21, no. 1 (2006): 61–75; Edlyn Vallejo Peña, Lissa D. Stapleton, and Lenore Malone Schaffer, "Critical Perspectives on Disability Identity," *New Directions for Student Services* 154 (2016): 85–96; Rebecca F. Spurrier, *The Disabled Church: Human Difference and the Art of Communal Worship* (New York: Fordham University Press, 2019), 134. See also the *Disability Language Style Guide*, National Center on Disability and Journalism: https://ncdj.org/style-guide/.

15 Philosopher Kevin Timpe suggests that a "unified concept of disability" cannot exist because no framework can sufficiently demarcate nondisabled people from those who are disabled ("Denying a Unified Concept of Disability," forthcoming in *Journal of Medicine and Philosophy*). Timpe draws upon the work of Elizabeth Barnes (*The Minority Body: A Theory of Disability*, Studies in Feminist Philosophy [New York: Oxford University Press, 2016]) but expands Barnes' focus on physical disability to consider a "full range" of disability identities, including intellectual disability.

16 Alison Kafer, *Feminist, Queer, Crip* (Bloomington: Indiana University Press, 2013), 6.

17 Kafer, *Feminist, Queer, Crip*, 6. However, Kafer's model does not entirely displace forms of medical or rehabilitative intervention in response to disability. For Kafer, interventions within the medical realm may be desired among some disabled people, especially to address realities such as chronic pain. Other scholars in disability studies seek to reimagine something like Kafer's framework for disability within explicitly medical settings. See Sarah Jean Barton, "A Critical Approach to Integrating Christian Disability Theology in Clinical Rehabilitation," *Journal of Disability & Religion* 21, no. 1 (2017); Susan Magasi, "Infusing Disability Studies into the Rehabilitation Sciences," *Topics in Stroke Rehabilitation* 15, no. 3 (2008); Susan Magasi, "Disability Studies in Practice: A Work in Progress," *Topics in Stroke Rehabilitation* 15, no. 6 (2008).

18 Rosemarie Garland Thomson, *Extraordinary Bodies: Figuring Physical Disability in American Culture and Literature* (New York: Columbia University Press, 1997), 8.

19 Lennard J. Davis, *Enforcing Normalcy: Disability, Deafness, and the Body* (New York: Verso, 1995), 24–27. Theologian Thomas E. Reynolds notes how normalcy also establishes particular norms as constitutive of a community's identity and sense of self. See *Vulnerable Communion: A Theology of Disability and Hospitality* (Grand Rapids: Brazos, 2008), 48.

20 Kafer, *Feminist, Queer, Crip*, 9.

21 Kafer, *Feminist, Queer, Crip*, 11.

22. Christian Scharen and Aana Marie Vigen, "Theological Justification for Turning to Ethnography," in *Ethnography as Christian Theology and Ethics*, ed. Christian Scharen and Aana Marie Vigen (New York: Continuum, 2011), 66.
23. Rowan Williams, *On Christian Theology*, Challenges in Contemporary Theology (Oxford: Blackwell, 2000), xii.
24. Mary McClintock Fulkerson, "Roundtable on *Ethnography as Christian Theology and Ethics*: Ethnography: A Gift to Theology and Ethics," *Practical Matters* 6 (Spring 2013): 2.
25. Swinton and Mowat, *Practical Theology and Qualitative Research*, 6.
26. For those readers eager for further methodological details, chapter 2 further contextualizes the research method and explores key research findings that inform each of the subsequent chapters. In brief, this project utilized an exploratory case study and narrative inquiry design involving in-depth, semi-structured interviews as well as participant observation within faith communities. A total of 33 adults from Christian faith communities in the state of North Carolina participated, with ages ranging from 24 to 77. Thirteen participants identified as adults with intellectual disabilities, 8 as parents or siblings of a person with intellectual disabilities, 5 as lay leaders, and 7 as clergy. Among these 33 participants, the Christian traditions represented included Churches of Christ, The Episcopal Church, the Southern Baptist Convention, Cooperative Baptist Fellowship, and The United Methodist Church. John W. Creswell and Cheryl N. Poth, *Qualitative Inquiry and Research Design: Choosing among Five Approaches*, 4th ed. (Los Angeles: SAGE, 2018), 121; Sharan B. Merriam and Elizabeth J. Tisdell, *Qualitative Research: A Guide to Design and Implementation*, 4th ed. (San Francisco: Jossey-Bass, 2016), 37–38; D. Jean Clandinin, *Engaging in Narrative Inquiry*, Developing Qualitative Inquiry (New York: Routledge, 2016), 18.
27. Swinton and Mowat, *Practical Theology and Qualitative Research*, 6.
28. Jennings, *Acts*, 139.
29. Deborah Beth Creamer, *Disability and Christian Theology: Embodied Limits and Constructive Possibilities*, Academy Series (New York: Oxford University Press, 2009), 31.
30. Brian Brock, *Wondrously Wounded: Theology, Disability, and the Body of Christ* (Waco, Tex.: Baylor University Press, 2019), xv.
31. The Episcopal Church, *The Book of Common Prayer and Administration of the Sacraments and Other Rites and Ceremonies of the Church: Together with the Psalter or Psalms of David According to the Use of the Episcopal Church* (New York: Seabury, 1979), 304–5.
32. Brock, *Wondrously Wounded*, xii.
33. John Swinton, "Disability Theology," in *The Cambridge Dictionary of Christian Theology*, ed. Ian A. McFarland, David A. S. Fergusson, Karen Kilby, and Iain R. Torrance (Cambridge: Cambridge University Press, 2010).
34. James I. Charlton, *Nothing about Us without Us: Disability Oppression and Empowerment* (Berkeley: University of California Press, 2000).
35. Charles Taylor, "The Politics of Recognition," in *Multiculturalism: Examining the Politics of Recognition*, ed. Amy Gutmann (Princeton, N.J.: Princeton University Press, 1994), 25. Though Taylor's account of identity formation vis a vis processes

of recognition depends on dialogical relationship (helpfully dismantling individualistic notions of identity), his reliance on the capacity for self-definition and self-reflection excludes many people with intellectual disabilities. Nevertheless, Taylor's thesis here offers a helpful diagnostic for issues related to representation, identity, and receiving witness. I will argue throughout this book that practices and theologies of baptism disrupt processes of misrecognition that underscore many practices of ecclesial exclusion that impact individuals with disabilities.

36 Harshaw, *God beyond Words*, 20.
37 Harshaw, *God beyond Words*, 70–77.
38 Harshaw, *God beyond Words*, 92.
39 Harshaw, *God beyond Words*, 95. Here, Harshaw is interacting with John Calvin's doctrine of Accommodation (or condescension).
40 In other work, Harshaw does commend a "prophetic role" among people with profound disabilities in Christian faith communities (see Jill Ruth Harshaw, "Prophetic Voices, Silent Words: The Prophetic Role of Persons with Profound Intellectual Disabilities in Contemporary Christianity," *Practical Theology* 3, no. 3 [2010]: 311–29). Here, I am critiquing her work by suggesting that through collaborative and relational means, ecclesial communities might (and should!) faithfully perceive, name, and learn from discrete acts of witness among people with profound intellectual disabilities.
41 Brock, *Wondrously Wounded*, 240.
42 Brock, *Wondrously Wounded*, xiv.
43 Benjamin T. Conner, "For the Fitness of Their Witness: Missional Christian Practices," in *Converting Witness: The Future of Christian Mission in the New Millennium*, ed. John G. Flett and David W. Congdon, 123–38 (New York: Fortress Academic, 2019), 129.
44 Conner, "For the Fitness of Their Witness," 126.
45 "The baptized body" to which I refer in this book's title, and throughout the book's content, describes the group of people inextricably caught up in one another by nature of their baptism into Jesus' death and resurrection life. Though Peter J. Leithart wrote a book sharing this same name (*The Baptized Body* [Moscow, Idaho: Canon, 2007]), his focus on debates of baptismal efficacy within Reformed Christian circles does not come to bear on my usage of this phrase throughout the arguments in this volume.
46 Examples of brief or anecdotal discussions in book-length projects include: Benjamin T. Conner, *Amplifying Our Witness: Giving Voice to Adolescents with Developmental Disabilities* (Grand Rapids: Eerdmans, 2012), 88–90; John M. Huels, "Canonical Rights to the Sacraments," in *Developmental Disabilities and Sacramental Access: New Paradigms for Sacramental Encounters*, ed. Edward Foley (Collegeville, Minn.: Liturgical, 1994), 96; Amy Jacober, *Redefining Perfect: The Interplay between Theology and Disability* (Eugene, Oreg.: Cascade Books, 2017), 7; Myroslaw Tataryn and Maria Truchan-Tataryn, *Discovering Trinity in Disability: A Theology for Embracing Difference* (Maryknoll, N.Y.: Orbis Books, 2013), 86. Relevant articles engaging the intersection of baptism and intellectual disabilities include Melissa Florer-Bixler, "Believers Baptism as Supported Decision," *Conrad Grebel Review* 38, no. 2 (2020): 135–46; Richard Cross, "Baptism, Faith

and Severe Cognitive Impairment in Some Medieval Theologies," *International Journal of Systematic Theology* 14, no. 4 (2012): 420–38; and Jason Reimer Greig, "Re-imagining Narratives: Anabaptist Baptismal Theology and Profound Cognitive Impairment," *Conrad Grebel Review* 38, no. 2 (2020): 120–34.

47 I share this concern regarding theological abstraction in disability theology with Jill Harshaw, who emphasizes the urgent need to address it in her book's conclusion (*God beyond Words*, 190). As I will address more specifically in chapter 1, several prominent texts in the field of disability theology that treat intellectual disability demonstrate limited connections and synthesis with central Christian practices, such as Molly Claire Haslam's *A Constructive Theology of Intellectual Disability: Human Being as Mutuality and Response* (New York: Fordham University Press, 2012) and Hans Reinders' *Receiving the Gift of Friendship: Profound Disability, Theological Anthropology, and Ethics* (Grand Rapids: Eerdmans, 2008).

48 Robert Bogdan and Steven J. Taylor, "Relationships with Severely Disabled People: The Social Construction of Humanness," *Social Problems* 36, no. 2 (1989): 139.

49 Peter Singer, *Practical Ethics*, 3rd ed. (Cambridge: Cambridge University Press, 2011), 160.

50 Stephen Jay Gould, *The Mismeasure of Man* (New York: Norton, 1996), 20.

51 Gould, *Mismeasure of Man*, 21.

52 Gould, *Mismeasure of Man*, 52.

53 Vocabulary from the early 1900s.

54 Dorothy E. Roberts, *Killing the Black Body: Race, Reproduction, and the Meaning of Liberty* (New York: Vintage Books, 1999), 63.

55 Douglas C. Baynton, "'These Pushful Days': Time and Disability in the Age of Eugenics," *Health and History* 13, no. 2 (2011): 59.

56 Baynton, "These Pushful Days," 45.

57 Baynton, "These Pushful Days," 48.

58 Among others with marked dependencies, such as older adults and those with various physical or sensory disabilities.

CHAPTER 1: ENTERING THE CONVERSATION

1 Harshaw, *God beyond Words*, 190.

2 Bethany McKinney Fox, *Disability and the Way of Jesus: Holistic Healing in the Gospels and the Church* (Downers Grove: IVP Academic, 2019), 186.

3 Dykstra and Bass, "Theological Understanding of Christian Practices," 18.

4 Rowan Williams, *Being Christian: Baptism, Bible, Eucharist, Prayer* (Grand Rapids: Eerdmans, 2014), vii.

5 Gordon S. Mikoski, *Baptism and Christian Identity: Teaching in the Triune Name* (Grand Rapids: Eerdmans, 2009), 4–5; Williams, *Being Christian*, vii.

6 Mikoski, *Baptism and Christian Identity*, 8, 67.

7 Alexander Schmemann, *Of Water and the Spirit: A Liturgical Study of Baptism* (Crestwood, N.Y.: St. Vladimir's Seminary Press, 1974), 12.

8 Lauren F. Winner, *The Dangers of Christian Practice: On Wayward Gifts, Characteristic Damage, and Sin* (New Haven, Conn.: Yale University Press, 2018), 14.

9 Kelly Brown Douglas, *The Black Christ*, Bishop Henry McNeal Turner Studies in North American Black Religion 9 (Maryknoll, N.Y.: Orbis, 1993), 17.
10 Douglas, *Black Christ*, 17.
11 M. Shawn Copeland, *Enfleshing Freedom: Body, Race, and Being* (Minneapolis: Fortress, 2010), 28.
12 Copeland, *Enfleshing Freedom*, 28.
13 Winner, *Dangers of Christian Practice*, 79; Joan R. Gundersen, *The Anglican Ministry in Virginia, 1723–1766: A Study of Social Class* (Hamden, Conn.: Garland, 1989), 111.
14 Willie James Jennings, "Being Baptized: Race," in *The Blackwell Companion to Christian Ethics*, ed. Stanley Hauerwas and Samuel Wells, 2nd ed. (Malden, Mass.: Wiley-Blackwell, 2011), 286.
15 Jennings, "Being Baptized," 286.
16 Winner, *Dangers of Christian Practice*, 112.
17 Winner, *Dangers of Christian Practice*, 16.
18 While these debates have become more frequent in the post-Enlightenment context, questions of the appropriateness of baptism and sacramental participation among people who lack some normative sense of "reason" began long before the rise of modernity. For example, Thomas Aquinas engages arguments from his contemporaries about the appropriateness of baptizing people with some notable absence of reason (see IIIa 68.12 in the *Summa Theologiae*).
19 Harshaw, *God beyond Words*, 122.
20 Tataryn and Truchan-Tataryn, *Discovering Trinity in Disability*, 87.
21 Medi Ann Volpe, *Rethinking Christian Identity: Doctrine and Discipleship* (Malden, Mass.: Wiley-Blackwell, 2013), 2. Volpe's daughter, Anna, has Down Syndrome.
22 Volpe, *Rethinking Christian Identity*, 225.
23 Volpe, *Rethinking Christian Identity*, 229.
24 Theo A. Boer, "Meaning of Life and Meaning of Care: A Christian Perspective," in *Meaningful Care: A Multidisciplinary Approach to the Meaning of Care for People with Mental Retardation*, ed. Joop Boer, Theo A. Stolk, and Ruth Seldenrijk (Boston, Mass.: Kluwer Academic, 2000), 62.
25 Myk Habets, "'Suffer the Little Children to Come to Me, for Theirs Is the Kingdom of Heaven.' Infant Salvation and the Destiny of the Severely Mentally Disabled," in *Evangelical Calvinism: Essays Resourcing the Continuing Reformation of the Church*, ed. Myk Habets and Bobby Grow (Eugene, Oreg.: Pickwick Publications, 2012), 320.
26 Amos Yong, *Theology and Down Syndrome: Reimagining Disability in Late Modernity* (Waco, Tex.: Baylor University Press, 2007), 172.
27 Yong, *Theology and Down Syndrome*, 173.
28 Colossians 1:15.
29 Yong, *Theology and Down Syndrome*, 180–81.
30 Reynolds, *Vulnerable Communion*, 177.
31 Reynolds, *Vulnerable Communion*, 179.
32 Reinders, *Receiving the Gift of Friendship*, 237.

33 See also Shane Clifton's *Crippled Grace: Disability, Virtue Ethics, and the Good Life*, Studies in Religion, Theology, and Disability (Waco, Tex.: Baylor University Press, 2018) and John Swinton's *Becoming Friends of Time*.
34 Reinders, *Receiving the Gift*, 131–32.
35 Reinders, *Receiving the Gift*, 162.
36 Reinders, *Receiving the Gift*, 224.
37 Reinders, *Receiving the Gift*, 283.
38 Reinders, *Receiving the Gift*, 284.
39 L'Arche International is an organization associated with over 150 communities across 38 countries. L'Arche communities, including residential homes where people with and without intellectual disabilities live life together, seek to celebrate people with intellectual disabilities by building communities of support with and around them. For more information, see L'Arche International's website: https://www.larche.org/en/welcome.
40 Jason Reimer Greig, *Reconsidering Intellectual Disability: L'Arche, Medical Ethics, and Christian Friendship*, Moral Traditions Series (Baltimore, Md.: Georgetown University Press, 2015), 5.
41 Greig, *Reconsidering Intellectual Disability*, 7.
42 Greig, *Reconsidering Intellectual Disability*, 8.
43 Greig, *Reconsidering Intellectual Disability*, 10.
44 A similar approach derived from the inclusion paradigm of special education can be found in the work of Barbara Newman, with her attention to cultivating environments where people with disabilities, especially intellectual disabilities, might grow more faithfully as disciples of Jesus. See Barbara J. Newman, *Accessible Gospel, Inclusive Worship* (Wyoming, Mich.: CLC Network, 2015), 3.
45 Erik W. Carter, *Including People with Disabilities in Faith Communities: A Guide for Service Providers, Families, and Congregations* (Baltimore, Md.: Brookes, 2007), 151.
46 Carter, *Including People with Disabilities*, 62–63.
47 Harshaw, *God beyond Words*, 52.
48 Harshaw, *God beyond Words*, 117. Harshaw illustrates this central claim by turning to historical accounts of the sacraments, the scriptural witness to the accommodative work of the Holy Spirit (particularly in Acts 10–11), as well as the tradition of Christian mysticism as supports for her arguments about the inclusive nature of the Triune God.
49 Swinton, *Becoming Friends of Time*, 104–8. Swinton's account of the body in connection to intellectual disability does not discount the intellectual aspects of discipleship embraced by many followers of Jesus, but rather seeks to illustrate a fuller picture of Christ's body and practices of discipleship. "The body of Christ is a place of embodied learning wherein the presence of profoundly intellectually impaired people reminds the body of the necessity and responsibility of revealing the love of God through the practices of love, practices that are not exhausted by the world that the intellect reveals" (108). Swinton, "Who Is the God We Worship?" 306.
50 Greig, *Reconsidering Intellectual Disability*, 179. A. M. Donald Allchin also reflects on the sacramental nature of community life in L'Arche. For Allchin,

the rituals of life in L'Arche communities affirm "the bodiliness of the human experience of God" (A. M. Donald Allchin, "The Sacraments in L'Arche," in *Encounter with Mystery: Reflections on L'Arche and Living with Disability*, ed. Frances Young [London: Darton, Longman, and Todd, 1997], 104).

51 Greig argues, "Foot washing reminds Christians of their true identity not as the autonomous monad of the choosing self, but rather the creaturely person of the ecclesial self" (184). For Greig, this sacramental centering of the body names the other as friend, and resists narratives focused on capacity and independence.

52 Yong, *The Bible, Disability, and the Church*, 111. Yong further offers a Pentecost-inspired vision where those with and without intellectual disabilities are "possible conduits for the Spirit's revelatory work," noting that since God engages us "through the multiplicity of our sensory capacities . . . what if the miracle of Pentecost isn't limited to speaking, hearing, and seeing, but also includes touching, feeling, and perceiving?" (70–73).

53 Yong, *The Bible, Disability, and the Church*, 139.

54 Elizabeth L. Antus, "Our Fragile Flesh: Sacramental Hospitality toward Persons with Intellectual Disabilities and Its Implications for Theology" in *Visions of Hope: Emerging Theologians and the Future of the Church*, ed. Kevin J. Ahern (Maryknoll, N.Y.: Orbis Books, 2012), 33.

55 Antus, "Our Fragile Flesh," 33.

56 Frances M. Young, *Arthur's Call: A Journey of Faith in the Face of Severe Learning Disability*, Face to Face (London: SPCK, 2014), 151, 157.

57 Stanley Hauerwas, "The Gesture of a Truthful Story," in *Critical Reflections on Stanley Hauerwas' Theology of Disability: Disabling Society, Enabling Theology*, ed. John Swinton (Binghamton, N.Y.: Haworth Pastoral, 2004), 77.

58 Hauerwas, "Gesture of a Truthful Story," 77.

59 For example, see Irma Fast Dueck, "It's Only Water: The Ritual of Baptism and the Formation of Christian Identity," *Vision: A Journal for Church & Theology* 14, no. 1 (2011): 22; Donald E. Healy Jr., "Rediscovering the Mysteria: Sacramental Stories from Persons with Disabilities, Their Families, and Their Faith Communities," *Journal of Religion, Disability & Health* 13 (2009); Huels, "Canonical Rights," 96; Jacober, *Redefining Perfect*, 7; Tataryn and Truchan-Tataryn, *Discovering Trinity in Disability*, 86.

60 Conner, *Amplifying Our Witness*, 9.

61 Don E. Saliers, "Toward a Spirituality of Inclusiveness," in *Human Disability and the Service of God: Reassessing Religious Practice*, ed. Nancy L. Eiesland and Don E. Saliers (Nashville: Abingdon, 1998), 30.

62 Lesslie Newbigin, "Not Whole without the Handicapped," in *Partners in Life: The Handicapped and the Church*, ed. Geiko Müller-Fahrenholz (Geneva: World Council of Churches, 1979), 23.

63 Jennie Weiss Block, *Copious Hosting: A Theology of Access for People with Disabilities* (New York: Continuum, 2002), 132.

64 Conner, *Amplifying Our Witness*, 88–90.

65 Miguel J. Romero, "Aquinas on the Corporis Infirmitas: Broken Flesh and the Grammar of Grace," in *Disability in the Christian Tradition: A Reader*, ed. Brian Brock and John Swinton (Grand Rapids: Eerdmans, 2012), 111.
66 Romero, "Aquinas on the Corporis Infirmitas," 102. See also Ivan Bankhead, "Thomas Aquinas on Mental Disorder and the Sacraments of Baptism and the Eucharist: Summa Theologica 3.68.12 and 3.80.9 Revisited," *Journal of Disability & Religion* 20, no. 4 (2016): 245.
67 Romero, "Aquinas on the Corporis Infirmitas," 106, 109.
68 Romero, "Aquinas on the Corporis Infirmitas," 112–13.
69 Romero, "Aquinas on the Corporis Infirmitas," 115. John Berkman makes a similar argument in his essay "Are Persons with Profound Intellectual Disabilities Sacramental Icons of Heavenly Life? Aquinas on Impairment," *Studies in Christian Ethics* 26, no. 1 (2013): 94.
70 Cross, "Baptism, Faith and Severe Cognitive Impairment," 430–31.
71 Cross, "Baptism, Faith and Severe Cognitive Impairment," 433–34.
72 Cross, "Baptism, Faith and Severe Cognitive Impairment," 435.
73 Cross, "Baptism, Faith and Severe Cognitive Impairment," 438.
74 Harshaw, *God beyond Words*, 123.
75 Harshaw breaks over Luther's baptism theology requiring a "later intentional commitment to the grace imbued at baptism."
76 Bankhead, "Thomas Aquinas on Mental Disorder," 123, 124. On this point she follows contemporary theologian Olli-Pekka Vainio, drawing a contrast with *fides infusa* which connotes "the actual effects of God in the human being."
77 For example, see the multitude of resources available from organizations such as The National Catholic Partnership on Disability (www.ncpd.org) and The United States Conference of Catholic Bishops (http://www.usccb.org/about/evangelization-and-catechesis/catechesis-with-people-with-disabilities.cfm), as well as specific Diocesan websites (e.g., The Catholic Diocese of Dallas, https://www.cathdal.org/Resources_for_Developmentally_Disabled_Individuals).
78 Paul J. Wadell, "Pondering the Anomaly of God's Love: Ethical Reflections on Access to the Sacraments," in *Developmental Disabilities and Sacramental Access: New Paradigms for Sacramental Encounters*, ed. Edward Foley (Collegeville, Minn.: Liturgical, 1994), 63.
79 Wadell, "Pondering the Anomaly," 64.
80 Mark R. Francis, "Celebrating the Sacraments with Those with Developmental Disabilities: Sacramental/Liturgical Reflections," in *Developmental Disabilities and Sacramental Access: New Paradigms for Sacramental Encounters*, ed. Edward Foley (Collegeville, Minn.: Liturgical, 1994), 83. For Francis, the fundamentally communal and celebratory nature of baptism challenges "the predominantly conceptual" mode of sacramental access preferred by many in the contemporary ecclesial scene (a mode of access often unattainable by many people living with intellectual disabilities). Francis identifies this highly conceptual perspective on baptism as problematic within the manualist (pre-Vatican II) tradition, particularly because the sacraments were administered in Latin with little to no lay understanding (82).

81 Francis, "Celebrating the Sacraments," 89.
82 Francis, "Celebrating the Sacraments," 90. Using an abundance of water (in parallel to bathing) is one example of linking the sacramental action of baptism to the practices of everyday life.
83 Huels, "Canonical Rights to the Sacraments," 95.
84 Joseph Bernardin, "Access to the Sacraments of Initiation and Reconciliation for Developmentally Disabled Persons," in *Developmental Disabilities and Sacramental Access: New Paradigms for Sacramental Encounters*, ed. Edward Foley (Collegeville, Minn.: Liturgical, 1985), 141.
85 Bernardin, "Access to the Sacraments," 142. Bernardin also stresses the "right" of participation among people with intellectual disabilities to engage the sacraments and to receive appropriate catechesis. With careful pastoral attention, Bernardin reminds those in positions of lay and clerical leadership that people with intellectual disabilities living in residential settings (particularly those without family members to help support their growth in a spiritual life) should be attended to by the local parish, through the provision of pastoral care and encouragement for full participation in the life of the local worshiping community (143).
86 Bernardin, "Access to the Sacraments," 143–44.
87 Melissa Florer-Bixler, "Baptism and Profound Disability," *ADNotes*, 2011.
88 Florer-Bixler, "Baptism and Profound Disability."
89 Florer-Bixler, "Baptism and Profound Disability."
90 Florer-Bixler, "Believers Baptism as Supported Decision," 135.
91 Made famous by the guardianship petition trial of Jenny Hatch, a young woman with Down Syndrome living in the United Kingdom, supported decision-making refers to the process of supporting individuals experiencing intellectual disabilities to maximally and actively participate in choices that affect their lives and wellbeing. More information about Jenny Hatch and supported decision-making can be found at this website: http://www.supporteddecisionmaking.org/.
92 Florer-Bixler, "Believers Baptism as Supported Decision," 136.
93 Greig, "Re-imagining Narratives," 128–31.
94 Jason D. Whitt, "Baptism and Profound Intellectual Disability," *Disability* (2012): 60.
95 Whitt, "Baptism and Profound Intellectual Disability," 62.
96 Whitt, "Baptism and Profound Intellectual Disability," 64.
97 Whitt, "Baptism and Profound Intellectual Disability," 65.
98 Whitt, "Baptism and Profound Intellectual Disability," 65.
99 Whitt, "Baptism and Profound Intellectual Disability," 65.
100 Whitt, "Baptism and Profound Intellectual Disability," 66.
101 Habets, "Suffer the Little Children to Come to Me," 315.
102 Habets, "Suffer the Little Children to Come to Me," 316. Here he gestures toward Galatians 2:20 as evidence of a thoroughly Christological narration of faith and election.
103 Charlton, *Nothing about Us without Us*.

CHAPTER 2: DRAWING FROM A MULTITUDE OF WITNESSES

1 Led by foundational work among the following theologians and ethicists (listed alphabetically): Luke Bretherton, Mary McClintock Fulkerson, Nicholas Healy, Mary Clark Moschella, Harriet Mowat, Emily Reimer-Barry, Christian Scharen, John Swinton, Aana Marie Vigen, Pete Ward, and Todd Whitmore.
2 Kyle B. T. Lambelet and Jon Kara Shields, "Introduction: Finding God in the Fieldnotes," *Ecclesial Practices* 8 (2021): 2.
3 Swinton and Mowat, *Practical Theology and Qualitative Research*, 6.
4 Michael R. Grigoni, "Beyond the Church and the Poor: Expanding the Subject of Ethnographic Theology," *Ecclesial Practices* 8 (2021): 95.
5 Swinton and Mowat, *Practical Theology and Qualitative Research*, 9.
6 Ryan Juskus, "Revealers, Skeptics, and Witnesses: Advancing a Witness Methodology in Ethnographic Theology and Ethics," *Ecclesial Practices* 8, no. 1 (2021): 26.
7 Nicholas M. Healy, *Church, World and the Christian Life: Practical-Prophetic Ecclesiology*, Cambridge Studies in Christian Doctrine 7 (Cambridge: Cambridge University Press, 2000), 38.
8 Existing theological literature that takes up the ethnographic turn in partnership with individuals with intellectual disabilities includes Lorraine Cuddeback-Gedeon's "'Nothing about Us without Us:' Ethnography, Conscientization, and the Epistemic Challenges of Intellectual Disability," *Practical Matters* 11 (2018), "How Fair Is Fair? Reflections on Informed Consent and Inclusive Research with the IDD Community," *National Catholic Bioethics Quarterly* 20, no. 2 (2020), and *The Work of Inclusion: An Ethnography of Grace, Sin, and Intellectual Disability* (forthcoming with T&T Clark); Rebecca F. Spurrier's *The Disabled Church*; and John Swinton, Harriet Mowat, and Susannah Baines' "Whose Story Am I? Redescribing Profound Intellectual Disability in the Kingdom of God," *Journal of Religion, Disability & Health* 15, no. 1 (2011). Other qualitative and mixed-methods studies at the intersection of intellectual disability and ecclesial life rely primarily upon nondisabled professional, academic, or caregiver perspectives for exploring religiosity among people with intellectual disabilities. Additionally, these studies typically emerge from disciplines outside of theology, such as special education and social work. Prominent examples include: Melinda Jones Ault, Belva C. Collins, and Erik W. Carter, "Congregational Participation and Supports for Children and Adults with Disabilities: Parent Perceptions," *Intellectual and Developmental Disabilities* 51, no. 1 (2013); Erik W. Carter, "A Place of Belonging: Research at the Intersection of Faith and Disability," *Review and Expositor* 113, no. 2 (2016); Erik W. Carter, "Supporting Inclusion and Flourishing in the Religious and Spiritual Lives of People with Intellectual and Developmental Disabilities," *Inclusion* 1, no. 1 (2013); Carter et al., "Congregational Participation of a National Sample of Adults with Intellectual and Developmental Disabilities"; Eleanor X. Liu et al., "In Their Own Words: The Place of Faith in the Lives of Young People with Autism and Intellectual Disability," *Intellectual and Developmental Disabilities* 52, no. 5 (2014); Victoria Slocum,

"Recommendations for Including People with Intellectual Disabilities in Faith Communities," *Christian Education Journal* 13, no. 1 (2016).
9 Swinton, Mowat, and Baines, "Whose Story Am I?" 16.
10 Devva Kasnitz and Russell P. Shuttleworth, "Introduction: Anthropology in Disability Studies," *Disability Studies Quarterly* 21, no. 3 (2001): 8; Heather E. Keith and Kenneth D. Keith, *Intellectual Disability: Ethics, Dehumanization, and a New Moral Community* (Chichester, West Sussex: Wiley-Blackwell, 2013), 173; Jonathan Perry, "Interviewing People with Intellectual Disabilities," in *The International Handbook of Applied Research in Intellectual Disabilities*, ed. Eric Emerson (Chichester, West Sussex: Wiley, 2004), 117; Swinton and Mowat, *Practical Theology and Qualitative Research*, 227.
11 Katherine E. McDonald et al., "Is It Worth It? Benefits in Research with Adults with Intellectual Disability," *Intellectual and Developmental Disabilities* 54, no. 6 (2016): 445.
12 Gerry Hendershot, "A Statistical Note on the Religiosity of Persons with Disabilities," *Disability Studies Quarterly* 26, no. 4 (2006): 1; Slocum, "Recommendations for Including People with Intellectual Disabilities," 110; Whitehead, "Religion and Disability," 389.
13 Tim Griffin and Susan Balandin, "Ethical Research Involving People with Intellectual Disabilities," in *The International Handbook of Applied Research in Intellectual Disabilities*, edited by Eric Emerson, 61–82 (Chichester, West Sussex: Wiley, 2004), 77.
14 Griffin and Balandin, "Ethical Research," 78; Colleen A. Kidney and Katherine E. McDonald, "A Toolkit for Accessible and Respectful Engagement in Research," *Disability & Society* 29 (2014): 1019.
15 Jan Blacher and Iris Tan Mink, "Interviewing Family Members and Care Providers: Concepts, Methodologies, and Cultures," in *The International Handbook of Applied Research in Intellectual Disabilities*, ed. Eric Emerson et al. (Chichester, West Sussex: Wiley, 2004), 135.
16 Charlotte Aull Davies, *Reflexive Ethnography: A Guide to Researching Selves and Others* (London: Routledge, 1999), 82; Kidney and McDonald, "A Toolkit," 1017; Katherine E. McDonald, "We Want Respect: Adults with Intellectual and Developmental Disabilities Address Respect in Research," *American Journal on Intellectual and Developmental Disabilities* 117, no. 4 (2012): 264–65; Katherine E. McDonald and Colleen A. Kidney, "What Is Right? Ethics in Intellectual Disabilities Research." *Journal of Policy and Practice in Intellectual Disabilities* 9, no. 1 (2012): 32; Ariel E. Schwartz et al., "'That Felt Like Real Engagement': Fostering and Maintaining Inclusive Research Collaborations with Individuals with Intellectual Disabilities," *Qualitative Health Research* 30 no. 2 (2020): 237.
17 Schwartz et al., "'That Felt Like Real Engagement,'" 236. Schwartz et al. understand "inclusive research" as an umbrella term that encompasses research approaches with disabled individuals including participatory action research, community-based participatory research, patient-engagement research, and emancipatory research.
18 Creswell and Poth, *Qualitative Inquiry and Research Design*, 121; Merriam and Tisdell, *Qualitative Research*, 37–38.

19 D. Jean Clandinin and F. Michael Connelly, *Narrative Inquiry: Experience and Story in Qualitative Research* (San Francisco: Jossey-Bass, 2000), 20.
20 Clandinin, *Engaging in Narrative Inquiry*, 18.
21 Blacher and Mink, "Interviewing Family Members," 135–36; Griffin and Balandin, "Ethical Research," 78; Perry, "Interviewing People," 120.
22 Kidney and McDonald, "A Toolkit," 1019.
23 Jocelyn Cleghorn, "The Ethnographic Method: A Case Study for Research among People with Severe Intellectual Disabilities," presented at the Australasian Society for Intellectual Disability Conference, Fremantle, Western Australia, 2014, 1–2; Cuddeback-Gedeon, "How Fair Is Fair?" 252–53; Irene Tuffrey-Wijne and John Davies, "This Is My Story: I've Got Cancer," *British Journal of Learning Disabilities* 35 (2006): 10–11.
24 Chris Taua and Tony Farrow, "Negotiating Complexities: An Ethnographic Study of Intellectual Disability and Mental Health Nursing in New Zealand," *International Journal of Mental Health Nursing* 18 (2009): 281.
25 Arthur J. Dalton and Keith R. McVilly, "Ethics Guidelines for International, Multicenter Research Involving People with Intellectual Disabilities," *Journal of Policy and Practice in Intellectual Disabilities* 1 (2004): 57; Perry, "Interviewing People," 118; Jackie Rodgers, "Trying to Get It Right: Undertaking Research Involving People with Learning Difficulties," *Disability & Society* 14 (1999): 426.
26 Griffin and Balandin, "Ethical Research," 70.
27 Cleghorn, "Ethnographic Method," 1–2; Tuffrey-Wijne and Davies, "This Is My Story," 10–11.
28 Griffin and Balandin, "Ethical Research," 72. Additionally, stories told about disabled individuals who were not participants in this study were recorded and represented with a pseudonym. Attempts to seek consent for inclusion of small portions of these individuals' stories were successful for all mentions of nonparticipants in this book's formal research process.
29 The Plain Language Action and Information Network, *Federal Plain Language Guidelines* (2011), https://plainlanguage.gov/guidelines/; CAST, "The UDL Guidelines," accessed October 30, 2018, http://udlguidelines.cast.org/; Kidney and McDonald, "A Toolkit," 1015; McDonald, "We Want Respect," 264; Helen Prosser and Jo Bromley, "Interviewing People with Intellectual Disabilities," in *Clinical Psychology and People with Intellectual Disabilities*, ed. Eric Emerson and Chris Hatton (Malden, Mass.: Wiley-Blackwell, 2012), 116.
30 Perry, "Interviewing People," 117.
31 Swinton and Mowat, *Practical Theology and Qualitative Research*, 222.
32 Michael V. Angrosino, "Participant Observation and Research on Intellectual Disabilities," in *The International Handbook of Applied Research in Intellectual Disabilities*, ed. Eric Emerson (Chichester, West Sussex: Wiley, 2004), 165; Cleghorn, "Ethnographic Method," 1–2; David Goode, *A World without Words: The Social Construction of Children Born Deaf and Blind* (Philadelphia: Temple University Press, 1994), 42.
33 Griffin and Balandin, "Ethical Research," 66; Kidney and McDonald, "A Toolkit," 1028; Katherine E. McDonald, "We Want Respect," 268–69; McDonald and Kidney, "What Is Right?" 32.

34 McDonald, "We Want Respect," 268.
35 Ages 18 years and older.
36 Johnny Saldaña, *The Coding Manual for Qualitative Researchers*, 3rd ed. (Los Angeles: SAGE, 2016), 44–45.
37 Saldaña, *Coding Manual for Qualitative Researchers*, 27.
38 Saldaña, *Coding Manual for Qualitative Researchers*, 76. Descriptive coding was initially utilized to establish a list of important topics and subtopics in the interview data.
39 Saldaña, *Coding Manual for Qualitative Researchers*, 77.
40 Saldaña, *Coding Manual for Qualitative Researchers*, 78.
41 Saldaña, *Coding Manual for Qualitative Researchers*, 231.
42 I utilized NVivo primarily as an organizational tool for my data, as well as an efficient instrument for noting important shared themes across the interview data and field notes (arising from my process of descriptive coding). As Swinton and Mowat advise, I additionally situated my data analysis in reflexive practices that helped me uncover and reflect upon my own assumptions and their impact on the research analysis (*Practical Theology and Qualitative Research*, 57). In addition to utilizing NVivo as a tool, I found my handwritten analytic memos as a very helpful source to draw upon the unique richness and meaning of various stories that did not fall within the shared themes across study participants. I explore these unique findings throughout the remaining chapters of this book.
43 Emily Reimer-Barry, "The Listening Church: How Ethnography Can Transform Catholic Ethics," in *Ethnography as Christian Theology and Ethics*, ed. Christian Scharen and Aana Marie Vigen (New York: Continuum, 2011), 101; John Swinton, "'Where Is Your Church?' Moving toward a Hospitable and Sanctified Ethnography," in *Perspectives on Ecclesiology and Ethnography*, ed. Pete Ward (Grand Rapids: Eerdmans, 2012), 83–84; Swinton and Mowat, *Practical Theology and Qualitative Research*, 59.
44 Swinton, "Where Is Your Church?" 57.
45 Swinton, "Where Is Your Church?" 84.
46 Donald E. Polkinghorne, "Validity Issues in Narrative Research," *Qualitative Inquiry* 13, no. 4 (2007): 480; Swinton and Mowat, *Practical Theology and Qualitative Research*, 222.
47 Willie James Jennings, "Grace without Remainder: Why Baptists Should Baptize Their Babies," in *Grace Upon Grace: Essays in Honor of Thomas A. Langford*, ed. Robert K. Johnston, L. Gregory Jones, and Jonathan R. Wilson, 201–16 (Nashville: Abingdon, 1999), 202.
48 Tuffrey-Wijne and Davies, "This is My Story," 10.
49 Pastor Ambrose notes that Eli rarely spoke throughout the years they knew each other. Eli's postbaptismal verbal response was one of only a few times Pastor Ambrose heard Eli speak.
50 The study was the foundation for my doctoral dissertation at Duke Divinity School.
51 Saldaña, *Coding Manual*, 38.
52 Clandinin, *Engaging in Narrative Inquiry*, 140.

53 Erin Stack and Katherine E. McDonald, "Nothing about Us without Us: Does Action Research in Developmental Disabilities Research Measure Up?" *Journal of Policy and Practice in Intellectual Disabilities* 11, no. 2 (2014): 89.
54 Swinton, Mowat, and Baines, "Whose Story Am I?" 6.

CHAPTER 3: THE BIBLE AND BAPTISM

1 The other accounts of Jesus' baptism in the canonical Gospels are found in Mark 1:9–11, Luke 3:21–22, and John 1:29–34.
2 Ronald P. Byars, *The Sacraments in Biblical Perspective*, Interpretation: Resources for the Use of Scripture in the Church (Louisville, Ky.: Westminster John Knox, 2011), 27.
3 Byars, *Sacraments*, 27.
4 Bryan D. Spinks, *Early and Medieval Rituals and Theologies of Baptism: From the New Testament to the Council of Trent*, Liturgy, Worship and Society (New York: Routledge, 2006), 4–5.
5 Byars, *Sacraments*, 23. Robin Jensen offers further Old Testament motifs parallel to Jesus' baptism, following the affirmations of early Christians (such as Origen, Gregory of Nyssa, Ephrem, and Cyril of Jerusalem): the Israelites following Joshua across the Jordan River to enter the Promised Land (Joshua 3:14–17), Naaman's healing in the river (II Kings 5), and the four rivers flowing from the Garden of Eden (Genesis 2:10–14). Jensen also reflects on potential connections between baptismal waters and the waters in Psalm 42, in light of common early Christian baptismal art that depicts a deer drinking at a pool. For Jensen, the gushing forth of water from the rock that Moses strikes in Exodus 17:1–7 also resonates closely with John's baptism of Jesus. Robin M. Jensen, *Baptismal Imagery in Early Christianity: Ritual, Visual, and Theological Dimensions* (Grand Rapids: Baker Academic, 2012), 184–86.
6 Pastor Daniel mentioned Henri Nouwen's book *The Life of the Beloved* as a formative text that emphasized this heart of belovedness at the center of baptismal identity both for Jesus and among all the baptized.
7 Byars, *Sacraments*, 92; Maxwell Johnson, *The Rites of Christian Initiation: Their Evolution and Interpretation*, rev. ed. (Collegeville, Minn.: Liturgical, 2007), 52.
8 Affirmed in the account of Jesus' baptism in the Jordan River, with the Holy Spirit portrayed as descending as a dove. Schmemann, *Of Water and the Spirit*, 42; Byars, *Sacraments*, 44.
9 Byars, *Sacraments*, 49, 62.
10 Winner, *Dangers of Christian Practice*, 112.
11 Grant Macaskill, *Autism and the Church: Bible, Theology, and Community* (Waco, Tex.: Baylor University Press, 2019), 108.
12 Spinks, *Early and Medieval Rituals*, 13. This Jesus-centered account of baptism in Paul's New Testament letters permeates his other key baptismal themes in Acts 2, Romans 6, 1 Corinthians 12, 2 Corinthians 5, and Galatians 3, including participation, exchange, life and death, and new creation (Spinks, *Early and Medieval Rituals*, 8).

13 Chapters of Pauline Epistles engaging baptism include (but are not limited to): Romans 6; 1 Corinthians 1, 6, 10, 12; 2 Corinthians 1; Galatians 3; Ephesians 1, 4–5; Colossians 2–3; 2 Timothy 2; and Titus 3. In comparison to other New Testament literature as well as nonbiblical first-century Christian texts, Paul offers the greatest volume of material attending specifically to baptism. Paul does not focus on offering a concrete rite or providing precise ritual guidelines for the Christian communities he corresponds with throughout the Near East. Instead, he seems to be in dialogue with communities who already practice baptism. Thus, Paul offers contextual teaching for communities who have embraced baptism and seek to have this particular Christian practice shape the witness of their community (Richard P. Carlson, "The Role of Baptism in Paul's Thought," *Interpretation* 47, no. 3 [1993]: 25; Nicholas Taylor, *Paul on Baptism: Theology, Mission, and Ministry in Context* [London: SCM, 2016], xvii–xviii, 25).
14 Drawing upon the larger context of Romans 5–8. New Testament scholar Rudolf Schnackenburg characterizes this passage from Romans 6 as the "locus classicus" on baptism in the New Testament, especially in its exemplification of baptism as an event that witnesses to a life of salvation, rooted in Jesus' incarnation, death, and resurrection (*Baptism in the Thought of St. Paul* [Oxford: Basil Blackwell, 1964], 30).
15 Everett Ferguson, *Baptism in the Early Church: History, Theology, and Liturgy in the First Five Centuries* (Grand Rapids: Eerdmans, 2009), 155.
16 Ferguson, *Baptism in the Early Church*, 156, 158; A. J. M. Wedderburn, "The Soteriology of the Mysteries and Paul's Baptismal Theology," *Novum Testamentum* 29 (1987): 50, 61.
17 John M. G. Barclay, "Under Grace: The Christ-Gift and the Construction of a Christian Habitus," in *Apocalyptic Paul: Cosmos and Anthropos in Romans 5–8*, ed. Beverly Roberts Gaventa (Waco, Tex.: Baylor University Press, 2013), 71.
18 Williams, *Being Christian*, 10.
19 Pelagianism is "the heresy that people can take the initial steps towards salvation by their own effort, apart from Divine Grace." E. A. Livingstone, *The Concise Oxford Dictionary of the Christian Church*, 3rd ed. (Oxford: Oxford University Press, 2013), 429.
20 "Christians die to sin because their baptism into Christ is a baptism into the salvific event of Christ's death. The upshot is that they no longer live in sin's dominion. Baptism is not merely an identifying with Christ . . . baptism into Christ, Paul says, is an inclusion into the event of Christ's death, an incorporation into the cross." Carlson, "Role of Baptism," 258.
21 Teresa Kuo-Yu Tsui, "'Baptized into His Death' (Romans 6:3) and 'Clothed with Christ' (Gal 3:27): The Soteriological Meaning of Baptism in Light of Pauline Apocalyptic," *Ephemerides Theologicae Louvanienses* 88, no. 4 (2012): 398.
22 Karl Barth, *The Teaching of the Church Regarding Baptism*, trans. Ernest A. Payne (1948; repr., Eugene, Oreg.: Wipf and Stock, 2006), 11; Carlson, "Role of Baptism," 262; Robert Jewett and Roy David Kotansky, *Romans: A Commentary on the Book of Romans*, Hermeneia, ed. Eldon Jay Epp (Minneapolis: Augsburg Fortress, 2006), 399; John A. T. Robinson, *The Body: A Study in Pauline Theology* (Chicago: Henry Regnery Company, 1952), 80; Schnackenburg, *Baptism in the Thought of*

St. Paul, 26; Samuli Siikavirta, *Baptism and Cognition in Romans 6–8: Paul's Ethics Beyond 'Indicative' and 'Imperative,'* Wissenschaftliche Untersuchungen Zum Neuen Testament (Tübingen, Germany: Mohr Siebeck, 2015), 88, 110; Taylor, *Paul on Baptism*, 23–24; Tsui, "'Baptized into His Death,'" 397.

23 Schnackenburg, *Baptism in the Thought of St. Paul*, 36.
24 Leander E. Keck, "What Makes Romans Tick?" in *Pauline Theology*, volume 3: *Romans*, ed. David M. Hay and E. Elizabeth Johnson (Minneapolis: Fortress, 1995), 25.
25 Jewett and Kotansky, *Romans*, 391–92; Taylor, *Paul on Baptism*, 58–59.
26 Macaskill, *Autism and the Church*, 146.
27 Williams, *Being Christian*, 6.
28 Siikavirta, *Baptism and Cognition*, 5.
29 Carlson, "Role of Baptism," 256.
30 Keck, *Romans*, 162.
31 Barclay, *Paul and the Gift*, 503.
32 Schnackenburg, *Baptism in the Thought of St. Paul*, 37.
33 Taylor, *Paul on Baptism*, 62.
34 Siikavirta, *Baptism and Cognition*, 117.
35 For a more detailed argument exploring questions of intellectual disability and participation in the realm of sin, see Michael Mawson, "The Sin of Disability: Why Disability Theology Needs a Doctrine of Sin," in *Knowing, Being Known, and the Mystery of God: Essays in Honor of Professor Hans Reinders: Teacher, Friend, and Disciple*, ed. Bill Gaventa and Erik De Jongh (Amsterdam: VU University Press, 2016).
36 Schnackenburg, *Baptism in the Thought of St. Paul*, 41.
37 Schnackenburg, *Baptism in the Thought of St. Paul*, 155.
38 Carlson, "Role of Baptism," 263.
39 Carlson, "Role of Baptism," 260; Siikavirta, *Baptism and Cognition*, 83.
40 Siikavirta, *Baptism and Cognition*, 6.
41 Siikavirta, *Baptism and Cognition*, 154.
42 Keck, *Romans*, 167. This theme of "becoming who I am/we are" resonates with baptism as foundational for identity among many participant reflections in the qualitative research project.

CHAPTER 4: A NEW CREATION

1 Susan Grove Eastman, *Paul and the Person: Reframing Paul's Anthropology* (Grand Rapids: Eerdmans, 2017), 4.
2 Eastman, *Paul and the Person*, 9.
3 Siikavirta, *Baptism and Cognition*, 161. Siikavirta supports this argument not only theologically but also by drawing upon Paul's textual construction of Romans 6, especially the tightly connected grammatical imperatives regarding baptism.
4 Siikavirta, *Baptism and Cognition*, 93.
5 Siikavirta, *Baptism and Cognition*, 116.
6 Eastman, *Paul and the Person*, 185.

7 Eastman, *Paul and the Person*, 2.
8 Eastman, *Paul and the Person*, 102.
9 Eastman, *Paul and the Person*, 153.
10 Eastman, *Paul and the Person*, 158.
11 Barclay, "Under Grace," 60.
12 Barclay, "Under Grace," 64–65.
13 Barclay, "Under Grace," 65.
14 Williams, *Being Christian*, 1–2.
15 Eastman, *Paul and the Person*, 145.
16 Macaskill, *Autism and the Church*, 97.
17 Robinson, *The Body*, 48.
18 Ernst Käsemann, *Perspectives on Paul* (Philadelphia: Fortress, 1971), 104; Romans 12:4 and 2 Corinthians 12:12.
19 Käsemann, *Perspectives on Paul*, 114.
20 Käsemann, *Perspectives on Paul*, 119.
21 Eastman, *Paul and the Person*, 181–182.
22 Eastman, *Paul and the Person*, 182.
23 Campbell, *Paul and the Creation of Christian Identity*, 154.
24 Carlson, "The Role of Baptism," 260.
25 Macaskill, *Autism and the Church*, 197.
26 Macaskill, *Autism and the Church*, 94–95.
27 Brock, *Wondrously Wounded*, 202.
28 Brock, *Wondrously Wounded*, 205.
29 Brock, *Wondrously Wounded*, 216.
30 Campbell, *Paul and the Creation of Christian Identity*, 165.
31 Campbell, *Paul and the Creation of Christian Identity*, 156.
32 Winner, *The Dangers of Christian Practice*, 98–99.
33 Eastman, *Paul and the Person*, 174.
34 Margaret E. Thrall, "The Second Epistle to the Corinthians," in vol. 1 of *The International Critical Commentary on the Holy Scriptures of the Old and New Testaments*, ed. J. A. Emerton, C. E. B. Cranfield, and G. N. Stanton (Edinburgh, Scotland: T&T Clark, 1994), 418.
35 Victor Paul Furnish, "II Corinthians," in *The Anchor Bible*, ed. W. F. Albright and D. N. Freedman, vol. 32A (Garden City, N.Y.: Doubleday, 1984), 329; Arthur J. Dewey and Anna C. Miller, "Paul," in *The Bible and Disability: A Commentary*, ed. Sarah J. Melcher, Mikeal C. Parsons, and Amos Yong (Waco, Tex.: Baylor University Press, 2017).
36 J. Louis Martyn, "Epistemology at the Turn of the Ages: 2 Corinthians 5:16," in *Christian History and Interpretation: Studies Presented to John Knox*, ed. W. R. Farmer, C. F. D. Moule, and R. R. Niebuhr (Cambridge: Cambridge University Press, 1967).
37 Martyn, "Epistemology at the Turn of the Ages," 285.
38 Susan Eastman, "Ashes on the Frontal Lobe" (paper presented at the Society of Biblical Literature, Chicago, 2012), 13. Eastman goes on to argue that Paul's

statement in 2 Corinthians 5:16 does not reject embodied knowledge, but rather, rejects knowledge about other persons "unmediated by being 'in Christ'" (14).
39 Williams, *Being Christian*, 3.
40 Thrall, "Second Epistle to the Corinthians," 423.
41 Ralph P. Martin, "2 Corinthians," in *Word Biblical Commentary*, ed. D. A. Hubbard and G. W. Barker, vol. 40 (Waco, Tex.: Word Books, 1986), 139.
42 Murray J. Harris, "The Second Epistle to the Corinthians: A Commentary on the Greek Text," in *The New International Greek Testament Commentary*, ed. I. H. Marshall and D. A. Hagner (Grand Rapids: Eerdmans, 2005), 436.
43 Thrall, "Second Epistle to the Corinthians," 430.
44 Martin, "2 Corinthians," 156.
45 Thrall, "Second Epistle to the Corinthians," 414.
46 Macaskill, *Autism and the Church*, 89.

CHAPTER 5: BAPTISMAL LITURGY AND DISABILITY

1 Stanley Hauerwas and Samuel Wells, "Christian Ethics as Informed Prayer," in *The Blackwell Companion to Christian Ethics*, ed. Stanley Hauerwas and Samuel Wells (Malden, Mass.: Blackwell, 2011), 6.
2 Kimberly Hope Belcher, *Efficacious Engagement: Sacramental Participation in the Trinitarian Mystery* (Collegeville, Minn.: Liturgical, 2011), 111.
3 David Ford, *Self and Salvation: Being Transformed*, Cambridge Studies in Christian Doctrine 1 (Cambridge: Cambridge University Press, 1999), 139, 144.
4 Schmemann, *Of Water and the Spirit*, 110.
5 Alan Jacobs, *The Book of Common Prayer: A Biography*, Lives of Great Religious Books (Princeton, N.J.: Princeton University Press, 2013), 46.
6 J. Robert Wright, "The Book of Common Prayer," in *The Wiley-Blackwell Companion to the Anglican Communion*, ed. Ian S. Markham et al., 81–90 (Malden, Mass.: John Wiley & Sons, 2013), 82.
7 Lesley A. Northup, "The Episcopal Church in the U.S.A.," in *The Oxford Guide to the Book of Common Prayer: A Worldwide Survey*, ed. Charles Hefling and Cynthia Shattuck, 823–42 (New York: Oxford University Press, 2006), 838.
8 Meyers, "Baptismal Covenant," 32; Colin Podmore, "The Baptismal Revolution in the American Episcopal Church: Baptismal Ecclesiology and the Baptismal Covenant," *Ecclesiology* 6 (2010): 30.
9 This is the first appearance of "covenant" language found in an Anglican prayer book, drawing upon a Reformed theological perspective on baptism. The Episcopal Church, *Book of Common Prayer*, 304–5.
10 The Episcopal Church, *Book of Common Prayer*, 302.
11 The Episcopal Church, *Book of Common Prayer*, 306–7.
12 The Episcopal Church, *Book of Common Prayer*, 306–7.
13 Kathy Black, *A Healing Homiletic: Preaching and Disability* (Nashville: Abingdon, 1996), 23; Nancy L. Eiesland, *The Disabled God: Toward a Liberatory Theology of Disability* (Nashville: Abingdon, 1994), 69–71; Amos Yong, *The Bible, Disability, and the Church: A New Vision of the People of God* (Grand Rapids:

Eerdmans, 2011), 51; Amos Yong, *Theology and Down Syndrome: Reimagining Disability in Late Modernity* (Waco, Tex.: Baylor University Press, 2007), 26.
14 William C. Gaventa, "Preaching Disability: The Whole of Christ's Body in Word and Practice," *Review and Expositor* 113, no. 2 (2016): 230; John Swinton, "Building a Church for Strangers," *Journal of Religion, Disability & Health* 4, no. 4 (2008): 30.
15 Marion J. Hatchett, *Commentary on the American Prayer Book* (New York: HarperCollins, 1995), 273.
16 The Episcopal Church, *Book of Common Prayer*, 303.
17 The Episcopal Church, *Book of Common Prayer*, 302–3.
18 The Episcopal Church, *Book of Common Prayer*, 304–5.
19 The Episcopal Church, *Book of Common Prayer*, 305–6.
20 The Episcopal Church, *Book of Common Prayer*, 308.
21 The Episcopal Church, *Book of Common Prayer*, 301.
22 The Episcopal Church, *Book of Common Prayer*, 308.
23 Michael Mawson, "Creatures before God: Bonhoeffer, Disability and Theological Anthropology," in *Christ, Church and World: New Studies in Bonhoeffer's Theology and Ethics*, ed. Michael Mawson and Philip G. Ziegler (London: T&T Clark, 2016), 135.
24 Mawson, "Creatures before God," 133.
25 Mawson, "Creatures before God," 133–35.
26 Dietrich Bonhoeffer, *Discipleship*, trans. Barbara Green and Reinhard Krauss, Dietrich Bonhoeffer Works—Reader's Edition (Minneapolis: Fortress, 2015), 216–17.
27 Mawson, "Sin of Disability," 99.
28 Bonhoeffer, *Discipleship*, 184–85.
29 Bonhoeffer, *Discipleship*, 186.
30 The Episcopal Church, *Book of Common Prayer*, 301.
31 Tom Greggs, "Bearing Sin in the Church: The Ecclesial Hamartiology of Bonhoeffer," in *Christ, Church and World: New Studies in Bonhoeffer's Theology and Ethics*, ed. Michael Mawson and Philip G. Ziegler (London: T&T Clark, 2016), 92.
32 Bonhoeffer, *Discipleship*, 184.
33 Bonhoeffer, *Discipleship*, 198.
34 Bonhoeffer, *Discipleship*, 5.
35 Bonhoeffer, *Discipleship*, 193–194.
36 Mikoski, *Baptism and Christian Identity*, 34.

CHAPTER 6: PRACTICING AND PROCLAIMING BAPTISMAL IDENTITY

1 Swinton, *Becoming Friends of Time*, 110.
2 Gordon W. Lathrop, *Holy Things: A Liturgical Theology* (Minneapolis: Fortress, 1993), 211. "Someone's station or rank is not the final arrival of God's intention. Indeed, while such a rank or place may be used as a good tool for work, work

that may yield fruits that the assembly itself employs, and while the assembly may pray for people in the work they do, the rank itself stays outside of the meeting and receives no eternal endorsement. The human being is larger, other, waiting for more, than the current social order can assign. There is thus no liturgical role for rich and poor, bosses and workers, professors and students, ethnic insiders and ethnic outsiders, even youth and age, as classes. That is why 'youth Sundays,' or the introduction of persons in the liturgy according to their vocations, wealth, or educational status, or a 'mass of the peasants' that prays against the 'bosses' can all be such profound violations of the sense of the liturgy ... no, in the assembly, there is only 'the people,' the personal/communal alternative vision of humanity standing together before God, which thoroughly relativizes all other human categories, setting the women and the peasants, but also the bosses and the men, free."

3 Fred P. Edie, *Book, Bath, Table, and Time: Christian Worship as Source and Resource for Youth Ministry*, Youth Ministry Alternatives (Cleveland, Ohio: The Pilgrim Press, 2007), 217.

4 Presbyterian Church (U.S.A.), *Invitation to Christ* (Louisville, Ky.: Presbyterian Church [U.S.A.], 2006), 7.

5 Rebecca F. Spurrier, *The Disabled Church: Human Difference and the Art of Communal Worship* (New York: Fordham University Press, 2019), 139.

6 Edie, *Book, Bath, Table, and Time*, 238.

7 Louis Weil, "Baptism as the Model for a Sacramental Aesthetic," *Anglican Theological Review* 92, no. 2 (2010): 266–67.

8 Edie, *Book, Bath, Table, and Time*, 187.

9 Healy, "Rediscovering the Mysteria," 208.

10 Johnson, *Rites of Christian Initiation*, 451–52.

11 Johnson, *Rites of Christian Initiation*, 451–52.

12 Maxwell Johnson expounds upon this role of baptism related to Christian identity within the whole of a worshiping community: "a welcome place in our constant experience of displacement, inviting us home always, always back home to re-claim, renew, reaffirm, and re-appropriate our baptism so that we might learn again to become who we are, the people God has already made us to be in Jesus Christ by water and the Spirit. Not only can we go home again, we must go home again! Our very identity depends on it." *Rites of Christian Initiation*, 477.

13 World Council of Churches, *Baptism, Eucharist and Ministry*, viii.

14 World Council of Churches, *Baptism, Eucharist and Ministry*, 3.

15 World Council of Churches, *Baptism, Eucharist and Ministry*, 2.

16 "The Word of God in the Life of the Church: A Report of International Conversation between the Catholic Church and the Baptist World Alliance," *American Baptist Quarterly* 31, no. 1 (2012): 69.

17 "Baptism and Incorporation into the Body of Christ, the Church," Lutheran-Mennonite-Roman Catholic Trilateral Conversations, 2012–2017, Mennonite World Conference, July 30, 2020, https://mwc-cmm.org/resources/baptism-and-incorporation-body-christ-church.

18 Weil, "Baptism as the Model for a Sacramental Aesthetic," 260–61.

19 Spurrier, *Disabled Church*, 76.
20 Harshaw, "Prophetic Voices, Silent Words," 319.
21 Christine Kelly, "Building Bridges with Accessible Care: Disability Studies, Feminist Care Scholarship, and Beyond," *Hypatia* 28, no. 4 (2013): 789.
22 Spurrier, *Disabled Church*, 210.
23 Kelly, "Building Bridges with Accessible Care," 791.
24 Susan Marie Smith, *Caring Liturgies: The Pastoral Power of Christian Ritual* (Minneapolis: Fortress, 2012), 37, 43. The contours of specific church communities necessitate attending to different "physical starting points" and pragmatic considerations (for example, accessibility for participation in baptismal practices in a specific church building), as well as clarifying the "intent or purpose" of baptismal practices (engaging communities in rich baptismal formation).
25 Gerald A. Arbuckle, *Grieving for Change: A Spirituality for Refounding Gospel Communities* (London: Geoffrey Chapman, 1991), 141.
26 Arbuckle, *Grieving for Change*, 142.
27 Arbuckle, *Grieving for Change*, 143.

CHAPTER 7: PRACTICES OF THE BAPTIZED BODY

1 World Council of Churches, *One Baptism: Towards Mutual Recognition: A Study Text*. Faith and Order Paper No. 210 (Geneva, Switzerland: World Council of Churches, 2011), 9.
2 Stanley K. Fowler, *More Than a Symbol: The British Baptist Recovery of Baptismal Sacramentalism* (Cumbria, UK: Paternoster, 2002), xiii.
3 Schmemann, *Of Water and the Spirit*, 16.
4 Schmemann, *Of Water and the Spirit*, 18.
5 Schmemann, *Of Water and the Spirit*, 18.
6 Christina Lappa et al., "Teaching the Christian Orthodox Mystery of Baptism to Adults with Moderate or Severe Intellectual Disability," *International Journal of Humanities and Social Science Invention* 7, no. 3 (2018): 64.
7 Lappa et al., "Teaching the Christian Orthodox Mystery of Baptism," 67.
8 Lappa et al., "Teaching the Christian Orthodox Mystery of Baptism," 73.
9 Gordon S. Mikoski also advocates for the pedagogical power of baptismal rites and services themselves, echoing John Calvin's emphasis on the pedagogical dimensions of Christian worship practices (*Baptism and Christian Identity*, 180).
10 World Council of Churches, *Baptism, Eucharist and Ministry*, 5.
11 World Council of Churches, *Baptism, Eucharist and Ministry*, 5.
12 Grant Macaskill, writing on church communities from a perspective of neurodiversity, underscores the great need for these practices of care, especially for individuals with intellectual disabilities and others who are nonspeakers: "We simply do not know how the Spirit is working in the hearts and neurons of those in our flock who are not yet verbal, who have not reached a point of typical cognitive development and may never do so. They remain part of the flock, however, and our care and hope for them should reflect this" (*Autism and the Church*, 197).

13 Jay Timothy Dolmage, *Academic Ableism: Disability and Higher Education* (Ann Arbor: University of Michigan Press, 2017), 131.
14 Lathrop, *Holy Things*, 219.
15 In partnership with disabled Christians, clergy and other church leaders must exercise practical wisdom to integrate needed accommodations within their church's liturgical life. Ashley Tindall, sharing her experience of baptism as a survivor of a traumatic brain injury who could not be fully immersed into water, illustrates the beauty of this practical wisdom in her blog post on baptism and accessibility: "Accessible Baptism (Guest Post)," Disability and Faith Forum, March 9, 2017, https://disabilityandfaith.org/accessible-baptism-guest-post/.
16 Gayle Carlton Felton, *By Water and the Spirit: Making Connections for Identity and Ministry* (Nashville: Discipleship Resources, 1997): a United Methodist resource for reflection on baptism, identity, and discipleship.
17 Mary Therese Harrington, "Affectivity and Symbol in the Process of Catechesis," in *Developmental Disabilities and Sacramental Access: New Paradigms for Sacramental Encounters*, ed. Edward Foley (Collegeville, Minn.: Liturgical, 1994), 116.
18 Harrington, "Affectivity and Symbol in the Process of Catechesis," 117.
19 Harrington, "Affectivity and Symbol in the Process of Catechesis," 117.
20 Harrington, "Affectivity and Symbol in the Process of Catechesis," 118–19.
21 Harrington, "Affectivity and Symbol in the Process of Catechesis," 122.
22 Mikoski, *Baptism and Christian Identity*, 37.
23 Through online dissemination of her Doctor of Ministry work, Kristin Adkins Whitesides provides a practical example of a disability-inclusive class focused on baptismal preparation: "Just As I Am: Believer's Baptism and Intellectual Disability," April 9, 2018, https://scholarblogs.emory.edu/candlerdmin/2018/04/09/just-as-i-am/.
24 World Council of Churches, *Baptism, Eucharist and Ministry*, 5.
25 Fowler, *More Than a Symbol*, 225.
26 World Council of Churches, *One Baptism*, 9.
27 Clergy and lay leaders might consider recording readings of these testimonies and making them available in accessible formats to further the proclamation of these baptismal testimonies.
28 Florer-Bixler, "Believers Baptism as Supported Decision," 145–46. Florer-Bixler's interaction with the broad category of baptismal testimony resounds with Neil Cudney and Keith Dow's own pragmatic reflections on baptizing individuals with intellectual and developmental disabilities within credobaptist contexts: "Should We Baptize People with Intellectual Disabilities?" Disability and Faith Forum, https://disabilityandfaith.org/should-we-baptize-people-with-intellectual-disabilities/.
29 Conner, "For the Fitness of Their Witness," 132.
30 Swinton, *Becoming Friends of Time*, 208.
31 John Swinton, *Dementia: Living in the Memories of God* (Grand Rapids: Eerdmans, 2012), 254.
32 Swinton, *Dementia*, 255.

33 Schmemann, *Of Water and the Spirit*, 93.
34 And as evangelical leader John Piper suggests, these kinds of accompaniment might provide the context where credobaptist churches come to welcome the baptism of individuals with profound experiences of disability, through coming to know the uniqueness of their witness and life of shared discipleship: Piper, "Believer Baptism and Mental Disabilities," Desiring God (blog), https://www.desiringgod.org/interviews/believer-baptism-and-mental-disabilities.
35 Young, *Arthur's Call*, 157.
36 Young, *Arthur's Call*, 157.
37 Swinton, "Building a Church for Strangers," 55.
38 Brock, *Wondrously Wounded*, 193.
39 Bonhoeffer, *Discipleship*, 240–41.
40 I use baptismal "remembrance" and "reaffirmation" interchangeably to signify the wide range of multimodal practices that communities engage with to affirm baptismal identity. These practices are not contingent on discrete cognitive skills related to memory.
41 James B. Torrance, *Worship, Community and the Triune God of Grace* (Downers Grove: IVP Academic, 1997), 85.
42 Goode, *World without Words*, 97.
43 Goode, *World without Words*, 97.
44 Bryan D. Spinks, *Reformation and Modern Rituals and Theologies of Baptism: From Luther to Contemporary Practices* (Burlington, Vt.: Ashgate, 2006), 210.
45 Spinks, *Reformation and Modern Rituals*, 211.
46 Spinks, *Reformation and Modern Rituals*, 211.
47 World Council of Churches, *Baptism, Eucharist and Ministry*, 6.
48 World Council of Churches, *Baptism, Eucharist and Ministry*, 5.
49 World Council of Churches, *Baptism, Eucharist and Ministry*, 5.
50 Weil, "Baptism as the Model for a Sacramental Aesthetic," 269–70.
51 While the United Methodist Church provides a formal liturgy of baptismal reaffirmation, liturgical scholars Mark Stamm and Lester Ruth recently crafted a liturgy of reaffirmation of faith for someone seeking rebaptism. The rite includes several ideas for enhancing the worship with multisensory avenues of participation: Derek Weber, "A New Ritual for Reaffirmation of Baptism," April 29, 2021, https://www.umcdiscipleship.org/articles/a-new-ritual-for-reaffirmation-of-baptism.
52 Johnson, *Rites of Christian Initiation*, 469.
53 Johnson, *Rites of Christian Initiation*, 471.
54 Gordon Mikoski considers how writing questions of baptismal promise relevant for a local church community might also supplement official liturgies to invite more expansive participation among the whole of the gathered worshiping body. For example, at St. Peter's (a Presbyterian church Mikoski utilizes as a case study), he writes that the minister asks the children present at baptisms: "Do you promise to be a friend to N.? If s/he needs directions will you show him/her the way? If s/he falls down will you pick him/her up? Will you play with him/her and share with him/her the stories of Jesus?" Parallel questions might

be developed to call churches to responsibility and reciprocal care in relationship with disabled members of the baptized body (*Baptism and Christian Identity*, 18).
55 William C. Gaventa suggests that when adults with intellectual disabilities are baptized for the first time, often after prolonged experiences of exclusion from church communities, this too constitutes an important instance of baptismal remembrance—a re-membering of this individual "as part of the body of the people of faith" (*Disability and Spirituality: Recovering Wholeness* [Waco, Tex.: Baylor University Press, 2018], 277).
56 Lathrop, *Holy Things*, 217

CONCLUSION

1 The Episcopal Church, *Book of Common Prayer*, 308.
2 Juskus, "Revealers, Skeptics, and Witnesses," 26.

Bibliography

Alcoff, Linda Martín. "The Problem of Speaking for Others." In *Who Can Speak? Authority and Critical Identity*, edited by Judith Roof and Robyn Wiegman, 97–119. Chicago: University of Illinois Press, 1995.

Alexander, J. Neil. "The Shape of the Classical Book of Common Prayer." In *The Oxford Guide to the Book of Common Prayer: A Worldwide Survey*, edited by Charles Hefling and Cynthia Shattuck, 173–92. New York: Oxford University Press, 2006.

Allchin, A. M. Donald. "The Sacraments in L'Arche." In *Encounter with Mystery: Reflections on L'Arche and Living with Disability*, edited by Frances Young, 101–18. London: Darton, Longman, and Todd, 1997.

American Association of People with Disabilities. "That All May Worship: An Interfaith Welcome to People with Disabilities." Washington, D.C., 2009.

Angrosino, Michael V. "Participant Observation and Research on Intellectual Disabilities." In *The International Handbook of Applied Research in Intellectual Disabilities*, edited by Eric Emerson, 161–77. Chichester, West Sussex: Wiley, 2004.

Antus, Elizabeth L. "Our Fragile Flesh: Sacramental Hospitality toward Persons with Intellectual Disabilities and Its Implications for Theology." In *Visions of Hope: Emerging Theologians and the Future of the Church*, edited by Kevin Ahern. Maryknoll, N.Y.: Orbis Books, 2012.

Arbuckle, Gerald A. *Grieving for Change*. London: Geoffrey Chapman, 1991.

Ault, Melinda Jones, Belva C. Collins, and Erik W. Carter. "Congregational Participation and Supports for Children and Adults with Disabilities: Parent Perceptions." *Intellectual and Developmental Disabilities* 51, no. 1 (2013): 48–61.

Bankhead, Ivan. "Thomas Aquinas on Mental Disorder and the Sacraments of Baptism and the Eucharist: Summa Theologica 3.68.12 and 3.80.9 Revisited." *Journal of Disability & Religion* 20, no. 4 (2016): 239–64. https://doi.org/10.1080/23312521.2016.1244502.

"Baptism and Incorporation into the Body of Christ, the Church." Lutheran-Mennonite-Roman Catholic Trilateral Conversations 2012–2017. Mennonite World Conference, July 30, 2020. https://mwc-cmm.org/resources/baptism-and-incorporation-body-christ-church.

Barclay, John M. G. *Paul and the Gift*. Grand Rapids: Eerdmans, 2015.

———. "Under Grace: The Christ-Gift and the Construction of a Christian Habitus." In *Apocalyptic Paul: Cosmos and Anthropos in Romans 5–8*, edited by Beverly Roberts Gaventa, 59–76. Waco, Tex.: Baylor University Press, 2013.

Barnes, Elizabeth. *The Minority Body: A Theory of Disability*. Studies in Feminist Philosophy. Oxford: Oxford University Press, 2016. https://doi.org/10.1093/acprof:oso/9780198732587.001.0001.

Barth, Karl. *The Epistle to the Romans*. Translated by Edwyn C. Hoskyns. New York: Oxford University Press, 1968.

———. *The Teaching of the Church Regarding Baptism*. Translated by Ernest A. Payne. 1948. Repr., Eugene, Oreg.: Wipf and Stock, 2006.

Barton, Sarah Jean. "A Critical Approach to Integrating Christian Disability Theology in Clinical Rehabilitation." *Journal of Disability & Religion* 21, no. 1 (2017): 5–13. https://doi.org/10.1080/23312521.2016.1269255.

Baynton, Douglas C. "'These Pushful Days': Time and Disability in the Age of Eugenics." *Health and History* 13, no. 2 (2011): 43–64. https://doi.org/10.5401/healthhist.13.2.0043.

Belcher, Kimberly Hope. *Efficacious Engagement: Sacramental Participation in the Trinitarian Mystery*. Collegeville, Minn.: Liturgical, 2011.

Berkman, John. "Are Persons with Profound Intellectual Disabilities Sacramental Icons of Heavenly Life? Aquinas on Impairment." *Studies in Christian Ethics* 26, no. 1 (2013): 83–96. https://doi.org/10.1177/0953946812466494.

Bernardin, Joseph. "Access to the Sacraments of Initiation and Reconciliation for Developmentally Disabled Persons." In *Developmental Disabilities and Sacramental Access: New Paradigms for Sacramental Encounters*, edited by Edward Foley, 141–49. Collegeville, Minn.: Liturgical, 1985.

Bevans, Stephen B. *Models of Contextual Theology*. Faith and Cultures Series. Maryknoll, N.Y.: Orbis Books, 2002.

Blacher, Jan, and Iris Tan Mink. "Interviewing Family Members and Care Providers: Concepts, Methodologies, and Cultures." In *The International Handbook of Applied Research in Intellectual Disabilities*, edited by Eric Emerson, Chris Hatton, Travis Thompson, and Trevor R. Parmenter, 133–59. Chichester, West Sussex: Wiley, 2004.

Black, Kathy. *A Healing Homiletic: Preaching and Disability*. Nashville: Abingdon, 1996.

Block, Jennie Weiss. *Copious Hosting: A Theology of Access for People with Disabilities*. New York: Continuum, 2002.

Boer, Theo A. "Meaning of Life and Meaning of Care: A Christian Perspective." In *Meaningful Care: A Multidisciplinary Approach to the Meaning of Care for People*

with Mental Retardation, edited by Joop Boer, Theo A. Stolk, and Ruth Seldenrijk, 51–63. Boston, Mass.: Kluwer Academic, 2000.
Bogdan, Robert, and Steven J. Taylor. "Relationships with Severely Disabled People: The Social Construction of Humanness." *Social Problems* 36, no. 2 (1989): 135–48. https://doi.org/10.1525/sp.1989.36.2.03a00030.
Bonhoeffer, Dietrich. *Creation and Fall: A Theological Exposition of Genesis 1–3*. Edited by John W. De Gruchy. Translated by Douglas Stephen Bax. Minneapolis: Fortress, 2004.
———. *Discipleship*. Translated by Barbara Green and Reinhard Krauss. Dietrich Bonhoeffer Works—Reader's Edition. Minneapolis: Fortress, 2015.
———. *The Collected Sermons of Dietrich Bonhoeffer*. Translated by Douglas W. Stott, Anne Schmidt-Lange, Isabel Best, Scott A. Moore, and Claudia D. Bergmann. Minneapolis: Fortress, 2012.
Bretherton, Luke. "Coming to Judgment: Methodological Reflections on the Relationship Between Ecclesiology, Ethnography and Political Theory." *Modern Theology* 28, no. 2 (2012): 167–96.
Brettler, M. Z., M. D. Coogan, and P. Perkins. *The New Oxford Annotated Bible: New Revised Standard Version: With the Apocrypha*. New York: Oxford University Press, 2010.
Brock, Brian. "How Can We Talk about Disability?" Lecture presented at the Summer Institute on Theology and Disability, Azusa, Calif., June 6, 2017.
———. "Introduction: Disability and the Quest for the Human." In *Disability in the Christian Tradition: A Reader*, edited by Brian Brock and John Swinton, 1–23. Grand Rapids: Eerdmans, 2012.
———. *Wondrously Wounded: Theology, Disability, and the Body of Christ*. Waco, Tex.: Baylor University Press, 2019.
Bromley, David G., and Lewis F. Carter. "Re-envisioning Field Research and Ethnographic Narrative." In *Toward Reflexive Ethnography: Participating, Observing, Narrating*, edited by David G. Bromley and Lewis F. Carter, 1–36. Oxford: JAI, 2001.
———. *Toward Reflexive Ethnography: Participating, Observing, Narrating*. Religion and the Social Order, vol. 9. Oxford: JAI Press, 2001.
Brown, Lydia. "The Significance of Semantics: Person-First Language: Why It Matters." Accessed August 3, 2021. https://www.autistichoya.com/2011/08/significance-of-semantics-person-first.html.
Butler, Judith. *Giving an Account of Oneself*. New York: Fordham University Press, 2005.
Byars, Ronald P. *The Sacraments in Biblical Perspective*. Interpretation: Resources for the Use of Scripture in the Church. Louisville, Ky.: Westminster John Knox, 2011.
Campbell, William S. *Paul and the Creation of Christian Identity*. New York: T&T Clark, 2008.
Carlson, Licia. *The Faces of Intellectual Disability: Philosophical Reflections*. Bloomington: Indiana University Press, 2009.

Carlson, Richard P. "The Role of Baptism in Paul's Thought." *Interpretation* 47, no. 3 (1993): 255–66.
Carter, Erik W. "A Place of Belonging: Research at the Intersection of Faith and Disability." *Review and Expositor* 113, no. 2 (2016): 167–80.
———. *Including People with Disabilities in Faith Communities: A Guide for Service Providers, Families, and Congregations*. Baltimore, Md.: Brookes, 2007.
———. "Supporting Inclusion and Flourishing in the Religious and Spiritual Lives of People with Intellectual and Developmental Disabilities." *Inclusion* 1, no. 1 (2013): 64–75.
Carter, Erik W., Harold L. Kleinert, Tony F. LoBianco, Kathleen Sheppard-Jones, Laura N. Butler, and Milton S. Tyree. "Congregational Participation of a National Sample of Adults with Intellectual and Developmental Disabilities." *Intellectual and Developmental Disabilities* 53, no. 6 (2015): 381–93.
CAST. "The UDL Guidelines," 2017.
Chappell, Timothy. "Knowledge of Persons." *European Journal for Philosophy of Religion* 5, no. 4 (2013): 3–28.
———. "On the Very Idea of Criteria for Personhood." *The Southern Journal of Philosophy* 49, no. 1 (2011): 1–27.
Charlton, James I. *Nothing about Us without Us: Disability Oppression and Empowerment*. Berkeley: University of California Press, 2000.
Clandinin, D. Jean. *Engaging in Narrative Inquiry*. Developing Qualitative Inquiry. New York: Routledge, 2016.
Clandinin, D. Jean, and F. Michael Connelly. *Narrative Inquiry: Experience and Story in Qualitative Research*. San Francisco: Jossey-Bass, 2000.
Cleghorn, Jocelyn. "The Ethnographic Method: A Case Study for Research among People with Severe Intellectual Disabilities." Presented at the Australasian Society for Intellectual Disability Conference, Fremantle, Western Australia, 2014.
Clifton, Shane. *Crippled Grace: Disability, Virtue Ethics, and the Good Life*. Studies in Religion, Theology, and Disability. Waco, Tex.: Baylor University Press, 2018.
Collins, Raymond F. "Second Corinthians." In *Paideia Commentaries on the New Testament*, edited by M. C. Parsons and C. H. Talbert. Grand Rapids: Baker Academic, 2013.
Conner, Benjamin T. *Amplifying Our Witness: Giving Voice to Adolescents with Developmental Disabilities*. Grand Rapids: Eerdmans, 2012.
———. *Disabling Mission, Enabling Witness: Exploring Missiology through the Lens of Disability Studies*. Missiological Engagements Series. Downers Grove: InterVarsity, 2018.
———. "For the Fitness of Their Witness: Missional Christian Practices." In *Converting Witness: The Future of Christian Mission in the New Millennium*, edited by John G. Flett and David W. Congdon. Lanham, Md.: Fortress Academic, 2019.
Cooper, Adam G. *Holy Eros: A Liturgical Theology of the Body*. Kettering, Ohio: Angelico, 2014.
Copeland, M. Shawn. *Enfleshing Freedom: Body, Race, and Being*. Innovations. Minneapolis: Fortress, 2010.

Cousar, Charles B. "Continuity and Discontinuity: Reflections on Romans 5–8 (In Conversation with Frank Thielman)." In *Pauline Theology, Volume III: Romans*, edited by David M. Hay and E. Elizabeth Johnson, III:196–210. Minneapolis: Fortress, 1995.

Creamer, Deborah Beth. *Disability and Christian Theology: Embodied Limits and Constructive Possibilities*. Academy Series. New York: Oxford University Press, 2009.

Creswell, John W., and Cheryl N. Poth. *Qualitative Inquiry and Research Design: Choosing among Five Approaches*. 4th ed. Los Angeles: SAGE, 2018.

Cross, Richard. "Baptism, Faith and Severe Cognitive Impairment in Some Medieval Theologies." *International Journal of Systematic Theology* 14, no. 4 (2012): 420–38. https://doi.org/doi:10.1111/j.1468-2400.2012.00652.x.

———. "Disability, Impairment, and Some Medieval Accounts of the Incarnation Suggestions for a Theology of Personhood." *Modern Theology* 27, no. 4 (2011): 639–58.

Cuddeback-Gedeon, Lorraine. "How Fair Is Fair? Reflections on Informed Consent and Inclusive Research with the IDD Community." *National Catholic Bioethics Quarterly* 20, no. 2 (2020): 251–62.

———. "'Nothing about Us without Us:' Ethnography, Conscientization, and the Epistemic Challenges of Intellectual Disability." *Practical Matters* 11 (2018): 1–18.

Dalton, Arthur J., and Keith R. McVilly. "Ethics Guidelines for International, Multicenter Research Involving People with Intellectual Disabilities." *Journal of Policy and Practice in Intellectual Disabilities* 1 (2004): 57–70.

Davies, Charlotte Aull. *Reflexive Ethnography: A Guide to Researching Selves and Others*. London: Routledge, 1999.

Davies, Douglas James. *Anthropology and Theology*. Oxford: Berg, 2002.

Davis, Lennard J. *Enforcing Normalcy: Disability, Deafness, and the Body*. New York: Verso, 1995.

Dewey, Arthur J., and Anna C. Miller. "Paul." In *The Bible and Disability: A Commentary*, edited by Sarah J. Melcher, Mikeal C. Parsons, and Amos Yong. Waco, Tex.: Baylor University Press, 2017.

Disability and Faith Forum. "Should We Baptize People with Intellectual Disabilities?" Disability and Faith Forum. https://disabilityandfaith.org/should-we-baptize-people-with-intellectual-disabilities/.

Disability Language Style Guide. National Center on Disability and Journalism. https://ncdj.org/style-guide/.

Dix, Dom Gregory. *The Shape of the Liturgy*. New edition. New York: Bloomsburg, 2005.

Dolmage, Jay Timothy. *Academic Ableism: Disability and Higher Education*. Ann Arbor: University of Michigan Press, 2017.

Douglas, Kelly Brown. *The Black Christ*. Bishop Henry McNeal Turner Studies in North American Black Religion 9. Maryknoll, N.Y.: Orbis, 1993.

Dueck, Irma Fast. "It's Only Water: The Ritual of Baptism and the Formation of Christian Identity." *Vision: A Journal for Church & Theology* 14, no. 1 (2011): 21–27.

Dykstra, Craig. "Pastoral and Ecclesial Imagination." In *For Life Abundant: Practical Theology, Theological Education, and Christian Ministry*, edited by Dorothy C. Bass and Craig Dykstra. Grand Rapids: Eerdmans, 2008.

Dykstra, Craig R., and Dorothy C. Bass. "A Theological Understanding of Christian Practices." In *Practicing Theology: Beliefs and Practices in Christian Life*. Edited by Miroslav Volf and Dorothy C. Bass. Grand Rapids: Eerdmans, 2002.

Eastman, Susan. "Ashes on the Frontal Lobe." Presented at the Society of Biblical Literature, Chicago, 2012.

———. *Paul and the Person: Reframing Paul's Anthropology*. Grand Rapids: Eerdmans, 2017.

———. "The Shadow Side of Second-Person Engagement: Sin in Paul's Letter to the Romans." *European Journal for Philosophy of Religion* 4/5 (2013): 125–44.

Edie, Fred P. *Book, Bath, Table, and Time: Christian Worship as Source and Resource for Youth Ministry*. Youth Ministry Alternatives. Cleveland, Ohio: The Pilgrim Press, 2007.

Eiesland, Nancy L. *The Disabled God: Toward a Liberatory Theology of Disability*. Nashville: Abingdon, 1994.

Emerson, Eric, and Chris Hatton, eds. *Clinical Psychology and People with Intellectual Disabilities*. Malden, Mass.: Wiley-Blackwell, 2012.

Episcopal Church, The. *The Book of Common Prayer and Administration of the Sacraments and Other Rites and Ceremonies of the Church: Together with the Psalter or Psalms of David According to the Use of the Episcopal Church*. New York: Seabury, 1979.

———. *The Book of Occasional Services*. Conforming to General Convention 2018. New York: Church Publishing, 2018.

Evans, William. "'I Am Not a Dyslexic Person I'm a Person with Dyslexia': Identity Constructions of Dyslexia among Students in Nurse Education." *Journal of Advanced Nursing* 70, no. 2 (2014): 360–72. https://doi.org/10.1111/jan.12199.

Felton, Gayle Carlton. *By Water and the Spirit: Making Connections for Identity and Ministry*. Nashville: Discipleship Resources, 2003.

Ferguson, Everett. *Baptism in the Early Church: History, Theology, and Liturgy in the First Five Centuries*. Grand Rapids: Eerdmans, 2009.

Fiddes, Paul S. "Ecclesiology and Ethnography: Two Disciplines, Two Worlds?" In *Perspectives on Ecclesiology and Ethnography*, edited by Pete Ward, 13–35. Grand Rapids: Eerdmans, 2012.

Fischer, Michael M. J. "Ethnicity and the Post-Modern Arts of Memory." In *Writing Culture: The Poetics and Politics of Ethnography*, edited by James Clifford and George E. Marcus, 194–233. Berkeley: University of California Press, 1986.

Fisher, Marisa H. "Heightened Social Vulnerability Among Adults with IDD: Findings, Perspectives, and Needed Interventions." In *Maltreatment of People with Intellectual and Developmental Disabilities*, edited by John R. Lutzker; Kate Guastaferro; Megan L. Benka-Coker, 139–62. Washington, D.C.: American Association on Intellectual and Developmental Disabilities, 2016.

Florer-Bixler, Melissa. "Baptism and Profound Disability." *ADNotes*, 2011.

———. "Believers Baptism as Supported Decision." *Conrad Grebel Review* 38, no. 2 (2020): 135–46.
Ford, David. *Self and Salvation: Being Transformed*. Cambridge Studies in Christian Doctrine 1. Cambridge: Cambridge University Press, 1999.
Fowler, Stanley K. *More Than a Symbol: The British Baptist Recovery of Baptismal Sacramentalism*. Studies in Baptist History and Thought, vol. 2. Cumbria, UK: Paternoster, 2002.
Fox, Bethany McKinney. *Disability and the Way of Jesus: Holistic Healing in the Gospels and the Church*. Downers Grove: IVP Academic, 2019.
Francis, Mark R. "Celebrating the Sacraments with Those with Developmental Disabilities: Sacramental/Liturgical Reflections." In *Developmental Disabilities and Sacramental Access: New Paradigms for Sacramental Encounters*, edited by Edward Foley, 73–93. Collegeville, Minn.: Liturgical, 1994.
Fricker, Miranda. *Epistemic Injustice: Power and the Ethics of Knowing*. Oxford: Oxford University Press, 2009.
Fulkerson, Mary McClintock. "Ecclesiology, Exclusion, and Sacraments." In *Ecclesiology and Exclusion: Boundaries of Being and Belonging in Postmodern Times*, edited by Dennis M. Doyle, Timothy J. Furry, and Pascal D. Bazzell, 239–46. Maryknoll, N.Y.: Orbis Books, 2012.
———. *Places of Redemption: Theology for a Worldly Church*. New York: Oxford University Press, 2007.
———. "Roundtable on *Ethnography as Christian Theology and Ethics*: Ethnography: A Gift to Theology and Ethics." *Practical Matters* 6 (Spring 2013): 1–9.
Furnish, Victor Paul. "II Corinthians." In *The Anchor Bible*, edited by W. F. Albright and D. N. Freedman, vol. 32A. Garden City, N.Y.: Doubleday, 1984.
Gaventa, William C. *Disability and Spirituality: Recovering Wholeness*. Waco, Tex.: Baylor University Press, 2018.
———. "Preaching Disability: The Whole of Christ's Body in Word and Practice." *Review and Expositor* 113, no. 2 (2016): 225–42.
Gernsbacher, Morton Ann. "The Use of Person-First Language in Scholarly Writing May Accentuate Stigma." *Journal of Child Psychology and Psychiatry* 58, no. 7 (2017): 859–61. https://doi.org/10.1111/jcpp.12706.
Goode, David. *A World without Words: The Social Construction of Children Born Deaf and Blind*. Health, Society, and Policy. Philadelphia: Temple University Press, 1994.
Gould, Stephen Jay. *The Mismeasure of Man*. New York: Norton, 1996.
Greggs, Tom. "Bearing Sin in the Church: The Ecclesial Hamartiology of Bonhoeffer." In *Christ, Church and World: New Studies in Bonhoeffer's Theology and Ethics*, edited by Michael Mawson and Philip G. Ziegler, 77–99. London: T&T Clark, 2016.
Greig, Jason Reimer. *Reconsidering Intellectual Disability: L'Arche, Medical Ethics, and Christian Friendship*. Moral Traditions Series. Baltimore, Md.: Georgetown University Press, 2015.
———. "Re-imagining Narratives: Anabaptist Baptismal Theology and Profound Cognitive Impairment." *Conrad Grebel Review* 38, no. 2 (2020): 120–34.

Griffin, Megan M., Lydia W. Kane, Courtney Taylor, Susan H. Francis, and Robert M. Hodapp. "Characteristics of Inclusive Faith Communities: A Preliminary Survey of Inclusive Practices in the United States." *Journal of Applied Research in Intellectual Disabilities* 25 (2012): 383–91.

Griffin, Tim, and Susan Balandin. "Ethical Research Involving People with Intellectual Disabilities." In *The International Handbook of Applied Research in Intellectual Disabilities*, edited by Eric Emerson, 61–82. Chichester, West Sussex: Wiley, 2004.

Grigoni, Michael R. "Beyond the Church and the Poor: Expanding the Subject of Ethnographic Theology." *Ecclesial Practices* 8, no. 1 (2021): 89–104. https://doi.org/10.1163/22144471-bja10027.

Gundersen, Joan R. *The Anglican Ministry in Virginia, 1723–1766: A Study of Social Class*. Hamden, Conn.: Garland, 1989.

Gunton, Colin E. *The One, the Three, and the Many: God, Creation, and the Culture of Modernity*. Cambridge: Cambridge University Press, 1993.

Gustavsson, Anders, Catarina Nyberg, and Charles Westin. "Plurality and Continuity–Understanding Self-Identity of Persons with Intellectual Disability." *Alter* 10, no. 4 (2016): 310–26. https://doi.org/10.1016/j.alter.2016.06.003.

Habets, Myk. "'Suffer the Little Children to Come to Me, for Theirs Is the Kingdom of Heaven.' Infant Salvation and the Destiny of the Severely Mentally Disabled." In *Evangelical Calvinism: Essays Resourcing the Continuing Reformation of the Church*, edited by Myk Habets and Bobby Grow, 287–328. Eugene, Oreg.: Pickwick Publications, 2012.

Hall, Amy Laura. "A Ravishing and Restful Sight: Seeing with Julian of Norwich." In *Disability in the Christian Tradition: A Reader*, edited by Brian Brock and John Swinton, 152–83. Grand Rapids: Eerdmans, 2012.

Haller, Beth, Bruce Dorries, and Jessica Rahn. "Media Labeling *versus* the US Disability Community Identity: A Study of Shifting Cultural Language." *Disability & Society* 21, no. 1 (2006): 61–75. https://doi.org/10.1080/09687590500375416.

Harrington, Mary Therese. "Affectivity and Symbol in the Process of Catechesis." In *Developmental Disabilities and Sacramental Access: New Paradigms for Sacramental Encounters*, edited by Edward Foley, 116–29. Collegeville, Minn.: Liturgical, 1994.

Harris, Murray J. "The Second Epistle to the Corinthians: A Commentary on the Greek Text." In *The New International Greek Testament Commentary*, edited by I. H. Marshall and D. A. Hagner. Grand Rapids: Eerdmans, 2005.

Harshaw, Jill. *God beyond Words: Christian Theology and the Spiritual Experiences of People with Profound Intellectual Disabilities*. Studies in Religion and Theology. London: Jessica Kingsley, 2016.

———. "Prophetic Voices, Silent Words: The Prophetic Role of Persons with Profound Intellectual Disabilities in Contemporary Christianity." *Practical Theology* 3, no. 3 (2010): 311–29.

Haslam, Molly C. *A Constructive Theology of Intellectual Disability: Human Being as Mutuality and Response*. New York: Fordham University Press, 2011.

Hatchett, Marion J. *Commentary on the American Prayer Book*. New York: Harper-Collins, 1995.
Hauerwas, Stanley. *Suffering Presence: Theological Reflections on Medicine, the Mentally Handicapped, and the Church*. Notre Dame, Ind.: University of Notre Dame Press, 1986.
———. "The Gesture of a Truthful Story." In *Critical Reflections on Stanley Hauerwas' Theology of Disability: Disabling Society, Enabling Theology*. Binghamton, N.Y.: Haworth Pastoral, 2004.
Hauerwas, Stanley, and Jean Vanier. *Living Gently in a Violent World: The Prophetic Witness of Weakness*. Resources for Reconciliation. Downers Grove: IVP Books, 2008.
Hauerwas, Stanley, and Samuel Wells. "Christian Ethics as Informed Prayer." In *The Blackwell Companion to Christian Ethics*, edited by Stanley Hauerwas and Samuel Wells, 2nd ed. Malden, Mass.: Blackwell, 2011.
———. "The Gift of the Church and the Gifts God Gives It." In *The Blackwell Companion to Christian Ethics*, edited by Stanley Hauerwas and Samuel Wells, 2nd ed. Malden, Mass.: Blackwell Publishing, 2011.
Hawkins, J. Barney, IV. "The Episcopal Church in the United States of America." In *The Wiley-Blackwell Companion to the Anglican Communion*, edited by Ian S. Markham, J. Barney Hawkins IV, Justyn Terry, and Leslie Nuñez Steffesen, 508–15. Malden, Mass.: John Wiley & Sons Ltd., 2013.
Healy, Donald E., Jr. "Rediscovering the Mysteria: Sacramental Stories from Persons with Disabilities, Their Families, and Their Faith Communities." *Journal of Religion, Disability & Health* 13 (2009): 194–235.
Healy, Nicholas M. *Church, World and the Christian Life: Practical-Prophetic Ecclesiology*. Cambridge Studies in Christian Doctrine 7. Cambridge: Cambridge University Press, 2000.
Hefling, Charles. "Introduction: Anglicans and Common Prayer." In *The Oxford Guide to the Book of Common Prayer: A Worldwide Survey*, edited by Charles Hefling and Cynthia Shattuck, 29–41. New York: Oxford University Press, 2006.
Hendershot, Gerry. "A Statistical Note on the Religiosity of Persons with Disabilities." *Disability Studies Quarterly* 26, no. 4 (2006): 1–8.
Hinchliff, Peter. "The Modern Period." In *The Study of Liturgy*, edited by Cheslyn Jones, Geoffrey Wainwright, Edward Yarnold, and Paul Bradshaw, 167–83. New York: Oxford University Press, 1992.
Huels, John M. "Canonical Rights to the Sacraments." In *Developmental Disabilities and Sacramental Access: New Paradigms for Sacramental Encounters*, edited by Edward Foley, 94–115. Collegeville, Minn.: Liturgical, 1994.
The International Handbook of Applied Research in Intellectual Disabilities. Chichester, West Sussex: Wiley, 2004.
Jacober, Amy. *Redefining Perfect: The Interplay between Theology and Disability*. Eugene, Oreg.: Cascade Books, 2017.

Jacobs, Alan. *The Book of Common Prayer: A Biography*. Lives of Great Religious Books. Princeton, N.J.: Princeton University Press, 2013.
James, Nancy Carol. "Liturgy in the Anglican Communion." In *The Wiley-Blackwell Companion to the Anglican Communion*, edited by Ian S. Markham, J. Barney Hawkins IV, Justyn Terry, and Leslie Nuñez Steffesen, 594–605. Malden, Mass.: John Wiley & Sons Ltd., 2013.
Jennings, Willie James. *Acts: A Theological Commentary on the Bible*. Belief: A Theological Commentary on the Bible. Unabridged ed. Louisville, Ky.: Westminster John Knox, 2017.
———. "Being Baptized: Race." In *The Blackwell Companion to Christian Ethics*, edited by Stanley Hauerwas and Samuel Wells, 277–89. 2nd ed. Malden, Mass.: Wiley-Blackwell, 2011.
———. "Grace without Remainder: Why Baptists Should Baptize Their Babies." In *Grace Upon Grace: Essays in Honor of Thomas A. Langford*, edited by L. Gregory Jones, Robert Johnston, and Jonathan Wilson, 201–6. Nashville: Abingdon, 1999.
Jensen, Robin M. *Baptismal Imagery in Early Christianity: Ritual, Visual, and Theological Dimensions*. Grand Rapids: Baker Academic, 2012.
Jewett, Robert, and Roy David Kotansky. *Romans: A Commentary on the Book of Romans*. Edited by Eldon Jay Epp. Hermeneia. Minneapolis: Augsburg Fortress, 2006.
Johnson, Maxwell. *The Rites of Christian Initiation: Their Evolution and Interpretation*. Rev. ed. Collegeville, Minn.: Liturgical, 2007.
Juskus, Ryan. "Revealers, Skeptics, and Witnesses: Advancing a Witness Methodology in Ethnographic Theology and Ethics." *Ecclesial Practices* 8, no. 1 (2021): 26–42. https://doi.org/10.1163/22144471-bja10011.
Kafer, Alison. *Feminist, Queer, Crip*. Bloomington: Indiana University Press, 2013.
Käsemann, Ernst. *Perspectives on Paul*. Philadelphia: Fortress, 1971.
Kasnitz, Devva, and Russell P. Shuttleworth. "Introduction: Anthropology in Disability Studies." *Disability Studies Quarterly* 21, no. 3 (2001): 2–17.
Keck, Leander E. *Romans*. Abingdon New Testament Commentaries. Nashville: Abingdon, 2005.
———. "What Makes Romans Tick?" In *Pauline Theology*, volume 3: *Romans*, edited by David M. Hay and E. Elizabeth Johnson, 3–29. Minneapolis: Fortress, 1995.
Keith, Heather E., and Kenneth D. Keith. *Intellectual Disability: Ethics, Dehumanization, and a New Moral Community*. Chichester, West Sussex: Wiley-Blackwell, 2013.
Kelly, Christine. "Building Bridges with Accessible Care: Disability Studies, Feminist Care Scholarship, and Beyond." *Hypatia* 28, no. 4 (2013): 784–800.
Kidney, Colleen A., and Katherine E. McDonald. "A Toolkit for Accessible and Respectful Engagement in Research." *Disability & Society* 29 (2014): 1013–30.
Kittay, Eva Feder. "Centering Justice on Dependency and Recovering Freedom." *Hypatia* 30, no. 1 (2015): 285–91.

Lambelet, Kyle B. T., and Jon Kara Shields. "Introduction: Finding God in the Fieldnotes." *Ecclesial Practices* 8 (2021).
Lappa, Christina, Ioannis Anastasiou, Constantinos Mantzikos, and Nicholas Kyparissos. "Teaching the Christian Orthodox Mystery of Baptism to Adults with Moderate or Severe Intellectual Disability." *International Journal of Humanities and Social Science Invention* 7, no. 3 (2018): 64–74.
Lathrop, Gordon W. *Holy Things: A Liturgical Theology*. Minneapolis: Fortress, 1993.
Leeb, Rebecca T., Jennifer W. Kaminski. "The Association Between Childhood Disability and Child Maltreatment." In *Maltreatment of People with Intellectual and Developmental Disabilities*, edited by John R. Lutzker, Kate Guastaferro, and Megan L. Benka-Coker, 11–81. Washington, D.C.: American Association on Intellectual and Developmental Disabilities, 2016.
Leithart, Peter J. *The Baptized Body*. Moscow, Idaho: Canon, 2007.
Linton, Simi. *Claiming Disability: Knowledge and Identity*. Cultural Front. N. Y.: New York University Press, 1998.
Liu, Eleanor X., Erik W. Carter, Thomas L. Boehm, Naomi H. Annandale, and Courtney E. Taylor. "In Their Own Words: The Place of Faith in the Lives of Young People with Autism and Intellectual Disability." *Intellectual and Developmental Disabilities* 52, no. 5 (2014): 388–404.
Livingstone, E. A. *The Concise Oxford Dictionary of the Christian Church*. 3rd ed. Oxford: Oxford University Press, 2013.
Macaskill, Grant. *Autism and the Church: Bible, Theology, and Community*. Waco, Tex.: Baylor University Press, 2019.
Magasi, Susan. "Disability Studies in Practice: A Work in Progress." *Topics in Stroke Rehabilitation* 15, no. 6 (2008): 611–17. https://doi.org/10.1310/tsr1506-611.
———. "Infusing Disability Studies into the Rehabilitation Sciences." *Topics in Stroke Rehabilitation* 15, no. 3 (2008): 283–87. https://doi.org/10.1310/tsr1503-283.
Marshall, Paul V. *Prayer Book Parallels*. New York: Church Hymnal Corp., 1989.
Martin, Ralph P. "2 Corinthians." In *Word Biblical Commentary*, edited by D. A. Hubbard and G. W. Barker, vol. 40. Waco, Tex.: Word Books, 1986.
Martyn, J. Louis. "Epistemology at the Turn of the Ages: 2 Corinthians 5:16." In *Christian History and Interpretation: Studies Presented to John Knox*, edited by W. R. Farmer, C. F. D. Moule, and R. R. Niebuhr. Cambridge: Cambridge University Press, 1967.
Matera, Frank J. "II Corinthians: A Commentary." In *The New Testament Library*, edited by C. C. Black, J. T. Carroll, and B. R. Gaventa. Louisville, Ky.: Westminster John Knox Press, 2003.
Matthews, Pia. *Pope John Paul II and the Apparently "non-Acting" Person*. Leominster, United Kingdom: Gracewing, 2013.
Mawson, Michael. "Creatures before God: Bonhoeffer, Disability and Theological Anthropology." In *Christ, Church and World: New Studies in Bonhoeffer's Theology and Ethics*, edited by Michael Mawson and Philip G. Ziegler, 119–40. London: T&T Clark, 2016.

———. "The Sin of Disability: Why Disability Theology Needs a Doctrine of Sin." In *Knowing, Being Known, and the Mystery of God: Essays in Honor of Professor Hans Reinders: Teacher, Friend, and Disciple*, edited by Bill Gaventa and Erik De Jongh, 93–103. Amsterdam: VU University Press, 2016.

McClintock Fulkerson, Mary. "Interpreting a Situation: When Is 'Empirical' Also 'Theological'?" In *Perspectives on Ecclesiology and Ethnography*, edited by Pete Ward, 124–44. Grand Rapids: Eerdmans, 2012.

McDonald, Katherine E. "'We Want Respect': Adults with Intellectual and Developmental Disabilities Address Respect in Research." *American Journal on Intellectual and Developmental Disabilities* 117, no. 4 (2012): 263–74.

McDonald, Katherine E., Nicole E. Conroy, Robert S. Olick, and the Project ETHICS Expert Panel. "Is It Worth It? Benefits in Research with Adults with Intellectual Disability." *Intellectual and Developmental Disabilities* 54, no. 6 (2016): 440–53.

McDonald, Katherine E., and Colleen A. Kidney. "What Is Right? Ethics in Intellectual Disabilities Research." *Journal of Policy and Practice in Intellectual Disabilities* 9, no. 1 (2012): 27–39.

McGrath, Alister E. "The Cultivation of Theological Vision: Theological Attentiveness and the Practice of Ministry." In *Perspectives on Ecclesiology and Ethnography*, edited by Pete Ward, 107–23. Grand Rapids: Eerdmans, 2012.

Meador, Keith G., and Joel James Shuman. "Who/se We Are: Baptism as Personhood." *Christian Bioethics* 6, no. 1 (2000): 71–83.

Merriam, Sharan B., and Elizabeth J. Tisdell. *Qualitative Research: A Guide to Design and Implementation*. 4th ed. San Francisco: Jossey-Bass, 2016.

Meyer, Paul W. *The Word in This World: Essays in New Testament Exegesis and Theology*. The New Testament Library. Louisville, Ky.: Westminster John Knox, 2004.

Meyers, Ruth A. "Rites of Initiation." In *The Oxford Guide to the Book of Common Prayer: A Worldwide Survey*, edited by Charles Hefling and Cynthia Shattuck, 1096–1133. New York: Oxford University Press, 2006.

———. "The Baptismal Covenant and the Proposed Anglican Covenant." *Journal of Anglican Studies* 10, no. 1 (2011): 31–41.

Mikoski, Gordon S. *Baptism and Christian Identity: Teaching in the Triune Name*. Grand Rapids: Eerdmans, 2009.

Miller, Valerie, and Camille Skubik-Peplaski. "A Systemic Review of Supports for Participation in Faith Settings for People with Disabilities." *Inclusion* 8, no. 2 (June 2020): 105–23. https://doi.org/10.1352/2326-6988-8.2.105.

Moschella, Mary Clark. *Ethnography as a Pastoral Practice: An Introduction*. Cleveland, Ohio: Pilgrim, 2008.

Newbigin, Leslie. "Not Whole without the Handicapped." In *Partners in Life: The Handicapped and the Church*, edited by Geiko Müller-Fahrenholz. Geneva: World Council of Churches, 1979.

Newman, Barbara J. *Accessible Gospel, Inclusive Worship*. Wyoming, Mich.: CLC Network, 2015.

Bibliography | 225

Northup, Lesley A. "The Episcopal Church in the U.S.A." In *The Oxford Guide to the Book of Common Prayer: A Worldwide Survey*, edited by Charles Hefling and Cynthia Shattuck, 823–42. New York: Oxford University Press, 2006.

Nouwen, Henri J. M. *Life of the Beloved: Spiritual Living in a Secular World*. New York: Crossroad, 2002.

O'Hanlon, Elizabeth E. "Religion and Disability: The Experiences of Families of Children with Special Needs." *Journal of Religion, Disability & Health* 17, no. 1 (2013): 42–61.

Parekh, Ranna. "What Is Intellectual Disability?" American Psychiatric Association, last modified July 2017, accessed October 15, 2018, https://www.psychiatry.org/patients-families/intellectual-disability/what-is-intellectual-disability.

Peña, Edlyn Vallejo, Lissa D. Stapleton, and Lenore Malone Schaffer. "Critical Perspectives on Disability Identity." *New Directions for Student Services* 154 (Summer 2016): 85–96. https://doi.org/10.1002/ss.20177.

"People First: Adults with Disabilities Speak for Themselves." Accessed August 3, 2021. https://www.factmo.org/people-first/#PeopleFirst.

Perry, Jonathan. "Interviewing People with Intellectual Disabilities." In *The International Handbook of Applied Research in Intellectual Disabilities*, edited by Eric Emerson, 115–31. Chichester, West Sussex: Wiley, 2004.

Piper, John. "Believer Baptism and Mental Disabilities." Desiring God (blog). https://www.desiringgod.org/interviews/believer-baptism-and-mental-disabilities.

The Plain Language Action and Information Network. "Federal Plain Language Guidelines," 2011.

Podmore, Colin. "The Baptismal Revolution in the American Episcopal Church: Baptismal Ecclesiology and the Baptismal Covenant." *Ecclesiology* 6 (2010): 8–38.

Polkinghorne, Donald E. "Validity Issues in Narrative Research." *Qualitative Inquiry* 13, no. 4 (2007): 471–86. https://doi.org/10.1177/1077800406297670.

Presbyterian Church (U.S.A.). *Invitation to Christ*. Louisville, Ky.: Presbyterian Church (U.S.A.), 2006.

Prosser, Helen, and Jo Bromley. "Interviewing People with Intellectual Disabilities." In *Clinical Psychology and People with Intellectual Disabilities*, edited by Eric Emerson and Chris Hatton, 107–20. Malden, Mass.: Wiley-Blackwell, 2012.

Reimer-Barry, Emily. "The Listening Church: How Ethnography Can Transform Catholic Ethics." In *Ethnography as Christian Theology and Ethics*, edited by Christian Scharen and Aana Marie Vigen, 97–117. New York: Continuum, 2011.

Reinders, Hans S. *Receiving the Gift of Friendship: Profound Disability, Theological Anthropology, and Ethics*. Grand Rapids: Eerdmans, 2008.

Reynolds, Thomas E. *Vulnerable Communion: A Theology of Disability and Hospitality*. Grand Rapids: Brazos, 2008.

Roberts, Dorothy E. *Killing the Black Body: Race, Reproduction, and the Meaning of Liberty*. New York: Vintage Books, 1999.

Robinson, John A. T. *The Body: A Study in Pauline Theology*. Chicago: Henry Regnery Company, 1952.

Rodgers, Jackie. "Trying to Get It Right: Undertaking Research Involving People with Learning Difficulties." *Disability & Society* 14 (1999): 421–33.
Romero, Miguel J. "Aquinas on the Corporis Infirmitas: Broken Flesh and the Grammar of Grace." In *Disability in the Christian Tradition: A Reader*, edited by Brian Brock and John Swinton, 101–51. Grand Rapids: Eerdmans, 2012.
"SABE USA." Accessed August 3, 2021. https://www.sabeusa.org/.
Saldaña, Johnny. *The Coding Manual for Qualitative Researchers*. 3rd ed. Los Angeles: SAGE, 2016.
———. *The Coding Manual for Qualitative Researchers*. 4th ed. SAGE, 2021.
Saliers, Don E. "Toward a Spirituality of Inclusiveness." In *Human Disability and the Service of God: Reassessing Religious Practice*, edited by Nancy L. Eiesland and Don E. Saliers, 19–31. Nashville: Abingdon, 1998.
Sampley, Paul J. "The Second Letter to the Corinthians." In *New Interpreter's Bible*, edited by L. E. Keck, Vol. 11. Nashville: Abingdon, 2000.
Schalock, Robert L., and David Felce. "Quality of Life and Subjective Well-Being: Conceptual and Measurement Issues." In *The International Handbook of Applied Research in Intellectual Disabilities*, edited by Eric Emerson, 261–79. Chichester, West Sussex: Wiley, 2004.
Scharen, Christian. "Ecclesiology 'From the Body': Ethnographic Notes toward a Carnal Theology." In *Perspectives on Ecclesiology and Ethnography*, edited by Pete Ward, 50–70. Grand Rapids: Eerdmans, 2012.
Scharen, Christian, and Aana Marie Vigen. *Ethnography as Christian Theology and Ethics*. New York: Continuum, 2011.
———. "Preface: Blurring Boundaries." In *Ethnography as Christian Theology and Ethics*, edited by Christian Scharen and Aana Marie Vigen, xvii–xxviii. New York: Continuum, 2011.
———. "Theological Justification for Turning to Ethnography." In *Ethnography as Christian Theology and Ethics*, edited by Christian Scharen and Aana Marie Vigen, 58–74. New York: Continuum, 2011.
———. "What Is Ethnography?" In *Ethnography as Christian Theology and Ethics*, edited by Christian Scharen and Aana Marie Vigen, 3–27. New York: Continuum, 2011.
Schmemann, Alexander. *Introduction to Liturgical Theology*. Crestwood, N.Y.: St. Vladimir's Seminary Press, 1966.
———. *Of Water and the Spirit: A Liturgical Study of Baptism*. Crestwood, N.Y.: St. Vladimir's Seminary Press, 1974.
Schnackenburg, Rudolf. *Baptism in the Thought of St. Paul*. Oxford: Basil Blackwell, 1964.
Schwartz, Ariel E., Jessica M. Kramer, Ellen S. Cohn, and Katherine E. McDonald. "'That Felt Like Real Engagement': Fostering and Maintaining Inclusive Research Collaborations with Individuals with Intellectual Disability." *Qualitative Health Research* 30, no. 2 (2020): 236–49. https://doi.org/10.1177/1049732319869620.
Siikavirta, Samuli. *Baptism and Cognition in Romans 6–8: Paul's Ethics Beyond 'Indicative' and 'Imperative.'* Wissenschaftliche Untersuchungen Zum Neuen Testament. Tübingen, Germany: Mohr Siebeck, 2015.

Singer, Peter. *Practical Ethics*. 3rd ed. Cambridge: Cambridge University Press, 2011.
Slocum, Victoria. "Recommendations for Including People with Intellectual Disabilities in Faith Communities." *Christian Education Journal* 13, no. 1 (2016): 109–26.
Smith, Susan Marie. *Caring Liturgies: The Pastoral Power of Christian Ritual*. Minneapolis: Fortress, 2012.
Spinks, Bryan D. *Early and Medieval Rituals and Theologies of Baptism: From the New Testament to the Council of Trent*. Liturgy, Worship and Society. New York: Routledge, 2006.
———. *Reformation and Modern Rituals and Theologies of Baptism: From Luther to Contemporary Practices*. Burlington, Vt.: Ashgate, 2006.
Spohn, William C. "Scripture." In *The Oxford Handbook of Theological Ethics*, edited by Gilbert Meilaender and William Werpehowski, 93–111. New York: Oxford University Press, 2007.
Spurrier, Rebecca F. *The Disabled Church: Human Difference and the Art of Communal Worship*. New York: Fordham University Press, 2019.
Stack, Erin, and Katherine E. McDonald. "Nothing about Us without Us: Does Action Research in Developmental Disabilities Research Measure Up?" *Journal of Policy and Practice in Intellectual Disabilities* 11, no. 2 (2014): 83–91.
Stevenson, Kenneth. "Worship by the Book." In *The Oxford Guide to the Book of Common Prayer: A Worldwide Survey*, edited by Charles Hefling and Cynthia Shattuck, 44–72. New York: Oxford University Press, 2006.
Stewart-Ginsburg, Jared H., Cynthia C. Baughan, JaneDiane Smith, and Belva C. Collins. "Sanctuaries, 'Special Needs,' and Service: Religious Leader Perceptions on Including Children with Disability." *Journal of Disability & Religion* 24, no. 4 (October 1, 2020): 413–30. https://doi.org/10.1080/23312521.2020.1776188.
Swinton, John. *Becoming Friends of Time: Disability, Timefullness, and Gentle Discipleship*. Waco, Tex.: Baylor University Press, 2016.
———. "Building a Church for Strangers." *Journal of Religion, Disability & Health* 4, no. 4 (2008): 25–63.
———. *Dementia: Living in the Memories of God*. Grand Rapids: Eerdmans, 2012.
———. "Disability Theology." In *The Cambridge Dictionary of Christian Theology*, edited by Ian A. McFarland, David A. S. Fergusson, Karen Kilby, and Iain R. Torrance. Cambridge: Cambridge University Press, 2010.
———. "The Body of Christ Has Down Syndrome: Theological Reflections on Vulnerability, Disability, and Graceful Communities." In *On Moral Medicine: Theological Perspectives in Medical Ethics*, edited by M. Therese Lysaught, Joseph Kotva, Stephen E. Lammers, and Allen Verhey, 613–18. 3rd ed. Grand Rapids: Eerdmans, 2012.
———. "'Where Is Your Church?' Moving Toward a Hospitable and Sanctified Ethnography." In *Perspectives on Ecclesiology and Ethnography*, edited by Pete Ward, 71–92. Grand Rapids: Eerdmans, 2012.
———. "Who Is the God We Worship? Theologies of Disability; Challenges and New Possibilities." *International Journal of Practical Theology* 14, no. 2 (2010): 273–307.

Swinton, John, and Harriet Mowat. *Practical Theology and Qualitative Research*. 2nd ed. London: SCM, 2016.
Swinton, John, Harriet Mowat, and Susannah Baines. "Whose Story Am I? Redescribing Profound Intellectual Disability in the Kingdom of God." *Journal of Religion, Disability & Health* 15, no. 1 (2011): 5–19. https://doi.org/10.1080/15228967.2011.539337.
Tassé, Marc J. "Defining Intellectual Disability: Finally We All Agree... Almost." *Spotlight on Disability Newsletter*. 2016. http://www.apa.org/pi/disability/resources/publications/newsletter/2016/09/intellectual-disability.aspx.
Taua, Chris, and Tony Farrow. "Negotiating Complexities: An Ethnographic Study of Intellectual Disability and Mental Health Nursing in New Zealand." *International Journal of Mental Health Nursing* 18 (2009): 274–84.
Taylor, Charles. "The Politics of Recognition." In *Multiculturalism: Examining the Politics of Recognition*, edited by Amy Gutmann, 25–73. Princeton, N.J.: Princeton University Press, 1994.
Tataryn, Myroslaw, and Maria Truchan-Tataryn. *Discovering Trinity in Disability: A Theology for Embracing Difference*. Maryknoll, N.Y.: Orbis Books, 2013.
Taylor, Nicholas. *Paul on Baptism: Theology, Mission, and Ministry in Context*. London: SCM Press, 2016.
Thomson, Rosemarie Garland. *Extraordinary Bodies: Figuring Physical Disability in American Culture and Literature*. New York: Columbia University Press, 1997.
Thrall, Margaret E. "The Second Epistle to the Corinthians." In vol. 1 of *The International Critical Commentary on the Holy Scriptures of the Old and New Testaments*, edited by J. A. Emerton, C. E.B. Cranfield, and G. N. Stanton. Edinburgh, Scotland: T&T Clark, 1994.
Tindall, Ashley. "Accessible Baptism (Guest Post)." Disability and Faith Forum. March 9, 2017, https://disabilityandfaith.org/accessible-baptism-guest-post/.
Torrance, James B. *Worship, Community and the Triune God of Grace*. Downers Grove: IVP Academic, 1997.
Tsui, Teresa Kuo-Yu. "'Baptized Into His Death' (Romans 6:3) and 'Clothed with Christ' (Gal 3:27): The Soteriological Meaning of Baptism in Light of Pauline Apocalyptic." *Ephemerides Theologicae Lovanienses* 88, no. 4 (2012): 395–417.
Tuffrey-Wijne, Irene, and John Davies. "This Is My Story: I've Got Cancer." *British Journal of Learning Disabilities* 35 (2006): 7–11.
Turner, Jennifer, and Jessica Schomberg. "Inclusivity, Gestalt Principles, and Plain Language in Document Design." *In the Library with the Lead Pipe*, 2016.
Volf, Miroslav, and Dorothy C. Bass. "A Theological Understanding of Christian Practices." In *Practicing Theology: Beliefs and Practices in Christian Life*. Edition unstated. Grand Rapids: Eerdmans, 2002.
Volpe, Medi Ann. *Rethinking Christian Identity: Doctrine and Discipleship*. Malden, Mass.: Wiley-Blackwell, 2013.
Wadell, Paul J. "Pondering the Anomaly of God's Love: Ethical Reflections on Access to the Sacraments." In *Developmental Disabilities and Sacramental Access: New*

Paradigms for Sacramental Encounters, edited by Edward Foley, 53–72. Collegeville, Minn.: Liturgical, 1994.
Ward, Pete. *Perspectives on Ecclesiology and Ethnography*. Studies in Ecclesiology and Ethnography. Grand Rapids: Eerdmans, 2012.
Weber, Derek. "A New Ritual for Reaffirmation of Baptism." April 29, 2021. https://www.umcdiscipleship.org/articles/a-new-ritual-for-reaffirmation-of-baptism.
Wedderburn, A. J. M. "The Soteriology of the Mysteries and Paul's Baptismal Theology." *Novum Testamentum* 29 (1987): 53–72.
Weil, Louis. "Baptism as the Model for a Sacramental Aesthetic." *Anglican Theological Review* 92, no. 2 (2010): 259–70.
Whitehead, Andrew L. "Religion and Disability: Variation in Religious Service Attendance Rates for Children with Chronic Health Conditions." *Journal for the Scientific Study of Religion* 57, no. 2 (2018): 377–95. https://doi.org/10.1111/jssr.12521.
Whitesides, Kristin Adkins. "Just As I Am: Believer's Baptism and Intellectual Disability." April 9, 2018. https://scholarblogs.emory.edu/candlerdmin/2018/04/09/just-as-i-am/.
Whitt, Jason D. "Baptism and Profound Intellectual Disability." *Disability* (2012): 60–67.
Williams, Rowan. *Being Christian: Baptism, Bible, Eucharist, Prayer*. Grand Rapids: Eerdmans, 2014.
———. *On Christian Theology*. Challenges in Contemporary Theology. Oxford: Blackwell, 2000.
Willimon, William H. *Worship as Pastoral Care*. Nashville: Abingdon, 1979.
Wimpenny, Peter, and John Gass. "Interviewing in Phenomenology and Grounded Theory: Is There a Difference?" *Journal of Advanced Nursing* 31, no. 6 (2000): 1485–92.
Winner, Lauren F. *The Dangers of Christian Practice: On Wayward Gifts, Characteristic Damage, and Sin*. New Haven, Conn.: Yale University Press, 2018.
"The Word of God in the Life of the Church: A Report of International Conversation Between the Catholic Church and the Baptist World Alliance." *American Baptist Quarterly* 31, no. 1 (2012): 28–122.
World Council of Churches. "Appendix II: The Life and Witness of the Handicapped in the Christian Community." In *Partners in Life: The Handicapped and the Church*, edited by Geiko Müller-Fahrenholz, 177–84. Geneva: World Council of Churches, 1979.
———. *Baptism, Eucharist and Ministry*. 25th anniv. ed. Geneva, Switzerland: World Council of Churches, 1982.
———. *One Baptism: Towards Mutual Recognition: A Study Text*. Faith and Order Paper No. 210. Geneva: World Council of Churches, 2011.
Wright, J. Robert. "The Book of Common Prayer." In *The Wiley-Blackwell Companion to the Anglican Communion*, edited by Ian S. Markham, J. Barney Hawkins IV, Justyn Terry, and Leslie Nuñez Steffesen, 81–90. Malden, Mass.: John Wiley & Sons, 2013.

Writing Culture: The Poetics and Politics of Ethnography. Berkeley: University of California Press, 2010.
Yong, Amos. *The Bible, Disability, and the Church: A New Vision of the People of God*. Grand Rapids.: Eerdmans, 2011.
———. *Theology and Down Syndrome: Reimagining Disability in Late Modernity*. Waco, Tex.: Baylor University Press, 2007.
Young, Frances M. *Arthur's Call: A Journey of Faith in the Face of Severe Learning Disability*. Face to Face. London: SPCK, 2014.
Zhang, DongDong, and Frank R. Rusch. "The Role of Spirituality in Living with Disabilities." *Journal of Religion, Disability & Health* 9, no. 1 (2005): 83–98.

Scripture Index

Genesis	
6:9–9:17	88
Exodus	
14	88
Isaiah	
1:16–17	88
Ezekiel	
36:25–28	88
Matthew	
3:13–17	88–93
29	75
Acts	
2	75
8	75
Romans	
5	75, 98
5–8	203n14
6	24, 110, 202n12, 203n13
6:1–14	75, 93–101
6:3	100
8:3–4	114
12	111
1 Corinthians	
1	203n13
6	203n13
10	203n13
11:29	111
12	111, 202n12, 203n13
12:12–13	111
12:13, 27	110
12:20	112
12:21–26	109
2 Corinthians	116
1	203n13
5	104, 113, 116–17, 202n12
5:16	205n38
5:16–21	113
5:21	114–15
Galatians	
2:20	113
3	112, 202n12, 203n13
3:13–14	114
3:28	115
Ephesians	
1	203n13
Philippians	
2:6–11	114
Colossians	
2–3	203n13
2 Timothy	
2	203n13
Titus	
3	203n13

Thematic and Author Index

Antus, Elizabeth, 36, 139
Arbuckle, Gerald, 149–50
Aquinas, Thomas, 37–38, 193n18

baptism, 2–3; baptized body/
community, 67–69, 71, 89–91,
106–19, 122–23, 131–36, 191n45;
ecumenism, 145–46; embodied,
71–72, 74, 172; sacrament,
39–40, 42–43; ordinance, 41–42;
participatory, 69–70; Bible, 75;
forgiveness, 90, 124–25, 133; Jesus,
65–67, 71, 88–92, 134–36, 202n12;
slavery, 25–28; water, 72–74; *see also*
baptismal practices; new creation
identity; Paul's baptismal theology
baptismal practices, 76–77, 139–79;
accessibility, 148–50; nurture,
157–59; preparation, 153–63;
reaffirmation, 171–78, 211n40;
testimony, 163–71
Bass, Dorothy, 3, 24
Belcher, Kimberly, 123
Bernardin, Joseph, 40, 197n85
Bonhoeffer, Dietrich, 131–37, 171–72
Book of Common Prayer (BCP), 121–37;
active verbs, 126–28; Baptismal
Covenant, 124–28; critiques of,
128–36
Brock, Brian, 12, 24, 111, 171

Carlson, Richard, 110
Carter, Erik, 34–35
Christian practices, 24–25, 36–43;
by denomination, 39–43; *see also*
baptismal practices
communion: *see* Holy Communion
Conner, Ben, 169
Cross, Richard, 38

disability, frameworks for: coalitional,
6–7; medical, 5, 189n17; minority,
5–6; political/relational, 6; social, 5
disability rights, 10, 45, 188n12
disability studies, vii, 5–7, 10–14, 17,
22–24, 30–44, 50–55, 62, 92, 139, 163,
181–85, 189n17, 192n47
discipleship, 65–66, 92, 95–96, 99–102,
157–58, 165–66, 169–70, 194n49
diversity, 112, 169
doctrine, 30–33
Dykstra, Craig, 24

Eastman, Susan Grove, 103–14
exclusion, 2, 22, 28, 81

Florer-Bixler, Melissa, 40–41, 168
Fowler, Stanley, 156
Francis, Mark, 39, 196n80
friendship, 33–34

Goode, David, 174–75
Greggs, Tom, 133–34

Greig, Jason, 33–34, 41

Harrington, Sister Mary Therese, 161–62

Harshaw, Jill, 11–12, 23, 34–36, 38, 191n40, 192n47, 194n48, 196n75

Hauerwas, Stanley, 33–34, 122

Holy Communion, 143–45

Huels, John M., 39

identity: baptismal, 76–77, 140–42, 176–78, 181; disability, 4, 6, 9, 16, 92, 99, 119, 130, 189n15; *see also* Paul; new creation identity

image of God: *see imago dei*

imagination, 14–15, 21, 23, 92, 122, 164, 169, 178, 183–84

imago dei: Christological understanding, 32–33; friendship framework, 31–34; relational understanding, 31–33; *see also* inclusion paradigm

inclusion paradigm, 21, 34, 194n44

intellectual disability: attitudes toward, 80–82; definition, 3–4

intelligence quotient (IQ) testing, 14–15

Kafer, Alison, 6, 189n17

Käseman, Ernst, 109

Lappa, Christina, 157

Lathrop, Gordon, 140, 162, 178

Lima Document, 145, 158, 163, 175

liturgy: embodied testimony, 167–69; PC (USA), 140; *see also Book of Common Prayer*

Luther, Martin, 38; Flood Prayer, 88

Macaskill, Grant, 92, 96, 107, 111, 116

Martyn, J. Louis, 114

methodology, 7, 12, 19, 44–46, 48–51, 183–84, 190n26, 198n8; limitations of, 83

new creation identity, 113–19, 126–28; disability, 115–19; cultural success, 117

Paul: baptismal identity, 97–101, 103–13; baptismal theology, 93–101; participation in Christ's death/union with Christ, 94–97; Jesus, 97–101; self, 104–6

prayer, 24, 61–63, 127–28, 130, 137, 156

qualitative research, 7–8, 47–86; critiques of, 11; data analysis, 60–61; interviews, 11, 50–60, 64–82; participants, 56–59; self-reflexivity, 9, 48, 55, 61–65; study-design, 52–56, 82–85; theological ethnography, 7–8, 48–52

Reinders, Hans S., 32–34

Reynolds, Tom, 32–33

Romero, Miguel J., 37–38

Schmemann, Alexander, 156–57, 162, 170

Schnackenburg, Rudolf, 95, 203n14, 203n22, 204n23, 204n32, 204n36, 204n37

Siikavirta, Samuli, 101–4

Simon, Menno, 41

sin, 25, 89–90, 94, 124–25, 132–34, 204n35

Smith, Susan Marie, 149

Spinks, Bryan, 93, 175

Spurrier, Rebecca F., 141, 148

supported decision-making, 41, 197n91

Swinton, John, 10–11, 61, 83, 139, 169–71, 188n10, 194n49

theological abstraction, 17, 21–24

theological anthropology: *see* identity

Thrall, Margaret, 115

understanding/unknowing, 77–80

Universal Design for Learning, 55, 159–63

vocation, 8, 33, 95, 110, 140, 166, 169–71

Volpe, Medi Ann, 30–31, 140

Wadell, Paul, 39

Weil, Louis, 142–43, 146, 176

Wells, Samuel, 122

Whitt, Jason, 41–42

Williams, Rowan, 94, 107

Winner, Lauren F., 27–28, 91–92, 112

World Council of Churches, 154, 166

Yong, Amos, 32, 35, 195n52

Young, Frances, 36, 170

Also Available in the SRTD Series

The Cerulean Soul: A Relational Theology of Depression
Peter J. Bellini

Accessible Atonement: Disability Theology and the Cross of Christ
David McLachlan

*Formed Together: Mystery, Narrative, and Virtue
in Christian Caregiving*
Keith Dow

Wondrously Wounded: Theology, Disability, and the Body of Christ
Brian Brock

Disability and Spirituality: Recovering Wholeness
William C. Gaventa

Crippled Grace: Disability, Virtue Ethics, and the Good Life
Shane Clifton

The Bible and Disability: A Commentary
Edited by Sarah J. Melcher, Mikeal C. Parsons, and Amos Yong

Pastoral Care and Intellectual Disability: A Person-Centered Approach
Anna Katherine Shurley

*Becoming Friends of Time: Disability, Timefullness, and Gentle
Discipleship*
John Swinton

Disability and World Religions: An Introduction
Edited by Darla Y. Schumm and Michael Stoltzfus

Madness: American Protestant Responses to Mental Illness
Heather H. Vacek

Disability, Providence, and Ethics: Bridging Gaps, Transforming Lives
Hans S. Reinders

Flannery O'Connor: Writing a Theology of Disabled Humanity
Timothy J. Basselin

*Theology and Down Syndrome: Reimagining Disability
in Late Modernity*
Amos Yong

www.ingramcontent.com/pod-product-compliance
Lightning Source LLC
Chambersburg PA
CBHW030120240426
43673CB00041B/1347